THE REINVENTION OF
OBSCENITY

THE REINVENTION OF
OBSCENITY

SEX, LIES, and

TABLOIDS in

Early Modern

FRANCE

JOAN DeJEAN

The University of Chicago Press
Chicago and London

The University of Chicago Press, Chicago 60637
The University of Chicago Press, Ltd., London
© 2002 by The University of Chicago
All rights reserved. Published 2002
Printed in the United States of America

11 10 09 08 07 06 05 04 03 02   1 2 3 4 5
ISBN: 0-226-14140-3 (cloth)
ISBN: 0-226-14141-1 (paper)

Library of Congress Cataloging-in-Publication Data
DeJean, Joan E.
    The reinvention of obscenity : sex, lies, and tabloids in early modern France /
Joan DeJean.
        p.   cm.
    Includes bibliographical references and index.
    ISBN 0-226-14140-3 (cloth : alk. paper) — ISBN 0-226-14141-1 (pbk. : alk. paper)
        1. French literature—17th century—History and criticism.   2. Erotic literature,
    French—History and criticism.   3. Sex in literature.   4. Censorship—France.
    I. Title.
    PQ245 .D38   2002
    840.9'3538'09032—dc21

                                                                            2002018007

♾ The paper used in this publication meets the minimum requirements of the American National Standard for Information Sciences—Permanence of Paper for Printed Library Materials, ANSI Z39.48-1992.

For Georges May,
with GRATITUDE

Contents

List of Illustrations   *ix*

Acknowledgments   *xi*

Introduction: "The Words That Shock So Much at First"   1

1   **Male Practices:** Théophile de Viau's "Sodomite Sonnet"   29

2   **The Heterosexual Turn:** *L'Ecole des filles* or, When (the) Sex Began to Talk   56

3   **Two-Letter Words:** Molière's *L'Ecole des femmes* and Obscenity Made Modern   84

Conclusion: Beyond Obscenity?   122

Notes   *131*

Works Cited   *183*

Index   *193*

Illustrations

1   First page of *Parnasse des poètes satyriques* (1622)   42

2   Advertisement for an English translation of *L'Ecole
    des filles*   58

3   *L'Origine du monde*, by Gustave Courbet (1866)   73

4   Title page and frontispiece (after François Chauveau)
    of the 1668 edition of *L'Ecole des filles*   80

5   Page 131 of *La Critique de "L'Ecole des femmes"* (1663)   104

6   Title page and frontispiece (by François Chauveau)
    of *L'Ecole des femmes* (1663)   111

7   Portrait of Molière by Nicolas Mignard (c. 1660)   113

8   Portrait of Molière by Charles Coypel   114

9   Molière in an anonymous French painting,
    Les Farceurs français et italiens (c. 1670)   116

10 *Molière in the Role of Arnolphe in* L'Ecole des femmes
    in the Year 1670, by Henry Lecomte   117

Acknowledgments

E-mail has made it possible to bother friends and colleagues with requests for information with an ease never before imaginable. In the course of this project's long, slow gestation over the past half-dozen years, I pestered Roger Chartier and Peter Stallybrass so often that my guilt level was usually off the charts. I never encountered a limit to either their knowledge or their generosity. "Thank you" just isn't enough.

Ralph Rosen discussed Roman obscenity, provided references, read several versions of parts of this manuscript, and even sent emergency faxes to Paris—all with great good humor and energy. Several friends—Herb Blau, David Hult, Michel Jeanneret, Christian Jouhaud, and Nancy K. Miller—also commented on drafts. Natalie Davis and Daniel Roche offered guidance in the ways of French archives. Paula Findlen and Ann Jones answered questions about Italian Renaissance material. Giulia Pacini generously helped translate some of this material and was imaginative in her manipulations of early modern Italian dictionaries. Lynn Festa saved me a trip to the place I love to hate, the new Bibliothèque Nationale de France, and, when I could no longer avoid going there, Amy Wyngaard guided me every step of the way. Christian Jouhaud also loaned books and was always there to answer questions. Numerous colleagues—John Baldwin, Lance Donaldson-Evans, Joe Farrell, Hope Glidden, François Lecercle, Deborah McGrady, Steve Nichols, and Etienne Van de Walle—discussed material far from my usual stomping grounds. Jonathan Goldberg and Michael Moon pushed me in new directions after I presented the material in lectures; and Neil Hertz (who wins the prize for the best obscene anecdote!) had great intuitions, even though he did force me to reread Garasse's endless, mad diatribe still again in order to test them. Dan Traister did all he could to get me information on the situation in England. Alan Thomas was, as always, the ideal editor—both supportive and rigorous. Jennifer Furlong, Marilyn Rackley, and Havivah Schwartz provided excellent research assistance. Gérard Jubert of the Archives Nationales went far beyond the call of duty to help me check the transcription of Théophile's trial. The librarians and staff of the Arsenal Library were quite simply superb. Finally, to June Hines, Brie Neff, and Philippe Taupin in particular, I owe a special thank-you: without them, I would quite literally not have written this book.

Early work on this project was completed during a leave made possible by the National Endowment for the Humanities.

Introduction

"THE WORDS THAT SHOCK
SO MUCH AT FIRST"

The words that shock so much at first don't shock at all
after a while. . . . Culture and civilization have taught us . . .
[that] the act does not necessarily follow on the thought.
—D. H. Lawrence, *A Propos of "Lady Chatterley's Lover"*

During the summer and fall of 1998, strange things were happening
in my health club on Rittenhouse Square in Philadelphia. It is a reasonably upscale place, with a membership older, more established,
and generally more reserved than those of other clubs I've frequented.
Since the conversation among members, when it exists at all, is most often
devoted to the market or to current events, the TVs are always tuned to
CNN. It was thus inevitable that we would live through the unfolding of
the Monica Lewinsky scandal together. And did we ever.

On the treadmill or the Stairmaster, while using free weights or a Nau-
tilus machine, there was no place to escape CNN's relentless repetition of
words and expressions that I had never dreamed I'd be hearing in such a
public context, much less be pronouncing myself in front of the mix of
lawyers, real estate agents, and the occasional professor with whom I
shared a work-out routine and little else. The day a Philadelphia lawyer on
an exercise bike said "blow job" loudly enough for all to hear, I realized that
speech about sexuality had probably reached a point of no return. By the
end of the year, when I left for France to begin writing this book, I thought
I had heard it all. It had also occurred to me that a crucial aspect of the
"Monicagate" scandal—the way it had so widely disseminated "dirty"
words—might one day be seen as a turning point in the process by which

what D. H. Lawrence called "the words that shock so much at first" came to lose the last remnants of their shock value. It is widely believed that, during certain periods (parts of the Middle Ages, for example), there was little prohibition against publicly pronouncing the words we now refer to as obscene. Today, we seem to be entering such an age, or at least another age destined to be thought of as lacking this prohibition against dirty words. The next generation of English speakers may no longer imagine that a class of words related to sexuality, a class of words that has been subject to censorship for over three hundred years, should continue to be judged obscene, because they will no longer believe in the obscene as we have known it. As if in anticipation of this linguistic turn, the word *obscene* may already be shifting onto new semantic terrain.

Of late, *obscene* seems to be moving beyond the meaning it slowly acquired in early modern French—"immodest," "indecent"—and to be taking on two new meanings: first, any subject that we find hard to look at and therefore do not want to see represented (thus, someone will say of a video documenting a death that it is obscene); second, as a semantic catchall for actions we consider morally indecent.

In these new usages, for the first time in its modern history, *obscenity* no longer has any essential affiliation with sexuality but refers instead to ethical issues.[1] Those who have observed the United States during and since the Clinton scandal could wonder whether the obscene's new semantic life means that we have reached the end of over three centuries of prohibition: the open declaration of sexual terms to be "obscene" may no longer function as a powerful repressive and creative force. In the following pages, I will re-create the trajectory as a result of which *obscene* first assumed the role it may now be losing. I will also re-create the unlikely collaboration that produced modern literary obscenity: the collaboration between the machinery of print culture and that of censorship.

In the popular imaginary, France has long had a particular affinity with sexual naughtiness. Paris was traditionally considered *the* center for the production of dirty books and dirty pictures. While this idea is certainly true, at least to a considerable degree, that truth is not what concerns me here. The legend of the intimate affiliation between things French and sexual impropriety originated—and I will use Samuel Pepys's diary to illustrate this origin—at the period I will discuss here. My subject is the causes and the consequences of this myth. Among the causes that I will foreground is the intense complicity between censorship and obscenity: the moment at which obscenity was reinvented witnessed the development of the modern book police and the first modern censorial machinery. Among the consequences, I find most significant the crucial role played by obscenity *not* as a factor that troubled or unsettled authorial authority—a charge against which an author (Ovid, for example) had to defend himself in order to be taken seriously—but rather as a foundation of that authority. Here, my argument will apply to Molière, the major author of the French tradition: I believe that he understood both the cause and the consequence I have just described and used obscenity to help found his career as print author. One could, however, extend this argument to numerous other pillars of the French tradition: Flaubert and Baudelaire, to name but two.

By claiming that obscenity was reinvented in seventeenth-century France, I am not denying the existence of obscenity *tout court* before this. I am arguing instead that modern literary obscenity is different from all its precursors. The concept of seeking to shock a literary public with language obviously did not originate in the mid-seventeenth century. However, modern obscenity redefined the nature of the representations designed to shock and titillate. In addition, it was both transmitted and received in radically new ways. Those differences in circulation explain why, in the space of a century, obscenity was transformed from a minor literary phenomenon available only within a restricted, elite audience into a veritable societal problem: literature that became the object of official, state-sponsored repression because it could be viewed as a threat to civic well-being.

Though modern literary obscenity was the first step on the way to pornography, it differs from it in crucial ways. I attribute particular significance to the fact that each of these terms—*obscenity, pornography*—began to be used at a particular moment, only when a type of literature significantly different from what had been previously available was being articulated. In each case, new terminology and new generic categories reflected the fact that there was suddenly more *there* there: sexually transgressive material was more public and more visible than ever before. What follows is an attempt to re-create a watershed in the history of "dirty" literature.[2]

Classical Latin had a vocabulary of obscenity, but that vocabulary disappeared along with the language, to be resurrected only in seventeenth-century France. The word *obscenity* reappeared at that time because of the simultaneous triumph of print culture in the vernacular and of modern book censorship. In midcentury, the book trade for the first time invested massively in publication projects both in French and in less expensive formats. Modern obscenity came into existence exactly as print culture was breaking into the first true mass markets. This meant that obscene material could, for the first time ever, circulate outside the public of elite male readers who, until then, had been virtually the sole audience for sexually transgressive literature. The obscene would never have become a censorable category had it not possessed this ability, unimaginable in antiquity, both to reach a large-scale audience of solitary readers and to become accessible to the lower orders of society.[3]

Once this uncontrolled circulation became possible, the French state invented structures—in particular, the modern writer's trial—that ever since have remained central to the prosecution of printed material. Any causality in my account is simple force of habit. In reality, it is often virtually impossible to distinguish cause from effect, to be certain, for example, that censorship assumed its modern guise in response to the new literary obscenity, rather than the other way around. The first scenario, while it might appear the more obvious, ignores one of the basic truths of the early modern French book trade, one that the authors of dangerous material quickly grasped: censorship sold books. Any volume the state tried to suppress instantly became eminently desirable. It is, therefore, more accurate to think of the simultaneous and interrelated development of mass-market print culture, of a new kind of obscene literature, and of modern censorial machinery.[4]

This book originated in one area of the complex relation between words and things. In its simplest formulation, the question that concerns me is this: Can a concept fully exist before the word we use to name it has been invented? Some cultural historians dismiss this type of inquiry as a simple chicken-and-egg issue. Those who are familiar with the debate about whether homosexuality as we know it existed before the word *homosexuality* was invented in the late nineteenth century will perhaps be prepared to take such questions more seriously. While I concede that the fact that a word does not exist does not mean that the concept behind it is completely nonexistent, I believe that the moment at which a term is created has particular significance. The period at which it is created experiences what might be called a *need* for a new concept. Once we have a sense of all the new words created in a given period, we have a much fuller picture of that period's defining character.

Walter Benjamin's *Arcades Project* provides a model for the type of cultural history I have in mind. Benjamin uses a group of words created in the 1820s—from *passage*, in the sense of a shopping arcade, to *spécialité*, the item featured in an individual store, to *réclame*, the advertisement that promoted a *spécialité*—to define the particular character of the city he calls "Paris, capital of the nineteenth century."

In similar fashion, *obscénité* began its active life in a modern language in a precise context, the Paris of the 1660s. This moment marked the beginning of Paris's reign as international cultural capital. Thus, two myths that have ever since remained central to the manner in which French culture is represented originated at the same moment—France as the quintessential land of style and France as the birthplace of dirty books. In addition, *ob-scénité* was created as part of a cluster of words, all of which subsequently became crucial to our modernity: among them, *nouvelle*, in the sense of the news that the modern periodical press was created to report, and *police*, used to designate the police force responsible for a city's orderly functioning and the repression of disorderly elements. At the inception of Paris's reign as international capital of fashion and style, the first incarnation of Benjamin's Paris, the modern press, the modern police, and modern obscene literature were simultaneously taking shape. Just in time to become an essential component in the French style that the European press resolutely promoted, obscenity received its modern literary form even as the police force given the power to suppress it was established.

No word, of course, springs to life, Athena-like, fully formed. The moment at which its official existence is clearly demonstrable—that is, when it has become familiar to native speakers of a language—is always preceded by a period during which it may be said to be preemergent, a period during which it is not yet commonly used, when the few who do use it are still uncertain about what exactly it will come to mean.[5] This is precisely the period in *obscenity*'s history that interests me: the century roughly from 1550 to 1663 during which the word and the concept it would come to designate were becoming ever more active presences on the French cultural scene but were not yet fully articulated.

Obscénité, however, is indeed a most curious key word. Unlike its near relative *pornographie*, it was not completely a modern invention but a term with a rich past in antiquity.[6] It is also different from the words such as *police* that have merely taken on new meanings in the course of their evolution. *Obscenity*'s history is both strange and somehow unfathomable. Once their role in Roman culture had been played out, the Latin words at the origin of our modern vocabulary—*obscenus, obscenitas*—simply disappeared; neither was carried over into medieval Latin or into intermediate languages such as Old French. Thus, even in the seventeenth century, when translators encountered the Latin words, they clearly did not know what precise content to give them and elected vague options such as *infamous* and *infamy*.

And yet, when the vocabulary suddenly resurfaced after centuries of dormancy, first in French and subsequently in other European languages, in every language it was reactivated in incarnations virtually identical to the Latin originals, *obscenus* and *obscenitas*.[7] This surface similarity could have encouraged anyone who knew Latin—and those who introduced the vocabulary into modern languages were all excellent Latinists—to assume that the words would, as it were, pick up where they had left off and mean, in seventeenth-century Paris (or London or Venice), just what they had meant in ancient Rome. This could help explain why, during the first century of the obscene's modern life, usage was so massively vexed.

The obscene's primary meaning in Latin, that of being "inauspicious, ill-omened, sinister," was briefly revived in mid-sixteenth-century France.[8] This may help us understand how it was that religious connotations clung stubbornly to the vocabulary of the obscene until the mid-seventeenth century, by which time the conditions that guaranteed its modern reinvention were in place. In secular usage, the Latin *obscenus* had a range of meanings—from "filthy" to "indecent"—that are more familiar to us today. Here, the obscene functions above all as a boundary marker, signaling the frontier between the indecent and the decent, the filthy and the clean, marking a boundary constantly in flux, redrawn in every culture and, within each culture, drawn differently at different moments. The major difficulty encountered in trying to understand obscenity as a transcultural concept is that of knowing just where a given society set those limits. In the history of literary obscenity that interests me, those limits are determined solely in legal terms. The most significant issue related to so-called sexually transgressive literature is not whether it actually offended its readers but whether political authorities were concerned enough about its spread to try to put an end to it.

In Roman culture, for example, it would appear that sexually transgressive literature encountered a large degree of tolerance as long as it remained confined to what Amy Richlin, in her groundbreaking study of Latin obscenity, terms "the garden of Priapus." Intention created a first form of confinement. Thus, obscenity was used by writers such as Martial above all as a personal insult, to embarrass the subjects whose vices or sexual peculiarities were being exposed. In this mode, obscenity can be understood as performing a function of shaming, rather than attempting to titillate. Writers also described their obscene work as having a function related to the Saturnalia and other festivals that Bakhtin evoked with his concept of the carnivalesque. These works, like the festivals, occupied a separate sphere in which, with the goal of protecting society from evil forces, traditional rules and values were reversed (Richlin, 10). The obscene was cordoned off inside well-maintained frontiers. As Richlin notes, even the vision of sexual transgressiveness that it flaunted conformed to a precise model: "male, aggressive, and bent on controlling boundaries" (xvi). It appears that, however crude its content, obscene literature was not judged offensive as long as it respected certain rules; certainly, from a legal standpoint, the Romans felt that it could be tolerated.[9]

In Rome it was possible to be both the author of highly sexually transgressive literature and an extremely successful patronage artist—witness the example of Martial. Nevertheless, the fact that Ovid's contemporaries circulated the story that he was persecuted because of the obscene quality of some of his work indicates that a charge of literary indecency was plausible, at least in the Augustan age.[10] In general, however, in antiquity sexually transgressive literature did not provoke anything like the intense passion that has surrounded modern obscenity trials. The state seems not to have been concerned with regulating or suppressing obscene literature, or at most to an extent that is by modern standards quite limited.

The obscene's far less troubled life in antiquity must above all be linked to the vastly more limited, and therefore more controllable, circulation of works in manuscript form and within scribal culture. This meant that obscene material could be seen as an insider joke to be shared among like-minded men, an audience not likely to be corrupted by the content of what it read. For obscenity to be a problem, it must be public. It must begin to circulate within the vastly less controllable and more public market of print culture. In antiquity, despite Plato's warnings about the public danger of the theater, literature's circulation was vastly more private.[11] In antiquity, therefore, the state might well not have found the regulation of obscenity a particularly pressing issue, whereas the conditions surrounding the circulation of "dirty" works, and literature in general, were beginning to change radically by the time the obscene found a second life in modern languages.

The greatest mystery in obscenity's complex history is that of the centuries-long disappearance of words used to designate the concept of sexually transgressive material, both in Rome and from the seventeenth century till today. This rupture in the history of *obscene* and *obscenity* surely means most obviously that the classical conception of the obscene was somehow no longer valid during the Middle Ages. The vocabulary's long suppression must also indicate the absence of a generally accepted concept of terms and content that writers felt obliged to avoid on the grounds that they were sexually indecent or out of the fear that their work would be regulated or suppressed.

In some ways, the situation was similar to that in antiquity. Material we might designate obscene was carefully confined: certain genres, those known as *courtois* (courtly) avoided crude sexual terminology, while other, more vernacular genres displayed it prominently. And yet, despite this abundant presence in medieval literature of material we would think obscene, there was no term specifically to designate such content. It was referred to as *non-courtois,* by opposition to the genres that refused it, and *vilain* ("common," in the sense of lower class, or "dirty"), a word with no particular affiliation with either words or literature.[12] There was practice without theory.

Nor is there evidence of any formal censorship of this material. Such displays were at times the object of intense disapproval, although even this unofficial censure tended to take place both late in the Middle Ages and on occasions when sexually transgressive material was employed outside the vernacular genres in which it flourished. The most notable instance of disapproval is now known as "the quarrel of the *Roman de la Rose*": the fifteenth-century writer Christine de Pizan took her thirteenth-century precursor Jean de Meun to task for his display of "licentious" language—specifically, what are now known as primary obscenities. She went so far as to contend that his linguistic vulgarity was reason enough for dismissing him from the ranks of the great authors.[13] Christine de Pizan, writing as she did just prior to the invention of print, which was destined to revolutionize the notion of authorship, may well have intuited some of the ways in which the foundations of literary authority were about to shift radically.[14] Indeed, by the time the line traditionally accepted as dividing the Middle Ages from the Renaissance had been crossed, both the modern concept of sexually transgressive literature and the modern conditions for its reception were clearly taking shape.

In the sixteenth century, in England, France, and Italy the history of print culture's involvement with obscenity began. In England and France, for the first time since antiquity, terminology specifically designed to designate indecent words and writing came into use. At the same moment, in Italy, for the first time ever, creators of such material became the object of official censorship.

In England and France, where vocabulary predated censorship, literary obscenity underwent one type of preemergence. By the early sixteenth century, English speakers had a word to designate something like the territory subsequently covered by the obscene: they could refer to "bawdy" language or poems. *Bawdy* did not have, however, *obscene*'s massively negative connotations: the term was not used in censorial fashion. The bawdy was clearly audacious, but it was neither socially threatening nor a problem the state sought to suppress. Writers used words considered bawdy without fear of censorship.[15]

Sixteenth-century French had no term used specifically to designate sexually transgressive words and writing. Writers such as Rabelais and Ronsard referred to the part of their work that modern readers would term obscene as *folastries*, a term without negative connotations. During the Renaissance, however, *obscene* entered a century-long transitional period during which it gradually acquired its modern meaning. At this point, the adjective functioned as a sort of semantic free radical, capable of playing dramatically different roles. In 1559, Jean Poldo d'Albenas discussed a passage from Martial, which describes Cato leaving a performance because it contained "obscene and indecent verse" (141). By making the neologism part of a semantic cluster containing the familiar adjective *indecent,* Poldo d'Albenas suggests to readers who knew classical Latin which of its meanings he had in mind and to other readers that the words are virtual synonyms.[16]

A 1579 appearance is the earliest sign that *obscène* was acquiring its modern meaning. In a preface to the second edition of Laurent Joubert's *Erreurs populaires,* the publisher, Simon Millanges, explained that, since the book describes childbirth, its author was obliged to "use words and terms which seem to be a little obscene"; readers—he lists possible categories, from nuns and priests to the unmarried—who prefer not to hear about "any shameful body parts" should just skip over these sections ("Au Lecteur," n.p.). Millanges announces two factors subsequently essential to obscenity's modern reinvention: first, the obscene is specifically tied to the body parts now known as primary obscenities; second, it became truly scandalous once obscene words began to circulate both in the vernacular and in print. As a printer-bookseller, Millanges was well-placed to know that works now had the potential to reach audiences never imaginable before the advent of print culture. Only one factor was still missing from the equation and, in France, would be added in the early seventeenth century: censorship.[17]

The third country, Italy, provides a very different story, for Italy had *I Modi.* The suppression of *I Modi* provides the first indication of the radically new way in which sexually transgressive representations were dealt with in the age of mechanical reproduction. This suppression was surrounded by so much secrecy that it has been reconstructed largely on the basis of hearsay and conjecture. In 1523 a celebrated painter, Giulio Romano, is said to have drawn sixteen highly erotic postures on the walls of the Sala di Constantino in the Vatican. The audience for those images was clearly highly restricted, so they provoked no outcry. The commotion began when they were reproduced in a series of sixteen engravings by the foremost engraver of the Italian Renaissance, Marcantonio Raimondi, and when those engravings—representing heterosexual couplings or postures so graphic that they are often described as athletic—appeared in print. The painter quickly decamped to Mantua, where he continued his career in brilliant fashion. The engraver, however, was thrown into the Vatican prison. He was released, it is said, only after the personal intervention of a future dei Medici Cardinal—and of the writer Pietro Aretino.

Shortly thereafter, Aretino made his involvement with the postures professional as well. He composed sixteen sonnets, known as the *Sonetti Lussuriosi*, to accompany the engravings and arranged to have them printed together. This, the broadest circulation yet for *I Modi*, was short-lived: it is said that the Pope himself ordered the destruction of all copies of the edition and of the plates of the engravings. A second edition met with the same fate. Aretino fell out of favor because of the affair but was not persecuted.[18]

The *I Modi* affair was the clearest warning that obscenity's modern reinvention was about to begin. This was the first case, in any culture and at any time, when we can be certain that sexually transgressive material was the object of something that we would call censorship, rather than mere censure. The newly radical tactic was clearly a direct response to the dramatically revised conditions for circulation made possible by mechanical reproduction: remember that the painter, to whose images accessibility could be controlled, got off scot-free, whereas the engraver, whose work could be made available to uncontrolled circulation, was imprisoned. Note that Aretino was also let off lightly: this may indicate that the affair was considered primarily a visual issue, perhaps also that the circulation of sexually transgressive images was considered a graver threat than that of sexually transgressive literature.

With the *I Modi* affair, sexually transgressive literature first took advantage of print culture's potential for diffusion. In its content, however, the volume is not yet part of modern literary obscenity: both engravings and sonnets are so massively Latinate, so close to classical precedent, that they are far removed from the material that emerged a century later.[19] Finally, this suppression carried out by the Catholic Church is a far cry from the secular censorship that was used to suppress the first classics of modern obscenity. *I Modi* surely served as a warning about what could happen now that mechanical reproduction had been added to the equation, but neither modern structures of censorship nor modern conditions for authorship were as yet in place.

By the time *obscène* next appeared in its new French usage, modern structures for censorship had begun to be established, as the writer who used the adjective knew from personal experience. In 1658 Guillaume Colletet devoted an important section of his "Traité de l'épigramme" to the "strict rules of modesty" (110) that poets must observe in order to steer satire away from the pitfall of the obscene. Colletet understood only too well why poets should respect society's sexual taboos, because thirty-five years earlier he had narrowly escaped prosecution in the first true writer's trial. The mature poet was able to offer this hard-earned advice: "The epigrammatic poet must not use obscene terms which represent things too freely and leave dirty images in the reader's mind. . . . There is a certain public decency which must never be violated. . . . Shouldn't we be ashamed to uncover that which we should keep secret, such as those parts of the body that propriety demands that we keep hidden?" (108–9).[20]

It was no accident that the boundary around the decent was beginning to be redrawn in the late sixteenth century. At that moment, under the influence of the Reformation and the Counter-Reformation, one complicity essential to obscenity's modern reinvention, the complicity between print culture and a revised vision of sexual transgressiveness, came to prominence. The Catholic Church had, of course, been made aware of the new technology's menace much earlier. Between 1517 and 1520, Luther's publications sold over three hundred thousand copies, making Lutheranism, in Arthur Dickens's phrase, "the first child of the printed book": "For the first time in human history, a great reading public judged the validity of revolutionary ideas through a mass-medium which used the vernacular languages together with the arts of the journalist and the cartoonist" (51).[21]

The Catholic Church had not needed this illustration to recognize the menace of print: the first Papal Bull requiring the prepublication screening of manuscripts dates from 1501. In response to Lutheranism's invasion of the French scene, the French state began to back up the Church's efforts by making the screening of all religious publications mandatory in 1521. Catholicism's response to the Protestant romp through the nascent print industry took a harder line at the Council of Trent in 1540.[22] It was then that the distinction was clearly drawn between Catholic and Protestant practice: just as print culture was spreading massively and as the Reformation was taking advantage of the new technology by promoting direct access to the scriptures through individual reading, the Council insisted on oral transmission of the Bible.[23] The Council also decided on what was in effect the first code governing the circulation of all publications dealing with "sacred matters." This was promulgated in the form of regulations included as a preface to the first edition of the infamous *Index of Forbidden Books* published in Rome in 1557. One of these regulations required all printers and booksellers, before printing any such books, to have the manuscript approved by their local authorities.[24]

Other rules focus on another area of concern: the vernacular. Permission to read the Bible in translation was among the most tightly regulated issues. Certain Catholic countries—notably Spain—simply virtually eliminated vernacular Bibles. For the French state, this became a particularly tricky issue following the Edict of Nantes (1598), when France became the only multiconfessional Catholic country. In response to this new wrinkle, the French Church devised a singular position, one neatly summed up in Nicolas Le Maire's *Le Sanctuaire fermé aux prophanes, ou la Bible défendue au vulgaire* (1651), in which he explains that all would continue to be well, as long as the Bible can be kept out of the hands of women and nonaristocratic male readers (331). Like print culture in general, sacred publications in French were an object of concern because of the possibility that information previously restricted to an elite male audience would now get into various types of wrong hands.

At first, both Church and state were anxious only about potential new access to religious materials. Amid the sweeping political and cultural turmoil unleashed by the Reformation and the Council of Trent, however, other types of material came in for scrutiny. Beginning in the 1560s, French monarchs began to extend the regulations originally formulated solely for sacred texts to all publications. For decades, however, nothing was done actually to enforce these new regulations. As soon as the state began to do so, the first modern machinery of censorship began to take shape.

In early modern France and England, censorship was initially solely in the hands of religious authorities.[25] The modern institution of censorship originated, however, only once civil authorities assumed control over its operation. In England the initial situation and its evolution are clear: religious courts and canon law had jurisdiction over all matters related to personal morality. Initially, the publication of works that tested the limits of decency was considered just such a matter; obscene publications continued to be regulated exclusively by religious authorities until the late seventeenth century. As of 1727, English common-law courts officially took over jurisdiction: from this point on, those held responsible for printed material pronounced obscene were considered to have committed a crime, a public offense, rather than a private act of personal immorality that would have come under religious jurisdiction. In the course of the debate that decided obscenity's legal fate in English law, the key factor in the equation was print: obscene books were judged too public to be regulated by spiritual courts.

In France the evolution was radically different. Religious jurisdiction began to be supplanted much sooner. Already in the 1620s, laws decreeing the establishment of secular censorship began to appear on the books. It is then that confusion sets in, a confusion that, I believe, helped make the publication of obscene books possible. In 1623, after the Sorbonne lost the monopoly given it by François I, ecclesiastical censors were shown only theological works. During the following decades, several rivals fought for absolute control: the Church, the university (the doctors of theology of the Sorbonne, also religious censors, although not all were priests), the Chancellery, and the Parisian Parliament.[26] Their struggle ended only with the creation of the book police. At this point, French censorship had been officially secularized and bureaucratized; it had assumed its modern form. Indeed, in the eighteenth century, the Church played an official role only on exceptional occasions, such as the censorship of the *Encyclopédie*. Nevertheless, in France civil censors never completely eliminated issues of personal morality from their decisions.

This fundamental ambiguity in the definition of French censorship may help explain why—unlike *obscene* which fell quickly into place—*obscenity* had to struggle to gain recognition in its French meaning. For 150 years, the word was unable to shake religious connotations. Witness *obscenity*'s inaugural appearance in a modern language, in the 1511 compilation, *Vies des saints Pères:* "Vesquit avec toutes luxures, obscénités et infamies." (He lived surrounded by all possible lust, obscenities, and infamy.) The volume's anonymous editor seems simply to have chosen the French equivalent of the Latin *obscenitas*, without considering that the noun had no modern meaning. As a result, *obscenity* becomes a mere subset of the sins of "lust" (*luxure*) or "shameful conduct" (*infamie*), a question of private morality, a religious offense. This was the dead-end path that delayed the term's reinvention until censorship and print culture together began to create a need for the neologism.

A little over a century went by before *obscenity* appeared again, this time in Father François Garasse's 1623 diatribe against contemporary freethinkers, *La Doctrine curieuse des beaux esprits de ce temps*, the catalyst for what proved to be the first trial on charges of literary obscenity. In his role as religious censor who hoped to have the freethinkers' works suppressed —he had in mind the poet Guillaume Colletet, who later introduced *obscene* in its modern usage and, in particular, Théophile de Viau, whose reorientation of the representation of sexuality will be the center of my first chapter—Garasse portrays the young libertines as guilty of "impieties, blasphemies, and obscenities" (85). The neologism is still an imprecise sin, although this time, rather than a sin of personal morality, it is a verbal offense, words forbidden because they violate religious taboos.

Another forty years elapsed before, in his 1663 *Critique de "L'Ecole des femmes,"* Molière finally used *obscénité* in a thoroughly modern manner, to provide a name for what his critics had found scandalous in *L'Ecole des femmes*. For the first time, Molière made obscenity's new nature clear: like blasphemy, it was a speech crime. However, he also indicated that the term should be freed from religious connotations; unlike blasphemy, modern obscenity was a purely secular offense.

Molière was obviously correct in his estimation of the emerging problem for which his contemporaries needed a name, for this time *obscenity* would stick, so much so that by the century's end, as the examples included in late-seventeenth-century dictionaries prove, it had become part of the language. All dictionaries make plain that it was by then free of religious connotations: "obscenities" are understood to be "dirty words," words that "offend modesty," rather than religious sensibilities.

It is hard to imagine that the Protestant-Catholic divide—England developed the first obscenity law, while France and Italy developed sexually transgressive literature well before they had laws to regulate it—was not operative in some way in all aspects of obscenity's reinvention. One area where I have difficulty understanding its role is that of modern obscenity's initial involvement with visual culture. In the Italian Renaissance, as *I Modi* and all subsequent sexually transgressive publications demonstrate, every prodding of the frontier around the decent featured either scandalous images or constant reminders of visual culture's seductive power: the sexual transgressiveness of this literature, in other words, is primarily a question of imagery.[27]

In a splendid essay, "Titian, Ovid, and Sixteenth-Century Codes for Erotic Illustration," Carlo Ginzburg describes the functioning, in Italy prior to the large-scale invasion of print culture, of two clearly separate "iconic circuits." The first consisted of all objects such as frescoes shown in places accessible to all. The second included the first but also artifacts such as small paintings that could be seen only in the homes of the elite (77). The first circuit was totally public and without social differentiation; the second was just the opposite. Intentionally lewd images circulated only within the second sphere, with rare exceptions—Ginzburg mentions decorations in brothels and taverns (79–80). Then, this clarity was, in Ginzburg's phrase, "disturbed" by print (92).[28]

In Renaissance France, the same neatly separated iconic circuits existed; their functioning was surely also troubled by print, even though early modern France did not witness any "disturbance" as spectacular as the *I Modi* affair. At the time of obscenity's reinvention, new types of imagery were undoubtedly put into circulation in each traditional circuit. What is remarkable and, to my mind, incomprehensible, however, is that, during the period when France became the center for the production of modern sexually transgressive print culture, there apparently was no parallel tradition of visual imagery. From the 1620s until well into the eighteenth century, there is no record of either the production or the prosecution of reproducible sexually transgressive images in France.[29] Thus, when *obscenity* first entered a modern language, it was completely free of visual connotations, and this for good reason: there was no contemporary tradition of image-making to which the term could be attached. The obscene's reinvention is a moment when the ability of the word—in this case, the printed word—to influence opinions and change the lives of an audience of anonymous readers was widely recognized—and just as widely feared. For the first modern censors, obscenity was exclusively a crime of the printed word.

Once broken, the complicity between sexually transgressive representations and visual culture was not soon reestablished. Indeed, it seems likely that Walter Kendrick's intuition is correct and that the connection that appears so natural to us today began to be forged only at the turn of the nineteenth century, when the word *pornography* was being created just as the first catalogues detailing the sexually transgressive visual artifacts recently discovered at Pompeii were published (26).[30] From that moment on and in increasingly spectacular fashion, obscenity has become more and more exclusively a visual affair. One has only to think of the outcry provoked by a long line of paintings, beginning, perhaps, with Manet's *Olympia* in 1865 and, more recently, by the work of various photographers, most visibly Robert Mapplethorpe. Indeed, in recent decades, the censure and censorship of material judged obscene has increasingly been confined to the visual media.

In the beginning, however, it was most emphatically not so.

Perhaps the most telling way in which the original literary obscenity confirmed the power of the printed word involves its massive display of what are now known as primary obscenities. Now I am not suggesting that trading on the shock value of this particular linguistic category was anything new or that it was presented as such. On the contrary, among the few constants in sexually transgressive literature from antiquity to the present day is the particular pleasure of foregrounding what the hero of *Les Liaisons dangereuses,* the Vicomte de Valmont, terms *le mot technique* (letter 110): it would appear that, in all cultures and at all periods, primary obscenities are perceived as having an unusually close connection with the thing they designate.[31]

The new literary obscenity called attention to this connection, to the peculiar physicality of these words; it did so by emphasizing that print has at its disposal the means to convey that raw blatancy. To this end, the early obscene classics use types of punctuation unavailable before print to make these terms, and these terms alone, as flagrantly evident as possible: they jump off the page. Thus, for example, the sonnet at the center of the trial I will consider in chapter 1 featured one of the earliest, perhaps even the earliest, use of what much later became known as the ellipsis, a mark that made the primary obscenities stand out so strikingly that the sonnet has a look of what it in some ways is: a poem about the new unprintability of these terms. Later, when Molière introduced *obscénité* as a fully secular term, he made its association with print evident by featuring in its inaugural scene another new form of emphasis, italics. *Obscénité* was reinvented as a child of the printed page.

When the printed word took control over the scene of sexual transgressiveness, both the content and the reception of that material were in rapid and radical flux. Here, we are dealing once again with a situation of mutual influence: it's impossible to separate the threads and to decide where it all began. This much, however, is clear: between the mid-sixteenth century and the mid-seventeenth, literary obscenity began to explore previously unexamined territory; during the same period, it began to reach previously untapped publics, and it became for the first time the object of official, public repression. First, the new conditions for its reception.

In the wake of the Reformation and the Counter-Reformation, radically new norms and expectations came gradually to be accepted regarding the representation of sexuality. In a Catholic country such as France, these were, of course, initially another part of the response to Protestantism's menace. Increasingly, however, they can also be seen as a preventive measure. By 1650—when Le Maire published his position paper forbidding the Bible in French expressly to women and nonaristocratic men—sexually transgressive literature was also finding a vernacular "translation": now written exclusively in French, it was about to invade for the first time the least classical of literary genres, the modern novel, the genre whose enduring success resulted from the fact that it appealed precisely to the new readers par excellence: women and the bourgeoisie.[32] And by the time the modern novel and a newly vernacular literary obscenity began to reach these new publics, the imposition of codes and regulations surely seemed far more urgent than before. It was at this moment that, for the first time ever, secular literature—literature without religious content—became the object, not of a form of censure, but of official, state-sponsored censorship.

Every institution goes through growing pains. As far as censorship in France was concerned, the confusion natural to a start-up period lasted for a long time, for it was only at the close of the seventeenth century that the process became truly bureaucratized and standardized. The period I will present here is part of this era when censorship was finding its way amid a great deal of confusion, first about who was in charge, but also about censorship's purview. I will re-create the period during which this institution —initially conceived to control religious publications and then, in the late sixteenth and early seventeenth century, occasionally used to suppress works with undesirable political content—had to broaden its scope.

From the 1620s on, it must have become increasingly evident that a category of dangerous publications that censors had not been concerned with before was taking shape. To this new censorial category belong the works in which we can see the development of our modern notion of literary obscenity.[33] The works I will consider here forced French censors to realize that they had a new problem on their hands: publications that could be considered a threat to public morality. In various ways, these works indicated what might be termed the secularization of sexuality, that is, sexuality presented not as a matter of personal morality, but rather a territory that, because it could be linked to a problem such as birth control in which the state had a big stake, could no longer be regulated by religious authorities. I will discuss at length the censorship of three works that helped secularize sexuality. These cases, truly the first modern writers' trials, functioned almost as workshops or laboratories, since they allowed the early state censors to feel their way through unfamiliar territory, to determine what the issues really were and where the limits should now be set—in short, to learn their trade.

Indeed, as I was working my way through their learning process, I came to realize that these cases were the first instances when we can be sure that book censorship had really functioned. True, the regulation requiring prepublication screening of religious books had sometimes been followed; some published books had also been suppressed. Never before, however, had officers of the state been assigned the task of evaluating a work and deciding whether it should be suppressed and on what grounds. Never before—and this is perhaps the most crucial factor—had these officers been obliged to confront the alleged authors of these works and assign responsibility for their existence. Prior to this, in cases of published books, when religious censors had asked the state to intervene, it was usually against printers and booksellers; officers of the state had not dealt with the individuals accused of having written the dangerous books.[34]

The trials I will consider functioned, therefore, not only as laboratories out of which the modern institution of censorship was shaped, but also as workshops that helped determine what a modern author would be—in particular, what his legal responsibilities and rights would be.[35] More than anything, it was this confrontation between the state and the author that forced the first modern censors to think about what it was that they were up to. Finally, this official recognition of authorial status in turn helped give literary obscenity the final push needed to make it a category whose existence could no longer be denied. Instead of a phenomenon carefully confined to the margins of the literary scene, work to be shared among wealthy, like-minded men and only behind closed doors, a tradition so ephemeral that we often no longer know whether a given period had any production with a content we would recognize as obscene, there was suddenly so much *there* there that the French state had to begin to give serious consideration to its potential consequences.

The fledgling censors, understandably, were caught short: they acted as though they were censoring sexually subversive material purely on religious grounds. Among their earliest realizations was the lack of vocabulary with which to designate that which they were seeking to suppress. At first, they used various terms, such as *impious,* with overt religious connotations. Eventually—the earliest usage I found is from a writer's trial in 1661—they settled on a rather inauspicious choice: *mauvais livres* (bad books), a term destined to remain in use throughout the eighteenth century. One aspect of their choice was consistent with the logic upon which French censorship was founded: "bad books" had been coined by religious authorities to denote books whose content could lead good Catholics astray.[36] The expression thus indicates the fundamental inability to disengage from its religious origins that continued to dog French censorship at least until the end of the Ancien Régime. Nowhere was this inability more evident than in the trial proceedings I will present here, for the original "bad books" were the first classics of modern literary obscenity.

A burgeoning censorial machinery in search of its mission, a book trade reaching out to publics never before part of literary culture, and Church authorities trying to maintain control over them both at the same time as they attempted to dictate new terms for the representation of sexuality: this was the backdrop against which unfolded the other major shift in the reception of sexually transgressive literature. This change in reception, perhaps more than any other factor, explains why I speak of obscenity's reinvention. With that phrase, I am trying to account for the most evident, and perhaps the most dramatic, shift in Western European standards for decency, as those standards applied to the representation of sexuality in literature. How else can we understand the fact that, in the late Middle Ages, Chaucer's work was apparently acceptable to the full contemporary audience for literature, whereas by the end of the seventeenth century, parts of it were expurgated because of their alleged indecency? How else do we understand the dramatic shift from the sixteenth century, when Boccaccio and Rabelais were censured for their anticlericalism, rather than for their lustiness, to the late seventeenth century, when their frank depictions of sexuality had become inconceivable?

Note that in these descriptions of the seventeenth-century evolution in standards, I am speaking not of censorship, but of a far more efficient form of repressive reception: the self-censorship performed by writers on their own production and by readers on the works they and those around them were consuming. Self-censorship, moments at which a broad reading public, rather than simply an inner circle of literati and professional critics, intervenes to police literary decency, may well be the ultimate proof of the power of Counter-Reformation standards for decency.

The furor unleashed by Molière's *L'Ecole des femmes* was a watershed for this self-censorship. It is because of this massive performance of self-censorship as much as because of the creation in France of secular censorial machinery that I argue that modern obscenity is fundamentally different from all earlier material in which writers may have been trying to shock people with words. In his next play, *La Critique de "L'Ecole des femmes,"* Molière made both official censors and this self-censoring public a gift of a term with which to designate the phenomenon they were seeking to banish from literature: *obscénité*. In Molière's usage, *obscenity* had three meanings: a particular representation of sexuality in literature; literature as legal problem, as the object of official censorship; and literature as a veritable social phenomenon, a force capable of unleashing and even of helping define society's newfound need to censor the representation of sexuality.

In this last sense, literary obscenity played a crucial role in a process that has been analyzed under a variety of names by commentators from Michel Foucault to Norbert Elias. I have in mind here what may be the most significant turning point ever in the history of the discourse of sexuality, the moment at which an extraordinary continuum from antiquity to the sixteenth century—because of which, for example, Richlin is able to characterize Roman portrayals of sexuality and the body as "Rabelaisian" (xvi)—finally came to an end. For Elias, the line ends where what he terms "the civilizing process" begins: initially in France and then gradually throughout Europe, a heightened emphasis was placed on the values of what was promoted as social refinement, with a concomitant condemnation of any behavior that could be seen as uncivilized. The civilizing process is perhaps above all a monument to the significance of taboos—concerning bodily functions in particular—that previously were neither clearly established nor universally accepted: taboos were a necessary condition of its existence; it solidified numbers of taboos. Logically, no area became more taboo-ridden than the discourse about sexuality.

In his *History of Sexuality*, Foucault calls attention to the moment at which the discourse about sexuality began to be forced underground: "At the beginning of the seventeenth century a certain frankness was still common. . . . Calling sex by its name thereafter became more difficult and more costly" (3, 17). For Elias, this evolution was proof of the advances of civilization; histories of reading would use it to explain Chaucer's—or Rabelais's—sudden unacceptability.

For Foucault, of course, this repression was only surface-deep, less interesting than that which it covered up, a vast "incitement" to discourse, as a result of which a discourse about sexuality resurfaced elsewhere, for instance, in the questions confessors used to guide penitents to knowledge of their sins. The modern strain of sexually transgressive literature I will present here can be seen as one of these resurfacings: it began to take form just as the discourse of sexuality was officially silenced; the tradition grew in importance in direct proportion to the imposition of standards regulating linguistic decency.[37]

In this literary resurfacing, readers were gradually confronted with what became the most dramatic revision in the representation of sexuality since antiquity. To begin with, modern obscenity signals the arrival of what Foucault terms "a discursive existence" for previously unexplored areas of sexuality (*History of Sexuality*, 33). In particular, female sexuality became, for the first time, central to the configuration of obscenity. It displaced the range of male sexual practice that is virtually the only sexuality considered by literature that confronts the limits of sexual decency in the early modern period prior to 1650 as much as in antiquity. The modern obscene marks both the first in-depth portrayal ever of female sexuality and the first major realignment in the portrayal of male sexuality since antiquity.

Until the beginning of the civilizing process, the image of desire operative in antiquity was seldom challenged. Men—for, with remarkably few exceptions, the desiring subject was male—desire what they find desirable, boy or girl (the desiring subject is invariably an adult and the object of his desire is far younger). In tandem with the modern concept of obscenity, a far more nuanced and far less clear-cut vision of desire gradually came to replace the long-dominant image. Here are some of the possibilities contained in this vision: the age imbalance disappears, so that, virtually for the first time ever, mature women become players on the scene of desire; women were placed in the role of desiring subjects, able to articulate their desire and to describe its objects. These new possibilities had in turn many consequences for the portrayal of the sexualized body and, therefore, for the way in which obscenity would be redefined. Most notably, for the first time ever the mature female body was represented in the full range of its sexuality and was portrayed as desirable: the obsession with female genitalia—at times, virtually the exclusive focus of modern sexually transgressive literature—had begun.[38] Once, because of the advances of print culture, obscenity gradually escaped from the special place to which it had been confined, its content was thus radically redefined. It is even possible to imagine that some of that new content was being tried out in an explicit attempt to reach the new readers, particularly women, then becoming for the first time a factor in the literary market.

I hope it is obvious that I am speaking here exclusively about literature. Until recent decades, virtually the only evidence on which to base our ideas of how desire was defined at a given moment is found in the period's literary texts. Some periods, classical Rome for instance, give the impression of a fairly uniform image. When we consider the evidence gathered from sexually transgressive literature, seventeenth-century France seems a period in transition, as though different faces of desire were being tried out, perhaps even proposed as models that might influence real-life practices. For we can never rule out the possibility that these authors were test-marketing new images of desire, particularly with a segment of the print industry as tied to economic concerns as this one had to be.

During the first half of the seventeenth century, literary obscenity can be seen in many ways as in search of itself. Censorship played a crucial role in that search. The very fact of starting to forbid a new type of work, or of tightening control over certain subject matter in all publications, seems to have influenced authors and printer-booksellers: desire's new image was thus partially a construct suggested by censorship's machinery. The high-profile censorial interventions I will present here, which involved the extensive and public use of force, made instant classics of the books they sought to suppress. At this early stage in the game, that success never translated into significant financial profits: these were small, shabby operations, a far cry from the eighteenth-century situation, when authors and printer-booksellers had a great deal to gain from the celebrity conferred on a work by a public suppression. Nevertheless, the decades I will be describing initiated a myth, tenacious until the end of the Ancien Régime, that a prohibited book was a guaranteed best-seller. I suspect that the censorship of Molière's works—the first time that an author had made a spectacular profit from such an encounter—was the origin of this belief. Before the watershed in the history of censorship that Molière represents, however, writers did not choose to take on the machinery of censorship.[39] One aspect of censorship's publicity value was surely unexpected: originally conceived to regulate the activities of those who made books, by the mid-seventeenth century the institution increasingly focused attention on those who wrote them.

We have thus come full circle to the two other words that were taking on new meanings at the time of *obscenity*'s reinvention: *news* and *police*. Precisely during the decades when modern literary obscenity was emergent, the first French newsmen were beginning to use *nouvelle* to mean the news about which the public deserved to be informed and, in particular, the latest news, the hottest stories. Thus, beginning with Théophile de Viau's, all writers' trials received immediate press coverage. By the time Molière staged the drama of obscenity in *L'Ecole des femmes,* the original newshounds were following his moves so closely that they even scooped one of them. The first newsmen to try to exercise their profession without interference from the French state and in print—previously, subversive news circulated *à la main,* in manuscript—sensed a natural affinity with obscenity: both were trafficking in the dangerous democratization of knowledge.

In the 1660s, when the periodical press was finding its modern definition, a commission led by the king himself and Jean-Baptiste Colbert began to meet. It was because of reforms that it initiated that the word *police* would definitively take on its dominant modern meaning.[40] Until then, French usage had followed Greek, and *police* referred to the art of guaranteeing that the inhabitants of the *polis* enjoyed an ordered and tranquil existence. In this sense, *police* is directly related to Elias's notion of a civilizing process; France's evolution to a more "policed" society can be seen as part of this trajectory. Beginning in the mid-sixteenth century, the word occasionally referred as well to the administration that oversees that civic order. Then, during the second half of the seventeenth century, it began to designate, first, the officers of the police and, then, the often repressive force that we have in mind when we now speak of "the police."

This semantic drift reflected real institutional change: roughly in mid-century, the beginning of a modern police force became visible. Under Louis XIV and Colbert's guidance, for the first time in history, such an institution was formally established; it was also, for the first time anywhere, a totally independent institution. Beginning in 1667, there was considerable debate over whether the police should be primarily charged with preventing problems from occurring and over the extent to which the police should be able to function as a repressive force (Anglade, 48). Thus, the die was cast: *police* could designate the repressive arm of the law. Among the areas over which Nicolas de La Reynie (first Lieutenant General of the Police) and his officers were given authority, few offered such spectacular opportunities for a show of repressive force as the often unruly, even wildly seditious Parisian book trade. *Police* came into its modern usage partly to reflect the possibility for repressive action on the part of the book police against those who wrote, made, and sold books.

From 1660 to 1669, the percentage of prisoners in the Bastille coming from the world of print culture was higher than at any other time during the Ancien Régime, with the exception of 1750–1779, the most dangerous years for the spread of the Enlightenment. It was then that the crown must surely have realized that the situation was out of control and that its haphazard methods were insufficient; it was time for the radical change that led to the first book police anywhere.[41] Because I am concerned with the process by which the crown came to realize that institutionalized civil censorship had become essential, this study ends just as the massive crackdown that culminated in the creation of the book police was in full swing.

In France, literary obscenity and civil censorship thus came of age together. Between the moment near 1620 to which both can trace the origin of their modern form and the early 1660s, when they truly came into their own, the friction between the two institutions caused literary obscenity to be reinvented as a legal problem. In what follows, I will not, therefore, document the full canon of sexually transgressive writing but will be concerned solely with moments when obscenity and censorship clashed, with what Roland Barthes termed "the underside of [French literary] history: the history of its censorship" (1242).

Commentators such as David Pottinger have denied that obscene publications influenced the development of censorship. In early modern France, however, the two institutions moved forward at the same moments and always after they had collided in some spectacular way. I will, therefore, reconstruct the early history of censorship as if obscenity's causal role in that history were certain. I will juxtapose the development of regulations designed to control the French book trade and the censorship of three books publicly pronounced sexually transgressive, but always with the following restriction: I will never claim that a particular law was formulated as a direct response to a precise book or that a particular author was censored because a new restriction had just been issued.

As I worked my way through the legal record, I came to realize just how precious the surviving writers' trials really are: they may well be the only window remaining onto the reality of the first civil censorship. In these cases, the word *trial* must be used advisedly. The proceedings then initiated against authors were far less public and far less governed by established procedure than those we designate by the term. Transcripts were drawn up, however, so that, in these few cases at least, it is possible to feel that we can know the machinery of censorship. The cases have the same format: the supposed authors of bad books are arrested and imprisoned for extended periods of time. They are interrogated, at length and repeatedly, on the subject of their relation to these forbidden books. Other witnesses are called in and a "confrontation" is staged—the prisoner listens to the witnesses' testimony and responds to it. All these proceedings were recorded— in the third person, so that they read roughly "the accused denied that he

. . . ," and so forth. Each case is closed when a higher authority signs the final sheet, which records the sentence handed down. These transcripts reduce human drama to pure legalese, but we should not forget that the stakes were high. In the first cases I present, little could be pinned on the writers, but this didn't stop the authorities from exiling them, confiscating their property, and burning their books. Had they been convicted, they would almost certainly have been executed.

Anyone who deals with early modern legal history is quickly obliged to confront a basic dilemma: Are we able to conclude anything about the actual enforcement of specific laws from the fact that they were on the books? To what extent, in other words, was the day-to-day reality of a book trade professional seriously affected by the increasingly numerous regulations created by civil authorities? In the end, I concluded that this question cannot be answered with certainty. I did not arrive at this position quickly or easily. Instead, I first spent months puzzling over how it could be that each account of censorship's early history gives an at least slightly different version of the way it was, in particular, of when existing laws were enforced.

There is good reason for this confusion, the most obvious being the glaring lack of primary sources. In key archives—in particular, those of the Bastille and the Chancellery (home to the primary precursors of the book police)—almost no material pertaining to the seventeenth century survives. This explains why (though this is rarely stressed) modern studies of Ancien Régime censorship present the institution as it functioned in the eighteenth century, when we know more or less how existing laws were enforced. (In the eighteenth century, censorship laws were often enforced with admirable efficiency—hence the myth of the rigors of French censorship.)[42] For the seventeenth century, and the fact cannot be adequately emphasized, almost no concrete evidence remains. The only sources we do have present a picture strikingly different from that suggested by the legal record.

My view of censorship fell into place when I discovered what I came to believe may be the only reliable source on the functioning of the book trade in seventeenth-century France, a remarkable 1694 volume by André Chevillier, *L'Origine de l'imprimerie de Paris*. As lifelong librarian of the Sorbonne, Chevillier was deeply implicated in the contemporary book trade and, in particular, in the struggle between religious and secular censorship that was crucial to obscenity's reinvention. Chevillier's is the only contemporary account that does more than merely list all relevant legislation: he also explains what motivated certain decisions. Most crucial, however, is his honesty: time and again, Chevillier cites a law only to admit that it was never enforced. Once my attention had been drawn to Chevillier's caveats, I began to take more seriously the almost incessant refrain found in seventeenth-century censorship law. Repeatedly, those issuing a new ordinance begin by saying that the crown is obliged to pass this edict because the previous one on the same subject has had no effect. By the time I had completed the research for this project, I had serious doubts about whether there had been anything more than short bursts of prepublication censorship before La Reynie came to power in 1667.

It is hard to know how to explain the chasm that apparently existed between legal record and legal reality. Many points seem to have been intensely and protractedly debated. Could this energetic debate have given some the impression that practical applications were in effect? Could some authorities have hoped that this impression alone might impose a certain order? Or is it possible that those with the authority to initiate censorship had reservations about this approach to regulating the book trade?

To illustrate just how tricky the situation can get, I will quickly present one example, that of what should have been the crucial tool of prepublication censorship, the official royal permission to publish. In February 1566, article 78 of the Edict of Moulins—issued in response to Protestantism's recent romp through the French print industry—decreed that, henceforth, no book could be printed "without our permission and letters of privilege granted by the Keeper of the Seal." The edict uses two terms, *permission* and *privilege*, that, in theory, designated distinct procedures with different goals. First, a manuscript was to be submitted to an officially designated reader or censor (from 1629 on, laws use these terms interchangeably) who, if the manuscript was found in no way objectionable, would grant a permission to publish. Once permission had been granted, someone—usually the would-be publisher but at times the author, who then negotiated with publishers—had to apply for the right to be the work's exclusive publisher, a monopoly granted for a fixed period of time and known as the privilege. From 1566 on, laws were issued and reissued at regular intervals, declaring that this process had to be respected and regulating one or another aspect of its enforcement. Any modern scholar could be forgiven for taking these increasingly detailed laws at face value, for believing that they knew what the rules were at any given moment, and what the penalties were for failing to observe them.

In point of fact, however, this clear process seems almost never to have functioned according to plan, principally because the basic distinction between permission and privilege was not maintained. In theory, censorship should have been confined to the permission-granting process, and the privilege should have functioned solely to protect publishers' rights. In actuality, however, there is no hard evidence that the permission had more than a sporadic existence before the eighteenth century. Particularly in late-sixteenth-century edicts, but persistently in seventeenth-century ones as well, the terms *permission* and *privilege* are confused. All too often, they seem to have been conflated. Throughout the seventeenth century, it appears to have been understood by practitioners and censors of the book trade alike that the privilege, without losing its economic function of granting a publication monopoly, at the same time conveyed a permission to publish.[43]

The next problem area is that of record keeping. In April 1653 the Parisian Parliament required all publishers to register privileges in the logbook of the Parisian Community of Printers. Predictably, there was a gaping hole between law and reality: registration did not begin immediately, and throughout the seventeenth century, it was carried out only occasionally. This means that, even if we accept that the privilege did function as a tool of censorship, little evidence has survived to document this role.[44]

Chevillier—who comments extensively on the privilege and obviously considers it the principal censorial mechanism—confirms the image left by the official logbook. He stresses on a number of occasions that, no matter how many laws concerning state-controlled prepublication screening were issued, "the Chancellor's office often made no effort to enforce them, particularly in war time" (396–97)—and we know how often France was at war during the seventeenth century! Chevillier also describes the many tricks devised by publishers for getting around the system when it was in effect, what he calls "surprising" the privilege; for instance, some printed fake privileges using fictive names (972–73).

In the long run, all surviving evidence relating to censorship's enforcement convinced me that, for the most part, in seventeenth-century France modern censorship was invented as a Potemkin village, a façade of bureaucratic efficiency. Its various dysfunctional aspects had important consequences for the development of the French book trade. Perhaps the most crucial result was that censorship and economic interests, which would have been kept apart had the permission system functioned as originally intended, became in fact intimately connected. The authors I will present here came in various ways to firsthand knowledge of this intertwinement: because the privilege system did not function properly, rapacious printer-booksellers published authors' works without their consent, thereby depriving them of any profits; at the same time, authors were often blamed for the dealings of printer-booksellers who considered only economic potential and never the author's safety.

Following Foucault's lead, recent commentators have asserted that censorship helped create the modern author, and I will have occasion to discuss ways in which this is true. In other ways, however, the ineffective censorship system forced this role upon French authors. Unless they assumed responsibility for their printed works—rather than simply being assigned authorial status as had happened to noted figures in earlier periods—they could suffer both important loss of revenue and serious legal consequences. By the early 1660s, when the situation had become so unruly that the crown began contemplating the creation of a police force, Molière was in a position to become the first modern writer because he understood three interrelated phenomena: the new ways in which the contemporary book trade was becoming profitable, the inevitability of a systematized institution of censorship, and the appearance of a new kind of transgressive literature. Thus, the celebrity of the most famous writer in the French tradition was partly founded on *obscénité*, that is, obscenity reinvented in a guise that—because it was intimately bound up with issues such as female genitalia and birth control—would surely have seemed incomprehensible to practitioners of literary obscenity in antiquity.

In the following pages, I will tell three stories. The first is that of a sonnet by Théophile de Viau that, through the combined machineries of censorship and print, became an early warning signal of the nascent taboos that would redefine the representation of sexuality. The second is that of the first work of modern literary obscenity, a novel called *L'Ecole des filles,* which kept censors scurrying for three decades. This novel introduced various new publics—from Samuel Pepys to the ladies-in-waiting of Louis XIV's court—to textual pleasures previously reserved for aristocratic males. The last is a double tale that took place just as Louis XIV was beginning the involvement with Versailles that would found French court culture and the civilizing process: Molière's run-in with rogue printer-booksellers led him to take on the issue of the nascent taboos that were helping define modern literary obscenity, and his decision in turn helped found tabloid journalism. With the plays Molière produced in 1663 and the furor they unleashed, we can watch a society redefining the limits it set around the printing of what D. H. Lawrence termed "the words that shock so much." By re-creating these stories, I hope to show that obscenity and censorship were constitutive experiences for what is known as the Golden Age of French culture. From there, truly inseparable, they began their relentless invasion of the scene of our modernity.

I

Male Practices

THÉOPHILE DE VIAU'S
"SODOMITE SONNET"

He viewed life as a four-letter word.
—Lenny Bruce's obituary,
Time Magazine, August 12, 1966

The trial of the poet Théophile de Viau in 1623 is a milestone both in the reinvention of obscenity and in the history of censorship. This was the moment at which censorship began to assume its modern form, becoming both secularized, an authority under state control, and institutionalized, an authority that followed established procedures. Théophile dallied with sexually transgressive literature at just the wrong moment: he thereby became the first writer to undergo a thoroughly modern writer's trial. To understand its modernity, one need only think of what seems the closest precedent to Théophile's case, the suppression in Italy, exactly a century earlier, of Aretino's *Sonetti Lussuriosi;* that censorship, controlled entirely by the Vatican, was anything but systematic.[1] Similarly, in France until the 1620s, the Church had exercised almost exclusive control over the institution of censorship: when writers were prosecuted, it was because of a perceived lack of religious orthodoxy in their work.[2]

With Théophile's case—surely more by accident than by design—a new model began to be put into place. Even though he was prosecuted at least partly because the subject matter of his work was considered heretical, and even though religious factions did exert influence on the proceedings, the case against Théophile de Viau was managed exclusively by civil authorities. In addition, although the case unfolded in a fashion that could hardly be considered systematic by subsequent censorial standards, it does provide the first clear evidence that censors were beginning to recognize the necessity of established procedures in their work. Both the grounds on which books could be suppressed and the terminology that could be used to justify those suppressions were obviously being reconsidered. Partly because of this nascent desire for censorial bureaucracy and partly because Théophile provoked further debate about the nature of the enterprise (his testimony indicates that he sensed that the sands of censorship were shifting around him and that this encouraged him to question his censors' tactics), the trial proceedings also provide a commentary on the first modern censorial machine even as it was being established. Théophile's trial is a monument in the history of censorship for still another reason: when it is considered in the context of the dramatic legal changes concerning that institution that were debated in the years just prior to and immediately following it, we see clearly how rapidly the desire to secularize censorship took root in France.

It is no surprise, therefore, that these legal proceedings are remarkably complex, nor that, despite obvious differences, they resemble something still recognizable as a writer's trial, even by today's vastly different standards for such enterprises. What is surprising, especially in view of the general state of seventeenth-century French archives relating to the suppression of books considered dangerous, is that the proceedings appear to be remarkably complete. In them are already evident the vexed issues that continue to dog the major French writers' trials (those of Baudelaire and Flaubert, to cite but the most spectacular): first, the question of whether the man is on trial at the same time as his work; and second, the problem of indecency's peculiar status as an offense somehow both religious and secular, a problem French law never successfully negotiated.

In the end, the state eliminated the man widely considered the leading freethinker of his generation. In so doing, Théophile's judges may truly have believed that they were following a model established by the Inquisition and thereby saving France from a threat to religious orthodoxy. After all, the landmark trials of freethinkers were hardly far in the past. Surely the spectacular case of Giordano Bruno's execution by the Inquisition in Rome on February 17, 1600, could not yet have been forgotten.[3] The judges appointed by the Parisian parliament were, however, hardly grand inquisitors; issues of religious orthodoxy were quickly and systematically displaced by the question of where the frontier defining sexual decency should be traced and, above all, by the issue of the types of sexual practice to be allowed to reside within those confines. Théophile proved to be the "example"—the term always used to justify the execution of those pronounced heretics—that allowed the first sexual inquisitors to indicate both that obscenity's modern era was about to begin and that censorship had begun to assume its modern guise.

During the four-year period from 1619 to 1623, near the end of his short life, Théophile de Viau (better known then as now simply as Théophile) was continually coming into conflict with both religious and secular authorities. Precisely at that moment, the crown was seeking to bring the French book trade under tighter control. Théophile was a recently converted Protestant. In addition, his trial took place relatively soon after the late-sixteenth-century wars of religion, during which Protestantism had become, as at no other time, a major threat to the French state religion and during which the powerful Protestant book trade constituted an important part of the religious menace. These facts cannot have been far from his accusers' thoughts.[4] Indeed, all the proceedings against him reveal the extent to which, prior to the establishment of the book police in 1667, it was difficult, at times impossible, to disengage the danger of literature from its menace to religious orthodoxy, even when the literature on trial was not dangerous on what we would now consider religious grounds.

Théophile's trial helps us pinpoint the confusion, between literature as religious threat and literature as secular threat, that was fundamental to the censorship of print culture in early modern France. It was the widespread and rapid circulation of Protestant literature *in French* subsequent to the previously unheard of print-runs and sales in German that prompted François I to impose strict controls on the nascent French print industry. It was this same sweeping success of Protestant publications *in French* that led, in 1544, to the establishment of the first French index of forbidden books. Thus, secular authorities and religious authorities began to clamp down on the French book trade at the same time and for the same reasons. For the next two and a half centuries, they continued to fight over the turf and never completely managed to sort out the limits of jurisdiction. Until the end of the Ancien Régime, for example, the index was often used to censor works whose threat was not only and not always primarily religious.[5] The first incursions of the obscene into print culture prove just how confused the situation had become, seventy-five years after the struggle for control over book censorship had begun.

The confusion between religious and secular issues that permeates the case against Théophile may have resulted in part because the same years during which Théophile was on trial—1619–1623—marked an essential, perhaps *the* essential moment in the early modern history of French print censorship for two reasons: (1) it was at this time that the authorities first seriously considered implementing rules and regulations, some of which had been on the books for a century or more; and (2) these years were significant in the transition from church to state control over print censorship—never again would the battle lines be so sharply drawn as at this time. The possibility of secular censorship was first considered during the second half of the sixteenth century. Finally, just as Théophile was going to trial and as the publications for which he was tried were appearing, the first lay censors were named to try to bring an increasingly unmanageable situation under control—and religious censors fought back. Thus, the case against the poet unfolded against the backdrop of a struggle for power over the institution of censorship.

Théophile's trial makes three things clear. First, the modern obscene would not have taken shape as it did, and perhaps not at all, without the decisive role of print culture. Second, whereas all censors, civil and religious alike, claimed to be interested only in religious issues, they were really more concerned with trying to convict Théophile of sexual crimes. Third, their obsession with Théophile's sexuality, in particular with what we would now term his sexual orientation, ultimately played a crucial role in giving obscenity its modern form.

Théophile's troubles began with his first exile, ordered by Louis XIII in 1619, an exile that appears not to have been enforced. In its account of the king's activities during 1619, *Le Mercure français* called Théophile an "atheist poet" and described his poetry as "unworthy of a Christian as much because of its beliefs as because of its filth" (*indigne d'un Chrétien tant en croyances qu'en saletés,* 65).[6] The double confusion that put the state's case against Théophile on a shaky foundation is already evident in this first attack. To begin with, the authorities were consistently unwilling or unable to distinguish between a threat to the religious order (*croyances*) and a threat to the moral order (*saletés*). In addition, in their attempts to condemn Théophile's work on any grounds *other* than religious, they were never able to get beyond vague terms such as *filth* or to define in any way his actual crime.

Théophile's trial is a significant moment in the history of bad books because his work is not particularly threatening according to any of the rules then governing the censorship of literary texts. Not only is Théophile's work not essentially blasphemous, but it should not have been perceived as sexually shocking in the contemporary context. In fact, Théophile may have been the initial victim of a fundamental shift in the standards for decency, a shift that played a key role in the invention of modern obscenity.

Théophile appears to have been the first French author whose career was amputated because of the awakening desire on the part of all would-be censors for the category now known as the obscene.

In late 1622 or early 1623, a collective volume, *Le Parnasse des poètes satiriques*, appeared without a privilege.[7] The volume belonged to a then reasonably familiar type, the various verse collections, usually called *parnasses* or *cabinets* (though sometimes also *délices* or *quintessence*), a series of which had been published, sometimes even with a privilege, in the late sixteenth century and until around 1615. Many volumes with similar names contain no sexually transgressive poetry; all those that do have the adjective *satirique* in their title. A specialist on French erotica, Pascal Pia, describes these "satirical" compilations as displaying "an exaggerated and joyful *gauloiserie*" (1:12), by which he means, just as was the case in England at the same time, that a degree of sexual explicitness which might seem surprising today was then acceptable. In Pia's view, this was the case because the so-called Gallic poetry, the French bawdy, was always accompanied by overtly comic intent.[8] This widely held view does nothing, however, to account for the bawdy's strange history in France, in particular for the fact that, comic or not, the tolerance for it suddenly came to an abrupt end.[9]

These compilations were apparently largely the work of the printer-booksellers who published them and sold them out of their bookshops; they were thus closely tied to market concerns. It appears that the publishers simply gathered together poems that had already circulated in print or in manuscript, generally without even notifying the poets responsible for them. Their casual attitude indicates that no one in the print world expected to encounter any difficulties with censorship because of these publications. Certainly this was true in the case of the 1622 edition of *Le Parnasse des poètes satiriques*. The publishers were so confident of doing business as usual that they had not even bothered to inform the author of a sonnet being published here for the first time, an author whose recognition value was such that, in a time-honored marketing strategy, his name was featured on the volume's first page, just before his poem: *Le Parnasse des poètes satiriques, ou dernier recueil en vers piquants et gaillards de notre temps. SONNET. Par le Sieur Théophile.*[10] As for the poet whose name was thus exploited, initially he clearly shared the view that this was a low-risk venture: Théophile eventually did get around to lodging a complaint against the publisher—he protested that his name should not have been used to promote a volume without his authorization—he did so, however, only months later, once the censorship process had already been initiated.

It's easy to see why no one thought that the 1622 *parnasse* would be treated differently from earlier collections of bawdy verse: it seems truly indistinguishable from those that no one had prosecuted. These collective volumes are all remarkably similar: they include numerous (several hundred) short poems, some of them attributed to well-known poets, most of them anonymous. The poems' content is varied; most seem in no way worthy of censorship. Among the daring ones, few try to scandalize in religious terms, whereas many are explicitly sexual. Of these, most are merely what might be called a bit risqué; only a minority are truly sexually transgressive. Those that are achieve this status by being totally *frontal*, centered on the overwhelming, unrelenting repetition of what are known in English as four-letter words: *fuck* (*foutre*), *cock* (*vit*), and *cunt* (*con*) are by far the most prominently displayed, with the first two occurring much more frequently than the third.

These four-letter words, primary obscenities, stand out as the principal mark of this bawdy poetry's sexual transgressiveness. With one exception, *cul* (ass), which was to become key in Théophile's case, they are never written out.[11] Instead, in an act of self-censorship that initially may have helped save the volumes from official prosecution, the words were abbreviated in various ways, and different types of punctuation were inserted to stand as a visual mark representing the suppressed content. This punctuation is the typographical equivalent of the fig leaves that began appearing in Renaissance engravings to veil male and female genitalia without fully hiding their contours.

The typographical fig leaves are, however, less efficient than their visual counterparts. A leaf painted on a representation of a human body means that the viewer, even though he or she obviously knows what presumably is there behind the cover-up, is nevertheless denied the right to see the offending sexual characteristics. In the case of a text, however, a reader—and there is no reason to imagine that seventeenth-century readers were any more conscious of these textual barriers than are their counterparts today—simply replaces the missing letters without a thought, so much so that he or she is immediately unaware that anything has been left out.[12] This is truly the zero-degree of censorship. Since, however, it obviously served an important function, I will consider it for a moment more. What follows may seem too detailed for this early stage of my argument, but its importance should soon become clear.

In sixteenth-century France, before secular censorship was even a theoretical reality and when the bawdy was in full flower, the problem of the four-letter word was negotiated in very different fashion. Poets twisted characters around within the words designating primary obscenities; confronted with a nonsense term, readers automatically rearranged the letters to reveal the four-letter word. Thus, to continue with the example of the term that became particularly problematic for Théophile, *cul* became *luc* in the expression *jouer du luc*. No letters were elided, so there was no need for any typographical symbol to designate an omission.

By the time the bawdy anthologies came along, the conventions for self-censorship were changing. Either poets or printers, or perhaps poets and printers together, decided to omit letters in the four-letter words whose status would, in the course of the *parnasses'* history and around Théophile's trial, be radically transformed.[13] From terms that, at the beginning of the seventeenth century, were considered inoffensive enough *to the audience for which these collections were intended* that they could be printed with only the most minimal of veils, these words became, before the century's end, totally unprintable—except, that is, in works certain to be immediately pursued by censorship. The brief span of time during which the "satirical" verse collections continued to appear marks a strange moment in the history of punctuation: once the decision was made to suppress some letters in each four-letter word, the need was clearly felt for a typographical code to guarantee that readers understood what was going on.

I first noticed this printerly creativity when I was looking for differences among the various collections, trying to understand why a type of sexually explicit poetry previously tolerated suddenly became intolerable. I noted only two changes, the first involving the punctuation of four-letter words. Prior to the moment when censorship was imminent, no effort was made to be systematic. Then, in 1618, just as Théophile's troubles were beginning, printers initiated the code that remained in place until the end of the collections' history. *Vit* (prick) and *con* (cunt) are simply truncated to v. and c., a typographical practice that remains invariable. The case of *foutre* (fuck) is, however, more interesting. From the beginning, printers decided that none of the then available forms of punctuation would do, probably because the poets intended, just as Lenny Bruce did three and a half centuries later, to display the word in its full grammatical range. They thus printed the initial *f* and the ending that allows the reader to tell if it is being used as noun, verb, or adjective.

This left one question: How to represent typographically the excised letters? At first, in the 1618 *cabinet*, for example, all sorts of combinations are found: two dashes, two periods, two dashes and a period. Then, beginning with the 1622 *parnasse*, the compilation that provoked secular censorship's first involvement with sexually transgressive literature, the visual mark that signaled suppressed content was standardized: "..." Thus, about a century before the ellipsis is thought to have existed in printing, at a time when the sign is not mentioned in treatises on punctuation, it was

invented by the printers and typographers who were in the process of trying to bring sexually transgressive literature out of the "secret *cabinets*" to
which its circulation had previously been confined and into the hands of a
broader audience.[14]

The printers responsible for this invention clearly believed, as did Lenny
Bruce, that *foutre* was the ur-obscenity, the most radical test case for typography and for censorship alike. Théophile's case was to prove them
both right and wrong. In thinking about the way he was brought to trial
for his poetry, it occurred to me that the systematization of the ellipsis may
have brought the abundant presence of four-letter words into sharper focus. The printers could thus have been signaling their awareness that the
printing of these terms with only the slightest typographical veil was soon
no longer to be a mere game, as it had been since the invention of printing.
Théophile's case was soon to prove that giving primary obscenities, the
names for the most private body parts, a public existence in print could
have potentially deadly consequences.[15]

Thus, the as yet nameless ellipsis—the typographical convention for an
intentional omission, in this case, the sign of a verbal taboo, of something
that cannot be printed—and modern censorship began to be tried out at
the same time. This simultaneity may have been entirely accidental; however, given that the ellipsis and secular censorship continued to share a history throughout the Ancien Régime, it is hard to think that this is entirely
true. The ellipsis, the substitution of a visual mark for suppressed content,
can be seen as calling attention both to that content and to the act of its
suppression. It is as if the printers were somehow asking for the official
censorship that came down on the volumes virtually as soon as the new typographical sign of intentional omission began to be standardized.

Their first censor clearly believed that this was the case. The Jesuit
Garasse, whose inspirational role I will soon retrace, saw the ellipsis as attracting his attention to the abundance of four-letter words. He charm-
ingly defined the typographical invention as typeface's revolt against the
task corrupt authors were attempting to assign it. The blanks in the text
were the sign of a resistance on the part of the characters that should have
spelled out the primary obscenities: "feeling ill at ease under the press,"
they had simply refused to ink out "the most indecent words."[16]

The causal relation between printing decisions and secular censorship
that the ellipsis may point to seems more certain in the case of a second
question relating to the volumes' appearance on the eve of Théophile's
trial. On a sheet added when the Arsenal library's copy of the 1618 *cabinet*
was rebound in the nineteenth century, the edition is described as "poorly
printed and on bad paper," to which a subsequent commentator added:

"Very badly printed on appalling paper." And so it is: even the 1666 Dutch Elzevier, hardly a luxury edition, used paper of far higher quality. This appears to have been the last edition of the *cabinet* before the watershed of Théophile's trial; related volumes from the same moment are of the same ilk. Thus, the 1620 *parnasse,* the final one *not* to have been prosecuted, is so poorly printed that it is full of lines of typeface on which the ink runs off. The copy of the 1622 edition (the one that was prosecuted) found in the French National Library has the most primitive title page imaginable; the title and the date are extremely crudely printed and placed far too high on the page. Indeed, the entire volume shows signs of having been hastily produced.[17]

The crude printing that characterizes these collections during the years just prior to the censors' intervention could well indicate an attempt to produce less expensive volumes, and thereby to reach out to a wider audience than had been imagined for the earliest collections. The pretrial compilations have none of the marks of more expensive editions destined for an elite readership in which early modern sexually transgressive poetry had previously appeared: no engravings adorn them; the 1613 edition is the last *cabinet* to have a frontispiece.[18] Unlike the previous prince of erotic poetry, Aretino, Théophile could never have hoped to see his sonnets linked to luxury engravings.

The notion of the intentional production of less expensive editions would help explain the biggest mystery surrounding these compilations— why, beginning with the 1622 *Parnasse satirique,* they became the target of censorship and why, from this point on, the French bawdy began to be judged indecent. It could be that *le gaulois* was tolerated by sixteenth- and early seventeenth-century authorities as long as it could be seen as conforming to its self-image: a discourse about sex for a public of like-minded men (hence the overwhelmingly phallic nature of the representation of sexuality). *Le gaulois* was the last erotic discourse created when literature still circulated only among the elite, within spaces to which they controlled all access. Many volumes of *gaulois* verse are called *cabinets;* on their title page others advertise their poetry as "coming from their authors' secret *cabinets*" (studies), indicating that they were earmarked for the private pleasures of gentlemen wealthy enough to enjoy them within the confines of spaces reserved exclusively for their private pleasures. This was thus a genre initially created for an audience both known and exclusive. To offer this verse to a nonelite audience, to unknown readers, in less expensive editions, was to make an insider sexual code available to outsiders and thereby to threaten to corrupt new publics. Certainly, after the recent Protestant romp through the French book trade, anxiety must have been high among authorities, both religious and secular, with regard to print's ability to produce converts. And in this case, if converts were produced, it would be in the realm of sexuality.

The first measures designed to regulate the French print industry had been a direct response to the Protestant menace (Martin, *Livre, pouvoirs et société*, 1:51). The most important of these early measures, the Edict of Gaillon, stipulated that printers and publishers had to institute preventive self-censorship: two printers and two publishers, chosen by their colleagues, would be entrusted with the task of preventing the publication of undesirable works. The Edict of Gaillon was issued in 1571, but no steps were taken to enforce it before 1618, when the Parisian Community of Printers, Publishers, and Binders (the guild equivalent to the English Stationers' Company) was founded, sixty-one years after its English counterpart. In the summer of 1618, the guild's statutes were registered with Parliament, which discussed their enforcement.[19]

As I stated in my introduction, we know next to nothing about the actual enforcement of prepublication censorship in seventeenth-century France. It is thus impossible to know whether any of the statutes to which I refer in this chapter, statutes designed to determine control over the institution, actually changed the modalities of censorship. The existence of these laws does mean, however, that, during the period between 1618 and 1623, civil authorities were concerned enough over recent developments in the book trade to imagine new measures that would attempt to tighten its regulation and that, in particular, they were concerned enough to decide that it was at long last time to wrest control over censorship out of the hands of religious authorities. In this chapter, I will track the heightened fears and anxieties that made more systematic, secular censorship first seem desirable. Whenever possible, I will expose the potential causes of those anxieties, such as the apparent publication strategy behind the *parnasses* that were the initial target of the new secular censors.

It is, therefore, par for the course that we don't know how seriously the 1618 statutes governing the new Printers' Guild were taken. (The answer seems to be: probably not very seriously.) They mark, nevertheless, the moment at which a number of measures were initiated that remained central to the regulation of print culture in France until the Revolution.[20] It was then, for example, that the authorities began to limit the number of master printers, a policy that would be ever more strictly enforced at the time of each new development in the creation of modern obscenity. (It was felt, in France as in England, that a large number of master printers would never find sufficient legitimate work and that limiting their number would help ensure that only approved manuscripts got into print.) It was also at this time that the elected representatives of the Community of Printers were assigned the task of making sure that no book was printed without an official royal permission to publish and that each printed book bore both a copy of the privilege and the name of its publisher. Before printing a book, the publisher was to register the title and the author's name in the register of the Community; he had also to show "the certificate given by those who have seen the book" (Bouchel, 61–63).

The 1618 statutes have a symbolic significance far greater than the sum of their parts: they marked the beginning of censorship's passage from religious to secular control. Prior to this point, it had been the exclusive domain of the doctors of theology at the university. From this time on, the king and his officers would assume ever greater responsibility. Power was not yielded without a struggle: several decades passed before a definitive solution was worked out, under which the Sorbonne retained the right to approve only theological publications. This long power struggle undoubtedly delayed the effective implementation of many new measures, those outlined in the 1618 code and subsequent ones as well. Nevertheless, already in July 1618 the writing was on the wall: the book trade was coming under secular control. And just as soon as censorship officially passed into secular hands, works of literature first began to be judged sexually indecent.

The 1618 code can help explain a number of nagging questions: why the 1618 edition of *Le Parnasse satirique*, published just before the statutes were registered, was the last one *not* to run into difficulty; why the next edition, in late 1622, was the first to be prosecuted; why Théophile began to be persecuted in 1619; and, finally, why, when he failed to heed the warning that persecution was intended to transmit and was again associated with dangerous publications in 1623, he was put on trial. The publications cited during his trial are just the kind the statutes were designed to prevent: they contained no privilege and their title pages mentioned neither author nor publisher.[21]

The moment at which the French bawdy was no longer tolerated and began to be repressed was a period when societal standards and cultural taboos related to the representation of sexuality appear to have been in flux, an essential origin of what Norbert Elias termed "the civilizing process." It was also a key moment in the history of French censorship. It's impossible to know which came first: Did the evolution in cultural standards bear some responsibility for the prominence suddenly given statutes first decreed a half-century earlier? Or did the conception of new standards for censorship help provoke the creation of taboos? This much is clear: rules and regulations first put on the books in response to the invasion of Protestantism finally began to be taken seriously in response to a new threat to print culture, that of sexually transgressive literature.

The earliest history of print culture in France, by André Chevillier in 1694, teaches us that the 1618 statutes did little to curb the unruly French book trade (573). In March 1623 Louis XIII, concerned over the lack of censorship, took another decisive step toward secularizing the institution: he made the first of a series of attempts to name official readers or censors (Chevillier, 396). He thereby set off an outcry on the part of the doctors of the Faculty of Theology. In December 1623, in fact, they published their own countercode in opposition to recent attempts to secularize censorship (Chevillier, 397). It is against this backdrop—of a perceived need for more effective censorship and of a struggle between secular and religious factions for the right to designate those who were to be in charge of the newly forceful institution—that Théophile and the *Parnasse satirique* became the first author and the first work to put the nascent system to a test.

The evolving language of censorship must have been responsible for some of the confusion that surrounded this first modern book trial. In 1571 the Edict of Gaillon provides for the censorship only of works judged "libelous" (*diffamatoires*). In 1586 the territory to be policed is enlarged to include works felt to be "heretical or against the Holy Catholic Church." In 1618 measures were to be taken to stop the printing of works in both these categories and a third as well, "scandalous books." It was in this as yet ill-defined middle territory that the French bawdy and Théophile's work were situated.

In France, Théophile's trial provided the definitive signal that the tolerance for the explicit expression of sexuality was coming to an abrupt end. The process that led to Théophile's involvement with censorship began three months before Louis XIII's decision to name official censors had set off a struggle between printers and priests, with the appearance of the December 1622 version of the *Parnasse satirique*, the first such compilation to include his work. The volume's lead poem, previously unpublished, is identified as a *sonnet par le sieur Théophile:*

> *Phylis, tout est ...outu je meurs de la vérole,*
> *Elle exerce sur moi sa dernière rigueur:*
> *Mon V. baisse la tête et n'a point de vigueur*
> *Un ulcère puant a gâté ma parole.*
>
> *J'ai sué trente jours, j'ai vomi de la colle*
> *Jamais de si grands maux n'eurent tant de longueur*
> *L'esprit le plus constant fût mort à ma langueur,*
> *Et mon affliction n'a rien qui la console.*

Mes amis plus secrets ne m'osent approcher
Moi-même en cet état je ne m'ose toucher,
Phylis, le mal me vient de vous avoir ...tue.

Mon Dieu, je me repens d'avoir si mal vécu:
Et si votre courroux à ce coup ne me tue,
Je fais voeux désormais de ne ...tre qu'en cul.

Phylis, everything is all ...ucked up; I'm dying of syphilis,
It's attacking me with all its might:
My C. lowers its head and has no strength
A stinking ulcer has spoiled my speech.

I sweated for thirty days, I vomited paste
Never did such great pains last for so long
The most steadfast spirit would have died from such languor,
And my affliction has nothing to console it.

My most intimate friends do not dare come near me
Even I do not dare touch myself in this state,
Phylis, I caught the disease from ...ing you.

My God, I repent of having so badly lived:
And if your anger does not kill me this time,
I swear from now on to ...ck only in the ass.[22]

Gaulois indeed. With this display of the verb *fuck* in all its forms, Théophile prefigures Lenny Bruce.[23] More precisely, the sonnet seems tailor-made to show off the new code for printing primary obscenities. It flaunts throughout the word considered most dangerous, the term for which the ellipsis had just been invented; it ends with a particularly spectacular display of the *cul*, the asshole, the one orifice whose name, according to the code then in place, could be written out. With the ostentatious distribution of four-letter words in his sonnet, Théophile makes it impossible for his reader to overlook the limit defining sexual decency, the distinction between that which could be printed and that which had to be replaced by a typographical convention. In the process, as the censors immediately understood, he turned the tables on customary wisdom.

That someone, probably the publisher, believed that *fuck* would be the key obscenity is evident from the decision to suppress, for the first time ever in French bawdy poetry, the initial *f* in *foutre*, as well as the central *ou*, so that, for once, the reader has to think just a bit before filling in the blank (see figure 1). Indeed, *foutre*'s initial appearance in the sonnet, in which

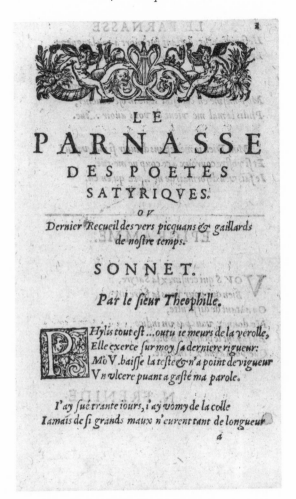

FIGURE 1   First page of *Parnasse des poètes satyriques* (Paris: A. de Sommaville, 1622). Courtesy of the Bibliothèque Nationale de France, Paris.

only the *f* is excised, seems to acknowledge this difficulty. Once the game has been made plain to the reader, the ellipsis replaces all but the final letters. The subsequent trial proceedings, however, confirm Théophile's instinct: this flaunting of the joy of printing *foutre* did not signal the beginning of modern obscenity. In this case, the gender-neutral orifice, the opening traditionally overlooked by French typographers because it was considered safe from censorship, became the truly dangerous body part. Indeed, the modern institution of censorship may well have been jolted into existence because of Théophile's flagrant display of the *cul*—and, in particular, because of his decision to attract attention to that orifice's poly-morphousness.

Given the sonnet's content—which Théophile himself described as *sale* (Prévot, 3)—the condemnation of *Le Parnasse satirique* on grounds of "im-piety and blasphemy" seems, to say the least, curious. Frédéric Lachèvre takes the charge at face value and portrays the trial's stakes as purely reli-gious, a skirmish in the battle to suppress freethinking in France. Those in charge of this case seem to have believed that the transition from religious to secular censorship would take place without difficulty, but they could hardly have been more wrong. In the course of his defense, Théophile forced them to confront some of the new anxieties responsible for the de-sire to put censorship under civil control.

But I am getting ahead of myself, because the bawdy compilation was not immediately condemned, and Théophile might have got off scot-free, had his publication record remained clean, at least for a time. In June 1623, however, just when the battle for control over censorship between religious and secular candidates was heating up, Pierre Billaine (who had also pub-lished several *Cabinets satiriques*) brought out the *Œuvres du sieur Théo-phile, seconde partie*. This slim volume contains at least one work, "Première journée" (a magnificent and perhaps unfinished first-person prose fiction), upon which it was just barely possible to hang the kind of charge—"impi-ety and blasphemy"—that would be leveled against the *Parnasse's* sexually crude verse. For example, in the "Première journée," the narrator describes his visit to the home of a woman said to be possessed (possession was just as highly charged an issue for seventeenth-century France as it was for the contemporary Anglo-Saxon world); in addition, he and one of his com-panions fail to remove their hats when a religious procession goes by.[24] Scenes such as these might not seem like much, but they at least do some-thing the sonnet to Phylis does not: provide a link, in print, between a known freethinker and a lack of religious orthodoxy—thereby encourag-ing the confusion, basic to these proceedings, between censorship on fa-miliar, religious grounds and censorship on unfamiliar, secular grounds.

The following month, a civil authority, the Parisian Parliament, issued an arrest order in which only *Le Parnasse satirique* was named. They went after several poets included in the collection, two of whom would be singled out for punishment: Théophile and Guillaume Colletet. (Some thirty-five years later, when this arrest order was just a bad memory, Col-letet first used *obscene* in its modern meaning, while warning poets of the dangers they faced if they indulged in sexually transgressive literature.) The two poets immediately fled Paris, thereby avoiding imprisonment (Lachèvre, 132). When it came time for sentencing, Colletet was banished for nine years, but Théophile, accused of having authored a series of bawdy poems that were featured in the volume (all had been published anonymously; none were by him), was condemned to death at the stake. Of course, since the authorities didn't have their hands on him, the death sentence could hardly have been carried out, so they simply burned him in effigy on August 13, 1623 (Lachèvre, 141).

All this was clearly just a ceremonial warning intended to send a message that limits would henceforth be enforced. No serious effort had been made to find the two poets, who hadn't even bothered to leave the country. But a self-appointed ecclesiastical censor, realizing that the civil authorities seemed to be planning to lay the matter to rest, was already poised to weigh in. The new attack on Théophile took a form appropriate for the age in which censorship began to manipulate print's power to influence public opinion: a Jesuit, Father François Garasse, made the matter public in a fat (1,028 pages) tome, *La Doctrine curieuse des beaux esprits de ce temps, ou prétendus tels*. This is the very book in which *obscenity* makes its second appearance in French, as a synonym for "impieties and blasphemies," the crimes upon which the secular authorities based their case against Théophile. Garasse had been preparing his attack for some time. On March 8, ecclesiastical censors—who, now that their role was under assault, were obviously working with zeal—approved his volume's religious content (Adam, 345). They thereby demonstrated that, while the new secular censors had failed to stop *Le Parnasse satirique*, their ecclesiastical counterparts could still run a tight ship.[25] The day before Théophile's symbolic execution was carried out, Sébastien Chappelet finished printing this work, which was put on sale a week later, on August 25.[26]

La Doctrine curieuse is rambling, bizarre, slightly mad. It is also a perfect illustration of the confusion between religious and secular issues out of which the modern obscene emerged. True, Garasse makes his case against the *beaux esprits* (read freethinkers) of the day largely in religious terms.[27] On the surface, he seems to be calling attention to the menace constituted by freethinking in general. From time to time, however, Garasse tips his hand and lashes out at Théophile in particular. At those moments, he both reveals his true motivation and establishes the terms, almost exclusively sexual, that would be followed in the upcoming civil case.[28]

Almost all of Garasse's outpouring is devoted to defining the *beaux esprits*, or "wits," of his volume's title. For Garasse, Théophile was clearly the most dangerous of them all. Garasse, however, did not accuse him of the sins one might expect to find featured in an attack on freethinkers authored by a Jesuit; Garasse's attack is motivated by a seemingly hysterical reaction to what he clearly viewed as various kinds of uncontrollable proliferation—from print culture to venereal disease. Thus, according to Garasse, Théophile was a menace to contemporary society because of his drunkenness, because of the definition of sexual desire proposed by his poetry, and because his personal behavior could be linked to the menace of print culture.

In Garasse's portrayal, freethinkers are creatures of the dark, who come into their own in drunken brawls in the cabarets or taverns that were central to the nightlife of early seventeenth-century Paris. The passage in which *obscenity* begins to acquire its modern meaning is typical of this tendency: according to Garasse, whenever the libertines find themselves in "one of their favorite cabarets, and drunk, they reveal completely their most mysterious secrets, and impieties, blasphemies, and obscenities come pouring out of their mouths" (85). Garasse makes two contributions that proved essential to creating the modern concept of obscenity. Rather than a synonym for the vaguely defined "filthy living" that was the term's function in its inaugural 1511 appearance in French, Garasse makes *obscenity* fully a speech crime: dangerous words pronounced by dangerous men of letters. What makes these obscenities dangerous, and obscenity a problem that the civil authorities need to suppress, is the fact that they are not pronounced inside private homes but publicly circulated, along with alcohol, among the patrons of the freethinkers' "favorite cabarets."[29] When he thus depicts the freethinkers in situ, spreading the contamination of their doctrine in the cabarets, Garasse suggests—as subsequent critics would, castigating men of letters for exchanging ideas in cafés—that speech crimes uttered in such promiscuous surroundings had the potential to corrupt an unpredictably diverse audience.

In addition, Garasse explains that the most dangerous freethinkers of all combine the promiscuity of public drinking spots and that of print. He felt compelled to write his tract the moment when, "three or four months earlier," he had come across *Le Parnasse satirique* "being sold openly" (780). He reveals familiarity with the recent civil prosecution of the volume when he denounces Théophile and Colletet as "its main authors" (781), though the compilation contains only one poem by Théophile. The Jesuit censor manages, however, to get a lot of mileage out of that poem.

For Garasse, the Phylis sonnet stands for the entire compilation, and the sonnet itself can be summed up by its last line. On the basis of that one line ("I swear from now on to fuck only in the ass"), the Jesuit pulls out all the stops: "In the past, the minute the word sodomy was mentioned, everyone began to talk about burning alive the person even suspected of it," whereas now "a book is being sold publicly which opens with a sonnet in which the author, who calls himself the sieur Théophile, repents because he has contracted an infamous disease from a prostitute, and swears to God to remain a SODOMITE all the rest of his days" (782). From this point on, whenever Garasse brings up Théophile, he invariably refers to him as a sodomite—and, lest there be any doubt about what he means by the term, he never misses the chance to describe the poet in suspicious male company.

Whereas the civil case may have influenced the religious censor, the influence in the opposite direction is plain—and nothing in Garasse's argument shaped Théophile's official trial more decisively than his reading of what, thanks to his intervention, came to be known simply as "the sodomite sonnet" (see, for example, Lachèvre, *Procès*, 281.) The state's proceedings against Théophile make a number of things clear—above all, the fact that the line delimiting sexual decency was being redrawn in the early 1620s. The category of the decent, as it was then redefined, relied in particular on the unqualified imposition of a demarcation never before operative in sexually transgressive literature: between desire for women and desire for men. On the basis of Théophile's trial, it could be argued that modern censorship came into existence in order, first, to impose a distinction between heterosexuality and homosexuality and, second, to declare that the representation of homoeroticism in print would henceforth be taboo. At the very least, it can be argued that among the first consequences of the transfer of censorship from religious to civil hands was the establishment of this distinction and of this taboo. And in this area, religious and civil censors found common ground. Their agreement inaugurated the process that resulted in the creation of the obscene as a censorial category. That process began when Garasse, in effect, declared that, whereas hundreds of poems that could be read as celebrations of heterosexuality would not be prosecuted, a single line that could be read as a choice of homoeroticism would.

Today, we tend to consider obscenity's success at cultural destabilization as indissociable from the desire of certain artists to force a confrontation with what can be thought of as emerging sexual issues—that is, societal "secrets" that their cultures would prefer not to face. *Obscenity* acquired its modern right to life, however, in a near reversal of this process: artists were initially censored for obscenity, when, like Théophile and Molière after him, they chose to represent, rather than the not yet representable, the no longer representable—issues that their culture had previously been able to confront, but that it was in the process of relegating to the realm of the taboo.

The misreading of Théophile's poem that Garasse initiated situates the

Jesuit censor on our side of the divide created by modern censorship: he saw only in terms of the categories that censorship began to enforce as soon as it came into existence. The so-called joyful representation of sexuality in the French bawdy is essentially a priapic cult. Female genitalia are mentioned—the word *cunt* is sprinkled throughout many of the genre's classic poems—but it is always clear that the only sexual organ that counts is the male one.[30] In the bawdy compilations, there is no sexuality other than male. This poetry is absolutely faithful to the model for Latin sexually transgressive literature as described by Richlin: "These texts manifest a Rabelaisian interest in the physical body, with the male genitalia serving as a source of bellicose pride, and the female genitalia as a source of (male) disgust" (xvi). Théophile's sonnet is plainly situated on the far side of the censorial divide; it belongs still to the world of classical erotic practice. To judge from his answers during his interrogations, Théophile clearly expected it to be evaluated according to those terms. He may have gone wrong because he chose to play with those terms, to indicate the beginning of a transition between classical practice and classical practice revisited by early modern authors.

The poetry in the satirical compilations, like the work of the erotic writers and artists of Renaissance Italy, was steeped in classical models and the influence of antiquity. Indeed, it may well be the last sexually transgressive literature to conform so overtly to the rules of Latin erotic literature.[31] All of Théophile's bawdy poems, and perhaps none more so than the sonnet chosen to open the 1622 volume, are highly literate, and highly Latinate, full of echoes of his Latin precursors, notably Catullus and Martial.[32] The elite male readers who undoubtedly formed the core of Théophile's first audience were surely sensitive to the sonnet's Latinate texture and would have heard the reminiscences of Théophile's Roman precursors. To this extent, the sonnet conforms perfectly to the model for sexually transgressive literature that had allowed that literature to circulate for centuries with no interference from censors: it was understood to be an elite product, never meant to pass beyond the restricted circle of the high-born and high-living, a form of transgression that knew its place and kept to it.[33]

Within this frame of reference, the sonnet's close, which sent Garasse into a furor whose frenzy could only be rendered by capital letters ("SOD-OMITE"), would not have been seen, as the Jesuit did, as a choice of what we would today term sexual orientation. It would not have been seen, as the Jesuit did, as based on the existence of two opposing models for male desire. On the contrary, in the sonnet the gender of the sexual object is irrelevant.

In this, Théophile, and the bawdy in general, are, once again, faithful to a classical model, according to which, in Foucault's phrase, "the same desire was directed at all that was desirable—boy or girl" (*L'Usage des plaisirs,* 209).[34] In this sonnet in particular, the choice Théophile is presenting has nothing to do with the opposition between women and men; he situates the sexual transgression of his work—as did each of the seventeenth-century authors singled out by censorship as test cases in the creation of obscenity as a category for policing literature—squarely in the domain of primary obscenities. The binary Théophile foregrounds is that of two three-letter words, *con,* which would have been subjected to an ellipsis and which he elides, and *cul,* the only term that could be fully spelled out.

Garasse was thrown off by Théophile's initial move, the apostrophe to Phylis. The Jesuit assumed that there was an actual person behind the name, and subsequent commentators all follow suit.[35] Here, too, Garasse's instinct is overly modern: no hard evidence proves the existence of a real woman behind the fantasy name; it seems likely that Théophile was once again following the example of his Latin masters such as Catullus and creating a generic figure of the beloved woman.

The poem gets its edge from Théophile's manipulation of this poetic convention. In early seventeenth-century pastoral literature, *Phyllis* was among the most common names for the object of the poet's desire. The only difference is that the name is usually written—as, for example, in Honoré d'Urfé's pastoral classic, *L'Astrée*—*Phillis.* In this sonnet, as in all the works that announced the reinvention of literary obscenity, the key is in the typography: by changing an *i* to a *y* and by cutting one *l,* Théophile made his sonnet sexually transgressive in another way. He transformed a conventional name for the beloved woman into an evocation of the first great sexual plague.[36] This, then, is the ultimate punch packed by the sonnet's last line. Since the *cul* was the less risky orifice for lovers as well as for typographers, this modern poet was weighing the risk of contamination, rather than the more traditional advantages of desire. Théophile thus simultaneously recalls the infamous close of Catullus 16 ("I will bugger you and I will fuck your mouths") and updates it with the threat of a contagious disease unknown to antiquity.[37]

Nothing suggests that either civil or religious authorities had any particular reason to be concerned about the syphilitic menace in the early 1620s. Nevertheless, Théophile's addition of the contamination of sexually transmitted disease to an already risky sexual equation could well have been the factor that set Garasse off on his rampage: to name the object of desire *Phylis* in a sonnet describing in disgusting detail the miseries inflicted by the pox and proclaiming (the end of) the type of promiscuity that spread it most effectively was, after all, to beg for just the type of contagious reading of sexual material that the censors were most inclined to favor.

Once again, Garasse misses none of Théophile's audacity: just before his initial accusation of sodomy, he proclaims his indignation that a poet would publish the fact of his having contracted "an infamous disease" (782). From then on, sodomy, syphilis (*la vérole*), and print almost always appear together in his tract (e.g., 935). The Jesuit makes by far his most telling evocation of the syphilitic menace, however, when he compares the threat of contamination posed by sexually transmitted disease to that of the printing press: he contends that the way in which Théophile "has made printing presses sweat" is only slightly "more decent" than the manner in which "he himself formerly sweated as a result of his promiscuousness" (782).[38]

Demographers have suggested a link between, as Johannes Fabricius puts it, "microbes and morals" (16), that is, that the syphilitic plague and the outpouring of commentary that both responded to and fueled anxiety about the disease's societal consequences contributed to the attenuation of the more liberal sexual climate of the late Middle Ages. Surely the rise of print culture, simultaneous with that of the syphilitic plague, must be factored into this equation, as Garasse does. Théophile's syphilitic sonnet might encourage us to believe in the connection between microbes and morals. It also played a vital role in provoking the invention of the modern category of obscenity, a category ultimately related—as cause or as effect, or as some combination of the two—to the creation of a newly strict vision of sexual decency in which, to include but two examples directly related to this case, four-letter words became the ultimate typographical taboo and certain visions of desire were pronounced off-limits for representation.

Richlin has suggested that, because "the term *obscenum* itself had a strong religious sense, this . . . may have promoted the special treatment of sexual material in Latin culture" (2). By the time Théophile was put on trial in 1623, any "special treatment" that might have allowed sexually transgressive literature to circulate with relative impunity in France was coming to an end. In this light, it is surely significant that it is during Théophile's trial that we find the first clear indications that the obscene had at long last begun to shed its religious connotations. Of course, it could be argued that this splitting off has never been successfully completed: one has only to think of the ability to scandalize a New York audience in the year 2000 possessed by some of the images in the "Sensation" exhibit at the Brooklyn Museum to realize that the bond may, even now, at times quickly be reactivated. Théophile's trial does, however, mark a crucial turning point in obscenity's history, the moment at which it first became possible to imagine a truly secular transgressive literature.

The unsettled state of thinking on issues at the intersection of religious and sexual transgression is clearly evident in the proceedings of Théophile's trial, which began in earnest shortly after Garasse's huge tome went on sale and immediately after September 15, 1623, when *Le Parnasse satirique* was once again reissued. On September 17, Théophile was arrested; he was confined to the Conciergerie Prison in Paris on September 28—thereby proving that the civil censors could lay their hands on someone quickly when they really wanted to do so. Théophile was locked up in the dark heart of the Conciergerie, perhaps the bleakest of the Ancien Régime's prisons, in a famous cell, the one in which Ravaillac had been left to rot in 1610 while awaiting his execution for regicide. This choice of holding cell indicates the seriousness with which the civil authority temporarily in charge of censorship was taking both its mission and Théophile's offense. Daylight reached this hellhole only for about two hours at midday; at other times, it was so dark, Théophile complained, that one could hardly tell the ceiling from the walls. Théophile was never able to obtain firewood. In a prison situated immediately on the river, deprived of daylight and heat, the cold and the damp must have been unbearable.[39]

Théophile was held under these conditions for nearly two years, during which time he was repeatedly interrogated and confronted with various witnesses for the prosecution. The presiding magistrates chosen by the Parisian Parliament, Jacques Pinon and François de Verthamon, presented two types of evidence: first, hearsay and rumors to the effect that Théophile was guilty of the crimes for which he was allegedly on trial, and, second, Théophile's writing, both published works and manuscripts they attributed to him. While the poet was easily able to defend himself against the accusations based on hearsay, those stemming from his own work necessitated a more complex defense: he argued that words were only thoughts, which could never be equated with criminal actions, and in addition that the first-person in a literary work could not be interpreted as a reference to the work's author and his personal beliefs and preferences.[40]

What is most puzzling about the case against Théophile, however, is not that the authorities used his work against him—it is that they did not put it to more effective use. Had the prosecution stuck to its alleged mission and concentrated on presenting evidence of impiety and blasphemy, the magistrates could have had a field day with Théophile, whose poetry is at times as dangerously irreverent as they could have wished. There is, for example, a second sonnet "To Phylis." This one turns on the intermingling of sacred and profane love with a consistently mocking tone. True, this sonnet was evoked several times, but only in passing and never with the kind of probing that would have made its subversiveness plain (see *Procès*, 32). After hearing testimony that he was the author of a poem mocking the Last Judgment, his interrogators asked the alleged author about the "dirty words" in the poem, rather than about its impiety (252). It seems, in fact, that Théophile's prosecutors were not sufficiently concerned with religious issues. Time and again, they got sidetracked by charges suggested to them by Garasse.

When we look at what the magistrates were actually trying to prove, rather than the charges they claimed to be prosecuting, it becomes clear that they returned obsessively to the two crimes—drunkenness and sodomy—that are at the heart of Garasse's demand that Théophile be silenced.[41] Furthermore, they understood quite clearly Garasse's implications. Thus, in "drunkenness" they saw the patronizing of cabarets and the dangerous promiscuity thus made possible, as well as the way this promiscuity facilitated the transmission of subversive literature. In particular, they saw that in the taverns of Paris sexually transgressive literature had finally begun to circulate outside the closed audience of elite readers to which it had previously been confined.[42]

This fear of social contamination explains some of the strangest characters called upon to testify for the prosecution, in particular, Pierre Guibert, a key player since he was the unique source for attributing by far the largest quantity of bawdy verse to Théophile. Guibert, as Théophile was quick to point out, was gifted with an unbelievably prodigious memory—he quoted long passages from poems he claimed to have heard recited seven to eight years previously, and on occasions when he had been drinking! The prosecution identified him as "a Parisian bourgeois" (414)—already indicating the spread of this dangerous work outside the more controllable elite—but Théophile corrected the record to show that he was in fact "the son of a butcher" (480). For Théophile, this meant that it was all the more unlikely that Guibert could have committed to memory so many lines of verse.[43] For his accusers, intent on proving Théophile guilty of "having committed debauchery *with servants* at the Pomme de Pin" (468; my emphasis), the nuance on Guibert's social status was surely only more evidence of the new promiscuity, the circulation within a nonelite audience of the representations of sexuality that, as Garasse intuited, was an early warning signal of the obscene's imminent reinvention.

It's easy to fast-forward to the lawyer for the prosecution, Griffith-Jones, on day one of D. H. Lawrence and Penguin Books's 1960 trial for obscene publication. Griffith-Jones, brandishing a copy of *Lady Chatterley's Lover*, inquired of the members of the jury: "Is this a book you would have lying around your own house? Is it a book that you would wish . . . your servants to read?" (Hyde, 62). Garasse consistently ended his accusations against Théophile by scoffing at his use of the title "sieur" and contending that only someone lowborn would have been "foolish" enough "to put down in writing" and "to confide to print" such "indecent words."[44] When faced with the possibility that absolute "nobodies" (*gens de néant*, as Garasse says) were both writing and reading such material, the civil authorities clearly became convinced that they had no choice but to put into place new mechanisms for censorship that would allow them to define, and then to police, the boundary between decent and indecent.

On no account should we underestimate the significance of Guibert's testimony. We know next to nothing about the identity of the early modern public for sexually transgressive literature. The Parisian butcher's son is the first known nonelite reader of this material. It is surely no accident that his testimony was solicited just as soon as modern censorship began its efforts to suppress sexually transgressive literature. Whether or not Guibert had been coached by the prosecution, his very presence at the trial surely must have seemed to prove that print was contaminating, syphilislike, with no regard for class lines. Obscenity was escaping from the barriers behind which, since antiquity, its circulation had been confined.[45]

The nocturnal scenes of "debauchery" that crossed class lines in a manner not often possible in the Paris of the 1620s were also threatening in another way, one just as crucial to the case against Théophile. They raised the possibility, to which the prosecution returns again and again, that these relations among men were literally, as well as literarily, sexual in nature. They never come up with any evidence proving the literal, so they are forced to focus on the literary, which they read as evidence of actual conduct. Théophile thus shared the lot of all sexually transgressive poets, from Catullus to Baudelaire: to be judged personally immoral because he was the author of poetry considered indecent. Witnesses such as Guibert repeat, ad nauseam, the last line of the "sodomite sonnet."[46] They also refer to the handful of other poems that lend themselves to the same distortion. In particular, witnesses cite again and again a line from a sonnet about masturbation ("Et tu me branleras la pique"; "And you will jack off my lance")—and their testimony was evidently considered damning only because all concerned clearly assumed that the "you" in question could only be male. Théophile protested against this, the prosecution's most flagrant attempt to confuse the man and his work. He pointed out that they were misreading his poetry and furthermore that, even if it meant what they said it did, "to write verse about sodomy doesn't make a man guilty of the deed; poet and pederast are two different occupations."[47]

It seems clear that his accusers would not have put themselves through two full years of proceedings had they not hoped, the second time around, to carry out a real rather than a symbolic execution. And yet, on September 1, 1625, Théophile was sentenced only to banishment from France in perpetuity—and even this relatively mild sentence was later reduced to simple banishment from the court. It could be said, however, that the civil censors did get their man: Théophile died in exile a year later, on September 25, 1626; it was generally agreed that his health had been broken by the harsh conditions of his long confinement.[48]

It could also be argued that the censors got their author. Théophile's trial marks the beginning of a phenomenon that will take on increasing importance in each chapter of this study: the way in which the author first becomes truly useful in print culture when, in the course of the struggle between print collectives (i.e., all those who collaborate to produce a work) and censorship, a name is needed on which to lay the blame for dangerous works. Before Théophile's trial, the state's most important incursion into censorship had been carried out against a publisher, Etienne Dolet. In Théophile's wake, however, modern censorship trials would always feature an author. Even those who put together the bawdy compilations seemed to sense the author's new importance in the business of shady literature. In 1625, the year of Théophile's sentencing, the 1622 *parnasse* was reissued, but with a title page that announced *Le Parnasse des poètes satiriques . . . par le sieur Théophile,* even though the volume was no more *by* Théophile than the compilation for which he had been tried. The publisher clearly realized that, since blame had been laid at the alleged author's feet and since, furthermore, he was still being held in prison, for the moment all eyes were on the author and the print collective had, therefore, nothing to fear.[49]

Théophile's trial was a landmark in the history of sexually transgressive literature in other ways as well. Because of the censors' truly obsessive focus in their questioning, they put body parts and genitalia at the center of the proceedings. In particular, they made *male* genitalia a central focus of censorial scrutiny. Théophile thus became the first author ever to have been prosecuted for naming in his work male genitalia, the obvious center of attention in all priapic depictions of sexuality. In this way Théophile's trial played an essential role in the process by which modern obscenity came to be identified with so-called four-letter words. It could, therefore, also have been seen as an implicit prohibition against the naming of genitalia, and male genitalia in particular. One of the more predictable consequences of these proceedings took the form of self-censorship: writers in the priapic, Rabelaisian, *gaulois* vein, such as Charles Sorel, immediately began dramatically to cut back on the explicit presence of male genitalia in their work.[50]

This perceived interdiction may have had far less predictable consequences as well. To begin with, from this moment on, male genitalia began
to be displaced from their virtually exclusive role in the spotlight of sexually transgressive literature. The next incarnation of erotic literature, which
came to prominence three decades later in the context of the second modern literary trial, played down the male organ and instead gave modern
obscenity a previously unheard of center of attention, female genitalia.
This double shift in the representation of the center of obscenity—on the
one hand, a dramatic attenuation in the focus on male genitalia and, on
the other, the beginning of the modern obsession with female genitalia—
produces a powerful message when it is seen in conjunction with the interdiction that comes across most forcefully in the course of Théophile's
censorship, the official intolerance of same-sex eroticism. When taken together, these factors can be seen as promoting a clear sexual vision: the
obligatory and officially decreed imposition of heterosexuality.

This was surely a far more comforting vision to the censors who faced
for the first time the possibility that this erotic literature, along with the
definition of "normal" male sexual practice that it conveyed, was in the hands
of a nonelite audience. It was also a more comforting vision for the society
that, during the second half of the century and the increasingly frequent
wars that put a strain on both France's finances and its manpower, witnessed the beginning of both an obsessive fear of a declining birthrate and
the science necessitated by that fear, demography.

Such speculation on the long-term consequences of forces set into
motion by Théophile's trial raises a question that looms large behind any
discussion of print culture's role in the reinvention of obscenity for the
modern age. At the same time as obscenity received a new lease on life, the
map indicating possible sexual behavior and the possible objects of desire
was dramatically redesigned. Who was responsible for this new design?
Did censors, answering to a monarchy fearful of any loss of control over its
subjects, succeed in imposing a new set of sexual desires? Or was the new
map the product of a vaguer set of forces, what can be called, for simplicity's sake, societal change—in this case, a sea change in the standards for
decency? Or was the new design for sexuality originally imagined by the
writers themselves, who succeeded thereby in at least predicting, if not
actually provoking, a complete reorientation in the portrayal of sexuality?
(Because I am dealing here with a history of representations, I don't feel
able to go farther than this. It is evident, however, that such a major revision in the depiction of sexuality had to have consequences on the ways in
which real people experienced their sexuality.)

Kendrick has characterized nineteenth-century obscenity trials as "laboratories" that made it possible for society to learn to distinguish transgressive literature, what society was in the process of naming "the pornographic," from its nontransgressive counterpart, the erotic or the merely realistic (68). A similar measuring of the standards for representational decency is already evident in the first modern writer's trial. In addition, Théophile's trial makes clear the extent to which these standards for representational decency are intermeshed with the issue of what I have been calling the map of sexual desire. The consequences of the remapping initiated during the proceedings against Théophile only become fully clear three decades later, in the first literature to establish the modern criteria for obscenity.

The authorities (and, in this case, civil and religious authorities were surely of one mind) may have believed that, by dictating the obligatory representation of heterosexuality, they were simultaneously eliminating the problem of sexually transgressive literature. Théophile's trial may well have helped put an end to the age—and it was a very long one, beginning as it did in antiquity—during which, in representation at least, male desire was polyvalent, desiring all that was desirable. The authorities surely could not have bargained for the form in which this type of bad book would next return, for the first time ever in a guise for which no one was prepared, since it was not predictable on the basis of classical precedent.

Obscénité began to take on its modern meaning in the context of a writer's trial. A bond seems thereby to have been forged, as a result of which the term has remained ever since a tool to be used in the policing of literature in order to bring it into conformity with current cultural norms and taboos. This newly available vocabulary, even the first hint of it, revealed a need in French culture that would be spectacularly realized some thirty years later with the first true obscenity trial. In the next case I will consider, the censoring authorities were so much more diligent than they had been in Théophile's case that they very nearly succeeded in destroying all the evidence and thereby covering up forever a work that they must have found truly threatening. With this case, I move beyond anything that could be considered, by any stretch of the imagination, simply *gaulois*. Few readers today would find *L'Ecole des filles* truly offensive; surely fewer still would see it as a threat to public morality. They would all clearly understand, however, why it—unlike Théophile's sonnet—could be categorized as obscene.

2

The Heterosexual Turn

L'ECOLE DES FILLES OR,
WHEN (THE) SEX BEGAN TO TALK

Obscenity in any company is a rustic uncreditable talent,
but among women 'tis particularly rude.

—Jeremy Collier, *Short View of the Immorality
and Profaneness of the English Stage*

Anyone convinced of the dangerous potential of print culture would have had ample cause for concern at the seventeenth century's midpoint. Its two dominant European centers, England and France, must have seemed poised on the same collision course. In England during the civil war and the Interregnum and in France during the civil war known as the Fronde, all systems that attempted to regulate the industry collapsed. At the same time, the demand for highly controversial publications of various kinds increased wildly. The 1640s and 1650s witnessed veritable outpourings of books and pamphlets taking sides in contemporary polemics. The demand was such, and the risks so low, that printers and booksellers outdid each other to expand their production and increase their profits. Numerous new print shops quickly began to take advantage of the situation. Then, on both sides of the Channel, the end of political unrest spelled the end of this new freedom; as soon as their rule was reestablished, both monarchies set about putting their houses in order.

Revolutions, even only would-be revolutions such as the Fronde, change much more than the political order and its modus operandi—though, given the fact that, in both countries, the modern state truly began to be put into place in the aftermath of these civil wars, that was already result enough.[1] In France, some of the most spectacular changes took place in the realm of literature: the immediate post-Fronde years formed a bridge between the literary culture of the Renaissance and that of the eighteenth century. In various genres and in various ways, literature became increasingly focused on women, increasingly middle-class, increasingly domestic. This new literary space—in which Rabelais's lustiness was disappearing and Richardson's eroticized propriety first stirring—is massively interior in its focus, often verging on the claustrophobic. To it belong different prototypes for what became known as the modern novel: among them, *L'Ecole des filles,* the first novel that can really be called obscene in the modern sense of the term—a novel so "modern" that specialists such as Foxon refer to it as "pornographic," even though that adjective was first used only well over a century later. In a (nearly) postrevolutionary moment, in an early sign of the movement by which literature began to represent the world as massively interior, a print collective with multiple connections to political sedition transferred its energies to this emerging field and reinvented sexually transgressive literature.

With this accomplishment in mind, Foxon stresses "the way in which pornography seems to have been born and grown to maturity in a brief period in the middle of the seventeenth century" (ix). He explains this phenomenon as a straightforward question of supply and demand: "if the demand had existed a hundred years earlier, something would have appeared to meet it" (50). I have no quarrel with this idea, but I do feel that it glosses over a crucial factor. Demand, there certainly was, probably in different European contexts: it can be documented with certainty in France and England. Supply, however, is altogether a different matter. It came from one source and one source alone: France.

This chapter will deal with the interrelated issues of the new demand and the new supply. The case of the butcher's son, Pierre Guibert, is the first documented case of the oral circulation of sexually transgressive poetry outside of an inner circle of high-born rakes. The example of *L'Ecole des filles* indicates that the new demand Foxon posits was largely a demand on the part of new book buyers and readers. For the first time, we know that this book was not only read but owned by precisely the new "classes" of readers who would prove to be essential to the popularity of the genre born in the wake of civil war, the modern novel. These were readers never before associated with erotic literature: middle-class, professional men—and women.

This radically different readership surely explains in large part the radically different nature of the new supply. The new publics—the first not to have shared in the classical education of upper-class men (for whom, for example, Martial's epigrams continued to circulate without alarming the

This Day is publiſh'd, Price (only) 3 s. 6 d.
Adorn'd with twenty-four curious Copper-Plate Prints, after the Manner of Aratine,

Being a true Engliſh Tranſlation, without thoſe innumerable Blunders which are to be found in every Page of the Iriſh Edition, merrily call'd a Dutch one, and ſold by the Iriſh Hawkers for 3 s. 3 d.

THE SCHOOL of VENUS, or the Lady's Delight, reduced into Rules of Practice; being a true Tranſlation of the French L'Eſcole des Filles. In two Dialogues between Frances, a married Lady, and Kitty, her Maid.

Sold at the Pamphlet ſhops over-againſt St. Clement's Church in the Strand; at the Royal Exchange, and by J. S. in Alderſgate-Street.

Note, Gentlemen who love to read Engliſh, are deſir'd to take Notice, not to aſk for the Iriſh, alias Dutch, Edition. At the above Shops the Iriſh Edition may be ſeen and compared.

FIGURE 2   Advertisement for an English translation of *L'Ecole des filles* from the *Daily Advertiser* (August 25, 1744). Courtesy of the Library of Congress, Washington, D.C.

censors)—acquired, appropriately, the first truly vernacular sexually transgressive literature: that is, both written in the vernacular and, unlike its precursors such as Aretino's dialogues, totally without classical models. The new erotic model was, furthermore, almost fully secularized: it eulogized pleasure for pleasure's sake, almost completely without religious reference. With *L'Ecole des filles*, we find ourselves suddenly far closer to *The Joy of Sex* than to Théophile's or Aretino's heavily Latinate poetry. Those responsible for the new erotic literature made its circulation ever more public: this novel was, for example, the first sexually transgressive book whose sale was advertised in a newspaper (see figure 2). This vernacular, secularized, increasingly available erotic literature obliged censorship to continue on the road to secularization; the reinvention of obscenity necessitated, in both France and England, the creation of the modern institution of censorship.

Lachèvre describes *L'Ecole des filles* as "the most fundamentally perverse literature that has ever seen or ever will see the light" (*Libertinage*, 82).[2] Eighty years after he wrote those words, notions such as "the most fundamentally perverse literature" have been given an entirely new spin. However, the next part of his assessment still holds true: "*L'Ecole des filles* is a work more than a century ahead of its time" (82). When confronted with this book, those attempting to police print culture in 1655 must have felt that time was out of joint. The slim volume, published, naturally, anonymously and with no privilege, can truly be said to have invented the problem of modern literary obscenity. With the case of *L'Ecole des filles*, we may be at an origin of the dangerous liaison that modern Western societies have been living ever since with one particular taboo, obscenity. The case may allow us to measure the limits assigned the original legal relation between tolerable and subversive, limits that different cultures have continuously redefined, for the past three centuries, and in different ways.

The thirty years that separated Théophile's prosecution from the next modern author's trial witnessed several attempted reforms in the regulation of print culture, reforms that brought about apparent changes but that left an overall situation not unlike that of 1623. These years during which the bawdy was on the wane and the obscene still dormant were marked first of all by an exacerbation of the issue whose origins can be traced to the moment in 1623 when the bawdy's prosecution began, the creation of prepublication censorship and the nomination of reader/censors to administer it. Chevillier's 1694 history of seventeenth-century print culture gives a blow-by-blow account of the mounting hostilities between various religious and civil factions striving for control over the new institution (395– 405).

In August 1624 the initial royal license, issued in March 1623, became law with the publication of the Edict for the Creation of Four Book Censors, a document so important that Chevillier quotes it in its entirety (398– 402). At this point, it would appear that the Faculty of Theology's initial outcry had been heeded and that all the positions would be filled by its members. Furthermore, it appeared that the theologians would examine mainly works with religious content. From the text of the Edict, it is not at all clear, as Chevillier points out, that Louis XIII had any intention of naming secular censors; the king appears to have viewed the Edict mainly as an attempt to underscore that something had to be done about the issue of censorship (573). The Faculty of Theology, however, obviously believed that this was the intention behind the Edict, because it offered such strenuous opposition that "the newly appointed censors refused to accept the nominations" (396).

The religious censors were once again successful in holding onto a function they seemed to have had little interest in exercising but which they, nevertheless, wished to keep out of secular hands. Preventive censorship thus remained largely a dead issue. Then, in January 1629, the king struck again—and this time he fulfilled the Sorbonne's worst fears. A new edict gave a civil authority, the Chancellor, complete control over preventive censorship (404). Two manuscript copies of every work for which a privilege was sought had to be submitted directly to him; he was to choose an appropriate reader/censor (405).[3]

It seems likely that those responsible for this edict understood one reason why reinforced secular censorship would soon prove essential: to the traditional categories of books to be suppressed, a new one was added and the phrase that remains to this day crucial to French prosecution of indecent material was first employed in a legal context: *corruption des mœurs* (corruption of morals; Isambert, 16:238).[4] Three years after Théophile's trial had effectively both sounded the death knell of the bawdy and alerted censorship to the growing threat of sexually transgressive literature, indecency received its first legal recognition. The next author's trial would be the initial test of the first category invented by secular censorship.

The 1629 edict continues the 1618 edict's attempt to guarantee that books would not be printed without a privilege by giving the state broader control over the process.[5] Louis XIII and Richelieu could hardly have picked, however, a more difficult time to crack down; before midcentury, in both domains in which print culture had traditionally been considered dangerous, all would-be regulators were confronted by crises of the highest order.

Perhaps the most serious and most tenacious challenge to orthodox Catholicism in the last century and a half of the Ancien Régime, that of the Jansenist movement, began in the early 1640s; its supporters were relentless in their attempts to keep Jansenist tracts and literature in circulation. Jansenism was the first heresy originating on French soil to be, like Lutheranism, "a child of the printed book." Its supporters circulated their ideas in print and, increasingly, in French.[6] Then, at the end of this same decade, France was plunged into the most serious political sedition prior to the Revolution, the civil war known as the Fronde (1648–1653), during which both sides vied for public opinion with a flood of clandestine pamphlets.[7] The situation in France surely seemed all the more dire, in view of the contemporary English context. The two courts were extremely close; the French monarchy anxiously monitored revolutionary activity across the channel.

Throughout these years of crisis, Pierre Séguier—who, as Lord Chancellor and Keeper of the Seal, was the government official ultimately responsible for the legality of publications—tried one measure after another to keep a lid on things. In February 1647, with the first flurry of Jansenist activity barely repressed and the Fronde clearly about to explode, he personally communicated to the Parisian printers the king's desire to stop the printing of books not marked with the royal seal (Martin, *Livre*, 1:573–74). As the civil war unfolded, laws decreeing the punishment of those linked to the circulation of seditious texts were issued. An October 1652 ordinance, for example, declared that the presses of any printers involved in the publication of such material would be seized and immediately sold (*Edit du roi*, 89). Mazarin, however, was no more successful than Richelieu had been at bringing the book trade under control; at the end of the Fronde, unlicensed publication was rampant (Barbiche, 377). Indeed, in all this tumultuous era for print culture, no moment at which it was possible to publish literary texts (virtually none appeared during the Fronde years) was more lawless than the immediate post–civil war years.[8]

In view of the spectacular instance of postpublication or repressive censorship that took place shortly after the crown at last took control over the regulation of literary texts, it is tempting to argue that the many laws that attempted to guarantee the functioning of prepublication censorship, just like those of the 1620s, have less to tell us about the history of French print culture than about the creation of sexual taboos and the increasing need for a clear category of what we would call indecent writing. *L'Ecole des filles* soon proved to be the test case that helped define both the taboos and the new type of writing.

Those who crafted *L'Ecole des filles* had learned invaluable lessons from the print industry's massive involvement with the production of seditious texts during the Fronde. This recent history could explain the fact that they chose to make this the first erotic work that was, as far as was conceivable at that time, intended for the contemporary equivalent of what we now term a mass audience. The collective that collaborated on the venture— authors, copyists, engraver, printers, and binders—made the decision to mass-market the text in a number of ways: with their choices of format, genre, and language and, above all, with their project of bringing a literature of sexuality far more into the open by giving it a radically new content.[9]

With each of these decisions, the collaborators proved that they had their fingers on the pulse of the French book trade, that they saw clearly both where it was headed and the problems confronting it. No issues were more critical than those that had been created by the proliferation of printing presses in Paris. In France, during the first two centuries of the printing press's existence, printing houses and presses were allowed simply to multiply in uncontrolled fashion. During the period just prior to the Civil War and just after it, there were no fewer than seventy-five printing houses operating in Paris alone, truly an enormous number for the period.[10] For the state, the existence of too many presses was a source of great anxiety; some print shops obviously had too little work, so the authorities worried about what idle printers' hands would be up to.

The Fronde years kept all the shops very busy doing just what the authorities feared most: turning out seditious pamphlets. This temporary prosperity ended along with the conflict. Faced with the return of hard times, some printers joined forces with the Jansenists. In early 1655 one print collective had another bright idea: they invented the modern obscene. Even as they did so, the beginning of the end of all this freedom was already in sight. Later that same year, for the first time, measures were taken to limit the number of Parisian printing houses on the grounds that fewer print shops would be more easily monitored and that this would guarantee that there would be enough legitimate work to go around. It is tempting to think that the obscene's first stirrings played a role in the establishment of this new policy.[11]

Before I consider the successful marketing of the obscene, however, here's the story, as it was reconstructed by Frédéric Lachèvre from the trial proceedings, of the attempts by French authorities to nip the phenomenon in the bud. Early in 1655 a writer or writers produced a manuscript entitled *L'Ecole des filles*. What is striking about the proposed candidates for authorship of this manuscript is that they were all ordinary men, men without patrons or protectors in high places. With this case, authorship moved away from previous practice, under which writers—Théophile, for example—always had influential patrons, and closer to the way of the modern world, in which authors rely mainly on the sale of their works to earn a living and thus act on their own, without protection.

Following Lachèvre's lead, recent critics agree that the principal author was the otherwise unknown Michel Millot—though, as I discuss later, this attribution is hardly certain. Two men, Millot and Jean L'Ange—a printer who continued to produce clandestine publications at least until 1657—acted as "agents" for the work, arranging its financing and its printing. Millot covered three-fourths of the cost, and the remainder was paid for by L'Ange.[12] The printing took place in the shop of Louis Piot, who naturally kept his name off the title page, which was marked only: "In Leyden." The seventeen-year-old Claude Le Petit—who clearly learned nothing from the experience, since he was destined to be burned at the stake seven years later because of his own bad books—helped correct proof. For the frontispiece, they went all out and hired François Chauveau, the century's most distinguished book illustrator.[13] In May the print-run was ready. Millot and L'Ange then played the role of booksellers in order to recoup their investment; they unloaded a few copies here, a few more there. Eight or nine, for example, were sold, presumably for resale, to a well-known author who had produced a good deal of subversive literature during the Fronde, Paul Scarron (whose wife, the former Françoise d'Aubignac, was later destined to become famous as Louis XIV's morganatic wife, Madame de Maintenon—it was a very small world indeed).

Up till this point, all was going well. Someone, perhaps the printer, Louis Piot, may have informed on them.[14] The authorities learned of the book somehow, and the situation degenerated quickly. L'Ange was arrested first, on June 12, when he arrived to meet the printer and bookseller Nicolas de La Vigne (who had marketed political pamphlets during the Fronde), who had been promised fifty copies for resale. L'Ange was then escorted back to his rented room on the rue des Rosiers, where some bound copies, as well as a manuscript of *L'Ecole des filles*, were confiscated.[15] The arresting officers, who represented the Chancellery (i.e., the Châtelet, the tribunal that handled police matters), next headed for Millot's place near Notre Dame. Either their knowledge of the case was quite shaky or they were still obsessed with the flood of seditious publications that had appeared during the Fronde; at first, they thought they were looking for someone who had authored pamphlets during the recent civil war (Lachèvre, *Le Libertinage au XVIIe siècle: Mélanges*, 95)! They eventually got around to questioning Millot about the right book and were able to confiscate enough unbound copies of *L'Ecole des filles* to require the services of a porter to carry them off.

The man, however, got away. In his report on the day's activities, the head officer repeats incessantly, thereby drawing our attention to the dubiousness of his claim, that he didn't have enough manpower to make an arrest (Lachèvre, *Le Libertinage au XVIIe siècle: Mélanges*, 97–98).[16] It was certainly convenient, in many ways, that the case unfolded in the absence of the individual declared by twentieth-century critics, following the lead of seventeenth-century censors, to be the author of the work being condemned.

Claude Hourlier, a magistrate representing the Châtelet, led the interrogations. In the proceedings, there are few traces of the new legal language that had been invented since Théophile's trial to prosecute indecency. The closest Hourlier comes to recently minted vocabulary is "contrary to good morals" (*contre les bonnes mœurs;* Lachèvre, *Le Libertinage au XVIIe siècle: Mélanges*, 104, 108), another phrase with a big future in the French prosecution of material judged indecent and the key phrase in the modern prosecution of all sex-related crimes. Usually, he uses the same tired language that had previously been applied to very different sorts of books—"against the honor of God and of the Church" (100), "impious" (116), and "contrary to Christian discipline" (116). When the obscene was finally reinvented, it caught the censors up short, and no one knew what to call it.[17]

Hourlier introduces the only real note of censorial modernity when he focuses the August 4 interrogation of L'Ange on the issue of the privilege. The question of requiring every book to contain a copy of its privilege, first stipulated in the 1618 Printers' Code (Saugrain, 376), had at last become a central concern for those seeking to regulate the French book trade in the decade preceding the publication of *L'Ecole des filles*. A November 1643 law outlawed the buying and the selling of books in which the privilege was not printed; the law was reissued in both 1649 and 1652. And as of April 1653, all printers were required by law to hand over the privilege to the Community of Printers before publication could begin—this ruling was reissued in August of the same year.[18] Granted, during the Ancien Régime laws were frequently repeated, but this is, within a limited time span, an extraordinarily high concentration of decrees focusing on the privilege. It is, therefore, hardly surprising to find Hourlier inquiring whether the printer had at least asked to see the privilege (Lachèvre, *Le Libertinage au XVIIe siècle: Mélanges*, 116).

What is surprising is that *L'Ecole des filles* was accompanied by a privilege—of sorts. The place where the official seal of approval should have been was taken up by the *bulle orthodoxe* (the orthodox bull, as in a papal bull or decree). This bull is a clear parody of the official privilege. It decrees, in the name of "our august Father Priapus" (rather than in that of the king), who should read this book and especially—in a perfect prediction both of all the clichés yet to be invented about the link between pornography and masturbation and of recent postmodern parodies of book apparatus—how it should be read.[19] To publish a work without a privilege at the end of a decade during which the authorities had been obsessed with this means of control was bad enough. To substitute instead a parody of the official permission was openly to taunt them—and Hourlier clearly got the message, because he devoted the same interrogation to the privilege and to the authorship of the bull (Lachèvre, *Le Libertinage au XVIIe siècle: Mélanges*, 115–16).

The bulk of the proceedings is pretty standard fare, except for the verdict, far harsher than that reserved for Théophile. The initially rather stiff sentence handed down against L'Ange (he was to have spent five years at hard labor) was quickly reduced to a bare minimum.[20] By far the harsher sentence was reserved for the absent "author," Millot. If found (hardly likely at that point), he was to be strangled and hanged. In Millot's absence, on August 9, 1655—less than three months after *L'Ecole des filles* had been printed—in a public ceremony on the Pont-Neuf, the punishment was carried out on his effigy. Around its neck, a sign explaining the author's crime was hung. Along with the effigy, all the copies of *L'Ecole des filles* that had been seized were burned—the decree even specified that the Orthodox Bull was to be burned, too.[21]

What was, in effect, the first obscenity trial thus ended in a rather unsatisfactory fashion. In particular, the authorities made no progress toward unsettling an idea that I find particularly appropriate: the author of *L'Ecole des filles*, as far as they were able to determine, was the print collective responsible for assembling, producing, and distributing the book. Twentieth-century commentators conclude from the fact that Millot received the stiffer sentence that he was the work's author. The trial proceedings, however, do not clearly establish authorship. The authorities could not have been convinced that the trial had put an end to the matter nor that they had found their man in Millot, because fifteen years later the book police were still torturing suspects, hoping at long last to learn the true story of *L'Ecole des filles*.[22]

Thus, on December 30, 1669, among the half-dozen *interrogations sur la sellette* or "interrogations on the hot seat" (the *sellette* was a small stool on which accused criminals were seated for their confrontations with the police) considered important enough that they took place in the presence of the head of the Parisian police, La Reynie, and other high-ranking officers in the Police Room of the Bastille Prison was that of a sixty-four-year-old named Lesoyeur, who had lived in Paris for thirty-seven years. He had been in prison since October 15 because the book police had found a manuscript of *L'Ecole des filles* in his handwriting, and they were trying to pin the work's authorship on him. Lesoyeur claimed to have copied it some ten years before; he insisted that he was not its author. The officials of the newly created book police nonetheless sentenced him to be flogged and to five years' banishment (Ravaisson-Mollien, 7:216–17).

The authorities did succeed in completing a process initiated by the proceedings against Théophile. They created a new type of author or a new definition of the author function: the author is the individual singled out for punishment when a work becomes the target of censorship. They thereby confirm Foucault's intuition that "books . . . really began to have authors . . . to the extent that authors became subject to punishment, that is, to the extent that discourses could be transgressive" ("What Is an Author?" 108). We might add that books began to have authors because the immediate precursors of the book police needed a name to identify the effigy central to the act of symbolic execution. That is, books began to have authors when censoring authorities decided to advance *authorship* as a regulatory principle rather than the visibly fragile institution of the privilege. It is also fitting that there remains so much uncertainty about Millot's authorship and, furthermore, that *L'Ecole des filles* was throughout its early history an anonymous classic. The authors of obscene literature, as Molière's dealings with the phenomenon would make amply clear, were those least protected by law; their works were always in a sense in the public domain.

In another way, the authorities were more successful: they, for once, almost completely suppressed a dangerous work. Not a single copy of the 1655 edition has come down to us. Of course, according to the well-known censorial cycle, the book's repression guaranteed its status as an underground classic. Somehow, either copies of the original edition or manuscripts were smuggled out of France.[23] The smuggling, furthermore, was a two-way street: copies of foreign editions of *L'Ecole des filles* were slipped back across the border to give French readers what could not be printed in France. Indeed, as late as 1700, French customs officers were still confiscating copies of the 1668 edition, proving that the original work of modern obscenity was not quickly outmoded. Because the work's appeal was also transnational, the obscene spread from France all over Europe, and France took over from Italy as the center of European erotic literature. And, whereas Italy's reign had been brief, France's would be long. Paris's status as the dominant center for the production of sexually transgressive literature was nearly uncontested virtually until the end of the nineteenth century. France's only real rival, England, did not enter this field until the mid-eighteenth century, with the publication of John Cleland's *Memoirs of a Woman of Pleasure* (1748–1749).[24] Because of *L'Ecole des filles*'s enduring appeal, the obscene was launched on its modern trajectory, in which it was to become no longer a series of isolated incidents such as Aretino's publications, but rather a true tradition.

L'Ecole des filles became the work that launched modern literary obscenity because the print collective that produced it happened along at the right time and because its members had their fingers on the literary pulse of the day and seemed to know just which innovations would characterize the post-Fronde revolution. The first mark of the work's modernity is their choice of prose. In Latin literature, obscenity almost never ventured outside the confines of poetry; the classics of the bawdy, such as Théophile's, are all in verse.[25] Their exceptional decision meant that *L'Ecole des filles* was part of a wave of experimentation in prose fiction during the immediate post–civil war years that proved to be one of the formative moments in the creation of the modern novel.

To cite but two examples of the works I have in mind: in 1654, the year prior to obscenity's launch, Madeleine de Scudéry—a known sympathizer of the antimonarchist faction during the Fronde—published the first volume of her new novel, *Clélie*. Like *L'Ecole des filles*, *Clélie* is markedly interior and feminocentric. With its exclusive focus on the mechanics of sex, *L'Ecole des filles* can be seen as a reversal of Scudéry's novel and in particular of its elaborate centerpiece, an allegorical map known as the Carte de Tendre, Scudéry's visual exploration of the emotions related to romantic love. The map was engraved by Chauveau, the artist responsible for the frontispiece of *L'Ecole des filles.*[26] Then, in 1656, just after he had tried to market eight copies of *L'Ecole des filles,* Scarron brought out the second part of his *Roman comique.* In 1651 the novel's first part had been, along with Scudéry's *Artamène,* one of the few works of literature to come off printing presses very much otherwise occupied with politics.

The *Roman comique* belongs to a small subset of the prose fiction produced in the mid-seventeenth century. It is one of a very few extraordinarily inventive works, all without immediate posterity, often not before the following century. Their authors launched what are now considered venerable novelistic traditions: the self-conscious novel, the epistolary novel, the historical novel. Collectively, they can be said to have invented the modern novel. *L'Ecole des filles* is just such a work. It is not clear that its authors had a category in mind for it, but today we would call it a novel. In the wake of the huge success of *L'Ecole des filles* and the novel's spectacular rise as the literary genre favored by the new reading publics, all the classics of modern obscenity would be novels.

Like all the works we now call novels and unlike some early obscene classics such as Chorier's *Aloysia Sigeae Toletanae satyra sotadica de arcanis amoris et Veneris, L'Ecole des filles* was written in French, also an auspicious decision, one that proved that the print collective was perfectly in sync with contemporary developments in the book trade.[27] Throughout Europe, the seventeenth century was the key moment in the nationalization of literary markets. The eclipse of Latin as the international language of print culture meant, of course, the consolidation of national literary traditions. In addition, it also dictated the definitive splitting up of the European book trade into a series of distinct national literary markets; whereas books printed in Latin could be printed anywhere, the same was not true of books printed in the so-called national languages. These interrelated developments necessitated, in turn, the nationalization of censorship and all forms of control over print culture. Finally, each language played a central role in the development of a sort of national image. This image was more or less mythic to the extent to which each language continued, well into the following century, to be spoken only by a cultural elite. Nonetheless, it was an essential image, that of persons united under the same monarch and by the same language sharing cultural ideals.[28]

In France, these related developments came together earlier than in any other country, just in time to set the stage for the invention of obscenity. To begin with, roughly the decade prior to the Fronde was an essential moment in the consolidation of a national tradition of French letters, a moment during which the state realized as never before that literature could play a role in a nation-building enterprise. At the same moment, many forms of knowledge—from medicine to theology to law—traditionally transmitted more readily in Latin, began to be communicated at least as readily in French, and often publication in French outstripped that in Latin.[29] Authors working in widely different domains seem more or less simultaneously to have accepted the fact that, henceforth, the major players on the French cultural scene would publish their works in French.

The statistics all confirm this changed situation for print culture in France. According to Martin, in the 1560s publication in French began at times to pull ahead of publication in Latin. In 1585 French finally outstripped Latin. At the end of the sixteenth century, however, between 1580 and 1600, Latin was on the rise again. In fact, during the entire first half of the seventeenth century, "Latin remained remarkably healthy" ("Classements et conjonctures," 1:449). What Martin terms "Latin's second death," that is, the moment at which publication in Latin definitively ceased to play a significant role in the Parisian book trade, took place only during the century's second half: "In 1641–1645, nearly a fourth of the books edited in the capital were written in the language of Cicero; in 1696–1700, [books in Latin] represented only 7 percent of all publications, and most of these were texts intended for schoolboys" (1:485).[30] As Martin concludes: "A fatal evolution: the beginning perhaps of mass culture" (Febvre and Martin, 495). It was surely no accident that, at the origin of mass culture, obscenity first invaded the modern literary scene.[31]

The nationalization of the book trade in the vernacular made inevitable the development of a more effective, more highly regulated system of censorship just at the moment of the obscene's invention. Censorship became all the more necessary because, at the same time as the book trade moved definitively into publication in the vernacular, the economic foundations of print culture were being decisively altered. The changes then implemented were designed to broaden the audience for print culture, thereby making it all the more inevitable that the crown would redouble its efforts to regulate the book trade. It was even more inevitable that the state would take censorship with increasing seriousness at a time when print culture was becoming ever more invasive. Dominique Julia points out that the first half of the seventeenth century saw a "spectacular rise" in the number of print editions: 600 in the year 1644 alone, as compared with only 150 for the entire decade 1600–1609 (259).

During the sixteenth and the first half of the seventeenth century, the most important editorial projects were both religious and monumental—multivolume and large formats, such as folios, that were expensive to produce but could also be sold for handsome sums (Febvre and Martin,

294). This type of publication became far less important in midcentury, undoubtedly partly because of the financial crisis that then threatened the book trade all over Europe (Martin, "Une Croissance séculaire," 2:96). Parisian editors were forced to realize that they had to find new ways of making print culture financially profitable.

The process of adaptation led them to reach out in different ways to new readerships. Febvre and Martin single out the decades 1640–1660 as the period during which, in a number of countries and in France and England in particular, the book trade invested massively in secular, less expensive projects: "Secular literature in the national languages, often intended for a public that did not read Latin, and for women in particular, first became fashionable. . . . From then on, editors begin to publish above all literary works that could be sold easily and quickly" (294–95).[32] Perhaps the easiest way to make this shift in direction was to print in small formats, since such volumes were infinitely less expensive to produce. Indeed, Martin's statistics show that, beginning in the 1660s, these less costly formats became a force to be reckoned with.[33] Thus, a number of factors came together to guarantee that, in the late 1650s and in the 1660s, the French language became, as never before, the cultural instrument through which the book trade, newly reoriented toward mass communication, began to conquer new types of readers. The stage was set for French to become Latin's heir, the new European cultural language.[34]

The obscene was inaugurated in French just as these manifestations of the nationalization and mass dissemination of print culture were being accomplished; the French obscene was thereby able to rise to European dominance on the wave of the French language and of the new print formats.[35] Unlike the classical obscene, and much more than the bawdy, modern obscenity was intended to be available to all; it was packaged to find as many unknown readers as possible. With the configuration that generated obscene literature, issues originated that are currently finding their logical culmination in the debate over material judged pornographic on the Web. In the terms of mid-seventeenth-century print culture, nothing signified availability as much as format, the infamous "small books."[36] The magistrates drawing up English law understood this: the first law allowing for civil censorship of obscene publications, in 1727, made the Latin *libellus*, a small book, synonymous with "an obscene little book."

These little volumes were as promiscuous as books get: made for easy circulation, they were designed to be slipped into a pocket or passed from hand to hand. Less expensive, they were priced to find new readers. Thomas describes the first English translations of *L'Ecole des filles*, in the late 1650s and the 1660s, as "cheaply produced" (20).[37] This was the ideal book form for the cafés that would begin to invade the Parisian scene just five years after modern obscenity. The English magistrates were correct in their appraisal of the situation. These less expensive, handy, "obscene little books" quickly found a broader, less exclusive readership than those for earlier forms of sexually scandalous literature. They arrived on the scene just as a number of factors indicate that the public for literature was both growing and opening up to new markets. For example, the *Bibliothèque bleue,* the inexpensive volumes sold by peddlers directly to the poorest public, went through a major period of expansion immediately after 1650. Just at this time, merchants, buying into the idea that cultural competence could enhance a person's worth, became increasingly eager to acquire the fundamentals of a literary education.[38]

And now, after all this build-up, the book that caused so much trouble. For today's readers, the plot will not seem worth the upheaval: Monsieur Robinet ("faucet" in French), the son of a rich Parisian merchant, is attracted to Fanchon, the sixteen-year-old daughter of a respectable bourgeois family. Fanchon—or so contemporary literary texts, and none more spectacularly than Molière's *L'Ecole des femmes,* tell us—was the girl of every French seventeenth-century bourgeois's dreams: beautiful, of course, and the product of such a sheltered upbringing that her absolute sexual innocence was a given. So perfect is the match that their families allow the young people to see each other freely. This is not enough, however, for our young Robinet, but Fanchon's ignorance is so complete that he can't make her understand what he has in mind. He therefore enlists the aid of Fanchon's more experienced cousin, Suzanne. Up to this point, we're in back story, set forth in a preface.

The work itself is in two parts, both dialogues between the two young women, and it begins with Suzanne's arrival to initiate Fanchon's education. The first part talks her through a presentation of male and female genitalia, followed by a discussion of how the various parts can be employed. It ends with the arrival of Robinet, eager to put this knowledge to the test. Time passes. Suzanne returns to Fanchon's comfortable bourgeois home and, in the second part, they discuss what Fanchon has learned under Robinet's capable tutelage. The story ends, as all good novels do, with a marriage on the horizon—not, however, that of our two young lovers, but rather Fanchon's union with a man who has recently begun, presumably with her parents' blessing, frequenting her home and flirting with her. The original "obscene little book" closes on a note of bourgeois domesticity: Suzanne once again offers her services, this time as a marriage broker.

In a number of his now classic works, Foucault links the silencing of the open expression of sexuality to "a formidable growth of the domain of confession" in the wake of the Reformation and the Counter-Reformation (*Les Anormaux,* 164). Beginning in the mid-seventeenth century, he documents a major recontouring of the institution of confession. Previously the confessor had focused his questions on the type of sexual relations the penitent had or had not enjoyed; from this point on, manuals teach him how to lead the penitent meticulously over all the relevant body parts. Together, confessor's questions and penitent's answers make up what Foucault calls "an anatomy of voluptuousness": "It's the body with its different parts, the body with its different sensations, that now defined the articulation of the sin of lust." The new type of confession that Foucault defines "had to follow a sort of sinful cartography of the body" (174). He calls this development "the appearance of the body of desire and of pleasure at the heart of the technique of spiritual direction" (187).[39]

At the moment when the manuals for confessors were being reoriented, the print collective imagined a related "anatomy of voluptuousness." Modern obscenity is quite clearly not mainly about action, but about talk of it—in a confessional mode. Note how the younger cousin comes clean to her wiser counselor, who interrogates Fanchon in the work's second dialogue about what she has been up to with Robinet. Here, the print collective could almost have been parodying one of the classic manuals for confessors. Thus, Suzanne begins her cousin's sexual awakening by inquiring whether any man has "ever touched her in any place" (187). In similar fashion, one of Foucault's key sources, Father Louis Habert, lists as the first question confessors are to ask about lust: "Have you ever performed any improper fondling" (*attouchements,* literally "touchings," 309). Thus, the original "obscene little book" and the confessor's manual conspire to give the impression of an age obsessively centered on a single problem, the relation between the hand and a few key body parts.[40] The first dialogue has been described as "a vocabulary lesson" (Camus, 165). In this area, the obscene seems like a hyperexaggeration of the bawdy.

Genitalia and sexual characteristics are named and renamed and nicknamed; lists of every possible synonym are carefully drawn up. Moreover, this work does not follow the conventions of earlier sexually transgressive literature in French; primary obscenities are neither scrambled nor replaced with an ellipsis. Instead, for the first time in the history of French printed books, all the words previously subjected to self-censorship—and, in Théophile's case, to actual censorship as well—are printed out, again and again, so often in fact that the novel could be taken for a treatise on four-letter words. It's made clear that calling a spade a spade, confronting the obscene word in its full force, is one of the particular joys procured by "obscene little books." The novel surely owed much of its initial success to the fact that it was the first work to profit from the new charge that four-letter words had acquired in the aftermath of Théophile's censorship. They had become absolutely taboo, and the print collective took evident delight in trafficking in this taboo. The novel thus played a key role in the process by which modern obscenity became synonymous with four-letter words. Witness the obscene's initial definition in French criticism, that given by Théophile's co-defendant Guillaume Colletet three years after *L'Ecole des filles*'s publication: obscene words are "those that name, and thereby uncover . . . those parts of the body that propriety demands that we keep hidden" (108–9).

When sex began a discursive existence in French, the discourse was radically different from any previous tradition of sexually transgressive literature. Most crucial is the fact that, when sex began to speak obscenity, it spoke as a woman. Robinet is given an almost exclusively off-stage role, while women do all the talking.[41] And when the young women talk, the great originality of their discourse about sex, the mark of its modernity, is that female genitalia are evoked as much as male; female genitalia are, moreover, *celebrated* in a fashion previously reserved for male organs. Thus, to return to Foucault's example of the all-important relation of the hand to the body, when Suzanne questions Fanchon about where men have tried to touch her, or later when she explains where men will touch her, with these questions, these "touchings," we are at a crucial turning point in the history of sexually transgressive literature. For the first time—unlike the evocations in Roman poetry, unlike the bawdy—female sexual characteristics are described without disgust, and the gesture of touching them is evoked as something that provokes both desire in the man and pleasure in the woman. Such a description might seem banal today, but it is one of the key distinctions separating the modern obscene from its precursors.

Of the obscene in Latin literature, Richlin remarks that "the strongest focus was on the genitalia" (26). She immediately adds a qualifier, reiterated whenever she mentions this subject, to the effect that female genitalia, unlike male, are evoked only rarely and that they are "almost exclusively described as disgusting" (26, see also 211).[42] From this perspective, the French bawdy can be seen as the last direct heir of Latin obscenity: priapic sex for an elite male audience. *L'Ecole des filles* breaks what was in effect the taboo within a genre that allegedly defined itself in opposition to all such taboos. In modern obscenity, female genitalia, for the first time in any erotic or transgressive literature, are portrayed not as disgusting but as a source of pleasure for both partners.[43] Obscenity began its modern existence when

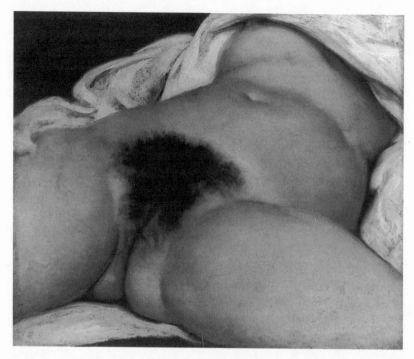

FIGURE 3   Gustave Courbet, *L'Origine du monde* (1866). Courtesy of the Musée d'Orsay, Paris.

authors decided both to free themselves from classical precedent and that female genitalia could be as much, or even more, of a turn-on as male.

This previously unheard of focus definitively altered the course of sexually transgressive literature. Indeed, until recent decades and with very rare exceptions—of which Sade's oeuvre is arguably the most striking—all subsequent obscene and pornographic literature follows this model and focuses the reader's attention on female genitalia. And once visual representations became central to the portrayal of eroticism, they shared this focus, generally even more relentlessly. One need only think of what might be considered the logical culmination of the road on which *L'Ecole des filles* launched obscenity, Gustave Courbet's 1866 canvas, *L'Origine du monde* (figure 3). Courbet's portrayal of female genitalia is so blatant and exclusive that it was thus described by one of its early viewers, Flaubert's close friend, Maxime Du Camp: "By some inconceivable forgetfulness, the artist . . . had neglected to represent the feet, the legs, the thighs, the stomach, the hips, the chest, the hands, the arms, the shoulders, the neck, and the head" (cited by Nochlin, 81).[44]

With *L'Ecole des filles*, we are at the origin of the modern erotic tradition that "forgets" all of a woman's body but the genitalia, thereby reversing the "forgetting" in Latin literature, the "blank space" its poets left "in the middle of the woman" (Richlin, 47). When it was first publicly exhibited in 1988, the Courbet canvas still possessed the capacity to shock an American audience that had had a great deal of exposure to this representational tradition. It is hard to imagine the impact its precursor must have had in 1655.

This change of focus, arguably the most dramatic in the history of erotic literature, had many other consequences for the representation of sexuality. The new focus on female sexuality resulted in a major realignment in the staging of male sexuality. In *L'Ecole des filles* and the other early classics of obscene literature, male sexual desire is no longer polyvalent, as it was in the bawdy. Following the dictates of Théophile's censors, the action has become resolutely heterosexual. Furthermore, male sexuality has become, as it were, beside the point; all attention focuses on the depiction of female sexuality. As soon as transgressive literature began to reach out to a wider readership, it sought to turn its readers on in an entirely new way; and, since nearly all early modern pornography repeats this new focus, it must have accurately predicted the nature of the new demand.[45]

From its portrayal of desire and because of its huge success, we can deduce that the first obscene novel managed to find, and perhaps helped to create, the audience that those who package pornography for a large audience today still imagine as their target: primarily men who will be turned on by any depiction of female sexuality, even female homosexuality, but turned off by any parallel focus on male genitalia—and most certainly by any hint of homoeroticism.[46] By highlighting the way in which the novel inaugurates modern pornography, I run the risk, however, of playing down the ways in which its portrayal of sexuality is not only unlike anything that had come before, but also unlike what was ahead.

To begin with, the novel does not mix various types of transgression. There is no trace in it of social or political satire, of abusive polemic or invective, areas in which all its precursors felt that obscenity was at home. The novel thus has no other focus to blunt its exposition of the means to sexual pleasure.[47] Politics and pornography would subsequently often be blended in the French tradition, particularly throughout the eighteenth century; because of its resolutely sexual focus, the work that reinvented obscenity seems more modern than its immediate successors.

The modern obscene marks a radical departure from prior erotica in another, equally radical way. If we step back from the lists of sexual organs and the uses to which they can be put to consider the context in which all this hot-blooded talk takes place, what is perhaps most striking is its "averageness"—Robinet and Fanchon are truly the boy and girl next door. In earlier erotic works, the protagonists are most often rigorously undefined—think of the example of the bawdy, in which there is no way of distinguishing any of the bearers of male genitalia from the mass of energetic lovers. When obscenity was partnered with the novel, the participants in its sexual scenes began to acquire various types of identity. In *L'Ecole des filles* the characters have proper names intended to be taken for real bourgeois names. Robinet is identified as "the son of a Parisian merchant"—a "very rich" merchant at that (Camus, 171).[48] Their story has a precise, nearly contemporary historical setting: "During the reign of Louis XIII" are its first words (171). The text is full of the type of small detail about daily life in a Parisian bourgeois household that could be called realistic—for example, the fact that women regularly attended vespers at 3 P.M. (240).[49] These characters read neither texts nor images; they need no outside stimulation. They are unusual precisely because they are so unexceptional, so thoroughly unsophisticated.

Their ordinariness is the signature of obscenity's modernity. Since antiquity sexually transgressive literature was allowed a virtually peaceful coexistence as long as it remained confined to certain clearly delimited areas. The message of *L'Ecole des filles* is that that order had now been overturned.[50] The obscene had escaped from the garden of Priapus, from the upside-down world of Bakhtin's carnivalesque. It had taken up residence within the everyday order.

In addition, the women of *L'Ecole des filles* cannot be identified by their flagrant sexual availability. By this, I mean that, unlike Aretino's heroines, they are neither sexy nuns nor courtesans nor simple whores; they belong to none of the categories of women who had sex for money and whose promiscuity was taken as a fact of life.[51] *L'Ecole des filles* is definitely not, as has often been said of Aretino's *Ragionamenti*, pornographic in the etymological sense of "writing about whores" (see, for example, Thomas, 17). Prior to *L'Ecole des filles*, when sexually transgressive literature has a precise setting, it is generally that of a brothel. Here, for the first time, a woman is initiated into her sexuality in a private home, her father's house. Here, also for the first time, a young man has sex with someone who is completely his social equal.[52] The novel stages the coming to sexual knowledge of an ordinary, bourgeois young woman. That was, for its readers, its principal turn-on and, for its censors, surely its principal threat: Fanchon could be any man's daughter; she could become any man's wife.

Nor is *L'Ecole des filles* pornographic in a now widely accepted sense of the term, that proposed most notably by Gloria Steinem. She defines pornography as a relation of unequal power: the man is dominant and the woman a victim; the victim is unclothed and vulnerable, while the male is clothed; female genitalia are on display "for the conquering male viewer"; sex takes place in a climate of both psychological and physical violence against women.[53] In *L'Ecole des filles*, the characters are there because they want to be; there is no imbalance of power—indeed, power is not an issue at all—and violence is never used. Fanchon is on display, not for her degradation, but just as Robinet is on display: for their mutual pleasure.

One thing *L'Ecole des filles* does share with pornography is the assumption that sexuality can and should be distinguished from generation. Steinem contends that Phyllis Schlafly's condemnation of the women's movement as "obscene" resulted from its failure to subordinate sex to procreation (36). In this context, it seems fitting that the first representative of our modern tradition of obscene literature may well also be the first printed volume to convey information on contraception. It also seems fitting that it does so in a manner that can be seen as empowering to women. In the long tradition of dialogues dealing with love and sexuality, male authors from Plato to Aretino elected a female protagonist as the principal voice of wisdom. When Suzanne takes on Fanchon's education, she makes room in the wisdom she imparts for subjects never before included in such discussions: a woman's right to sexual pleasure and, above all, the means that allow her to have that pleasure without risk of pregnancy.

Perhaps the most surprising consequence of *L'Ecole des filles*'s unparalleled display of four-letter words is the link thus established between the role traditionally assigned them, that of scandalizing, and this new one, that of imparting information in an area until then not part of the domain of print culture. Demographers and historians of sexuality stress that the earliest evidence of the practice of birth control in France was printed only in the second half of the seventeenth century, and in England that evidence appears only later, in the eighteenth century.[54] The fact that this information began to circulate in print in mid-seventeenth-century France confirms Foucault's hypothesis that, once censorship began to repress the explicit references to sexuality in literary texts, this discourse found a new home in a burgeoning scientific and medical literature dealing with issues related to sexuality. This literature quickly became increasingly specialized; as Foucault remarks, the displacement provoked by censorship was at the origin of numerous new discourses, today known as demography, biology, and so forth. Foucault situates at this period one further related consequence: the official realization on the part of emerging modern states that they were dealing not simply with a people (*peuple*) but with a population. This realization prompted the beginning of an official policing of sexuality, in the sense of public policy on sexuality.[55]

Naturally, some of the information the novel presents as fact seems ludicrous today—the claim, for instance, that out of a hundred cases of unprotected intercourse, fewer than two will result in pregnancy (263). Also, the contraception described—a "small cloth" (*un petit linge*) to be placed over the penis—seems by today's standards less than foolproof.[56] When, however, the novel presents this information as an essential part of every sexual education, it was making available information that early modern public policy sought to suppress. What was simultaneously most "obscene" (in Schlafly's view) and most unruly (in terms of policing) about its presentation was that it directed the information to those most directly affected by conception. Thus, when coitus interruptus is explained, the woman is told when and how to initiate it (262). In contrast, when the practice resurfaces in eighteenth-century libertine literature, it is always fully a male prerogative. Similarly, when the novel presents what may be the earliest printed information on sex aids, any reader familiar with their use in subsequent pornographic texts is caught up short: the description is divided equally between sex toys for men and those for women. Those for women are characterized as "diverse inventions by which women can have pleasure with no fear of pregnancy" (180; see also 260–61).[57] When it gave these issues their first public airing, the novel featured sexuality as independent of the moral and religious context from which it had previously been inseparable. The process of obscenity's secularization had been completed.

Sex moved from the brothel into the private home, sex intimately related to the realities of everyday life, of marriage and the family. The novel's message to women seems clear: they were responsible for their bodies and their sexuality. They had a right to pleasure; they could learn how to have it without fear of pregnancy—and even without men. *L'Ecole des filles* uses obscenity to promote the individual's right to information about sexuality and reproduction, on the grounds that this knowledge would allow sexual independence. The print collective thus showed that the heterosexuality made compulsory during Théophile's trial had its own capacity for subversiveness. The novel's program for female empowerment was surely particularly unwelcome because it appeared on the heels of the Fronde, during which women—and none more spectacularly than the duchesse de Montpensier, at whose court in exile L'Ange found work as a printer as soon as the *L'Ecole des filles* affair was over—had been particularly influential members of the rebel coalition.[58]

Was all this revolutionary content a sign that the print collective sensed that the male-focused, desire-all-that-is-desirable line was no longer valid in a world in which the print industry was opening up to new publics? For once, we possess a good deal of information about the work's initial readers. The variety of those attracted to the little book surely signifies that its authors had guessed correctly that there was a demand for what they were prepared to supply.

I'll begin with the least surprising of those readers. Only one copy of the novel's original edition is known to have survived the censors' bonfire. It was confiscated, some six years after the book trial, at the time of the arrest of Nicolas Fouquet, Louis XIV's finance minister, on charges of fiscal corruption.[59] He had kept the little book multiply locked away, inside a house with a secret entrance used to receive his mistress, inside his secret study, and in a locked chest (Lachèvre, 82). This reading is typical of lewd literature's controlled, noncontaminating circulation as long as its readers were, like Fouquet, elite, extremely wealthy males.

Our second reader, though today equally predictable, is significantly more modern. Thanks to this reader's habit of keeping a diary, we know precisely how his copy was purchased (in 1668, so it was probably the Roger Bon Temps edition) and how it was read. Thus, on January 13, 1668, Samuel Pepys recorded that, at the end of a day's work, he stopped at his bookseller's, Martins, where he perused a copy of *L'Ecole des filles*. Pepys, however, decided against buying what he described as "the most bawdy, lewd book that ever I saw," declaring that he "was ashamed of reading it"; he returned home to have dinner and put his accounts for the next day "in good condition" (9:21–22).

But the industrious civil servant did not manage to forget the lewd little book. The following month, on February 8, he paid another visit to Martins, once again after a long day at the office. This time, he stayed a full hour, and he left having "bought that idle, roguish book, *L'Ecole des filles*" (9:57). Pepys had worked out a most ingenious compromise to justify this purchase. It was "not amiss for a sober man once to read [it] over to inform himself in the villainy of the world." Nevertheless, he "resolve[d], as soon as I have read it, to burn it, that it may not stand in the list of books, nor among them, to disgrace them if it should be found." Ever thrifty, as well as respectable, Pepys decided to keep costs down on this purchase: he bought it "in plain binding (avoiding the buying of it better bound)." That evening's supper with his wife was a happy occasion: his sister had made a good match; so "that care will be over" (9:58).

The following day, he made effective use of his purchase. He spent the morning in his office, alternating business and the "mighty lewd book." In the afternoon and evening, he was at home, in the company of four male friends, singing and drinking his "good store of wine." When they left, Pepys retired "to his chamber," where he read *L'Ecole des filles* through again—allegedly "for information's sake," though obviously for pleasure as well, since he records (using his own brand of self-censorship) that "it did hazer my prick para stand all the while, and una vez to decharger." True to his word, Pepys then burned the volume, so "that it might not be among my books to my shame" (9:59).

Foxon describes "Pepys in his role as the first great middle-class civil servant" as emblematic of the new readership for dirty books: "remember that it has probably been the apparently respectable . . . professional man who has provided the bulk of the demand for pornography over the years" (50). Certainly Pepys's reading of the novel is very different from previous consumption of sexually transgressive literature. His relation to the ob-scene is most obviously financial, clearly inscribed into a bourgeois rather than an aristocratic economy: in his diary, it is interwoven with his relation to the accounts that were the center of his professional life; he carefully calculates what the volume is worth to him. It is also more ordinary: his reading takes place in his home, as part of his daily routine. Finally, Pepys's relation to the obscene is more public: he finds the book in a shop; he en-joys it as an extension of a boisterous moment of male companionship.

In one aspect at least, these two readings were alike. Though they were worlds apart socially, Fouquet and Pepys, both known for their amorous adventures, undoubtedly were interested in more or less the same content. In the case of the third recorded reading, however, we are in all likelihood dealing with a public just as unexpected as the book's view of female sexu-ality.

On November 19, 1687—at a time when the book police were still try-ing to ferret out the novel's author—the comte de Bussy-Rabutin, himself the author of sexually scandalous literature, wrote his cousin, the marquise de Sévigné, with an anecdote: "Madame de Montchevreuil [a governess], having found in the room of the ladies [*filles*]-in-waiting of the dauphine a book entitled *L'Ecole des filles*, went to make a complaint to the king."[60] With *L'Ecole des filles*, the *filles de Madame la dauphine* received a kind of education unheard of for unmarried women of the day. Late at night in their shared room, when their official duties were done, following the ex-ample of the novel's frontispiece (figure 4), they read together about sex toys, boy toys, and contraception. When he learned what they were up to, the king summarily dismissed them (Lachèvre, 87 n. 1). Small wonder. Along with servants, women were the potential audience for sexually transgressive literature most feared by the authorities at all periods. Thus,

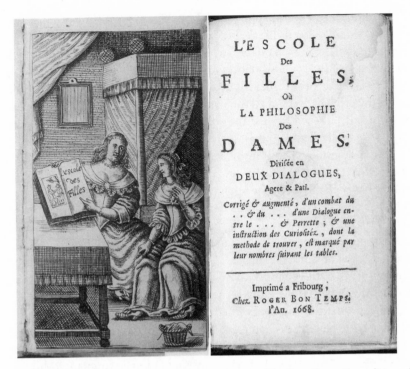

FIGURE 4   Title page and frontispiece of *L'Ecole des filles,* from the earliest edition of which a copy has been traced (1668). Frontispiece is believed to copy François Chauveau's for the original 1655 French edition. Probably printed in Holland. (British Library no. PC29a16.) Reprinted by permission of the British Library, London.

before questioning the members of the jury at Lawrence's obscenity trial about how they would feel if their servants read *Lady Chatterley's Lover,* the lawyer for the prosecution asked whether they would want their "young daughter or their wives to read it" (Hyde, 62).[61]

The sea change in the nature of erotic literature initiated by *L'Ecole des filles* parallels the general reorientation that would shortly be taking place in French literature (and English as well), a reorientation dictated by its changed audience. The fifteen years that separated *L'Ecole des filles* and Molière's most bourgeois comedy, *Le Tartuffe,* marked a crucial moment in the passage from literary genres designed to be appreciated above all by a male, classically educated public and new or recontoured forms that featured a domestic, middle-class world. This new focus was designed to appeal to the new classes of readers then entering the literary marketplace in important numbers—in particular, to the two groups whose reading of *L'Ecole des filles* is attested: the bourgeoisie and women.

Benedict Anderson describes vividly the particular nature of the bond between the bourgeoisie and print culture. He evokes the example of two factory owners in different cities who were not related, as contemporary aristocrats were, because of shared kinsmen or because they married each other's daughters. Instead, they negotiated their cohesion as a class through print culture in the vernacular, what Anderson calls "vernacular print-capitalism" (76). They "c[a]me to visualize in a general way the existence of thousands and thousands like themselves through print-language. For an illiterate bourgeoisie is scarcely imaginable. Thus in world-historical terms bourgeoisies were the first classes to achieve solidarities on an essentially imagined basis" (77). The new literary genres—in particular, the novel—that rose to prominence in the postrevolutionary decades of the second half of the seventeenth century played a crucial role in the process by which the bourgeoisie negotiated its cohesion. Modern obscenity had its role to play in this process. *L'Ecole des filles* seems a case of sexually transgressive literature recontoured expressly for the bourgeoisie's "imaginings."

The frontispiece François Chauveau designed for the original edition speaks to erotica's new life in the little book's reaching an expanded readership (see figure 4).[62] The setting is resolutely domestic and average. The engraving represents a scene set in a well-to-do bourgeoise's bedroom. Within that everyday setting, the two women turn to intellectual matters. They are seated in the narrow space beside the bed, called a *ruelle*, and defined since the 1620s as the space in which women carried out intellectual discussions. The frontispiece makes it clear that the women are abandoning traditional activities for a newer pursuit: a workbasket sits on the floor at a distance from them; all their attention is concentrated on a book.[63]

The older woman is drawing her companion's attention to the book's title, *L'Ecole des filles*. Even for those unfamiliar with the volume's content, the frontispiece shows that it intends to reach the new readers par excellence, women. The fact that the image is bookish rather than erotic could indicate an awareness that what was dangerous about what the two women are doing is sharing, and therefore spreading, knowledge. For those who know the book's content, the image suggests that the newly nationalized print culture in French will spread the message that obscenity is set to invade everyday life in bourgeois households like the one depicted in the engraving. It will carry into those households information directed at their "womenfolk," knowledge that can give them new control over all aspects of their sexuality. When modern obscenity escaped the boundaries within which its classical precursor had been confined, it immediately gave the authorities a set of completely modern concerns.

In England, the novel's circulation, both in French and in English, began just as, in the aftermath of the Restoration, the crown tried to tighten
up on the print industry. The 1662 Licensing Act, in particular, decreed the
strict enforcement of all earlier laws. Perhaps because the book was once
again marketed in a postrevolutionary climate but by printers used to operating under revolutionary conditions, it once again forced the censors'
hand. The novel, known in English as *The School of Venus*, played a key role
in the early modern history of obscenity law and in the definitive secularization of censorship in England. English translations were prosecuted
twice, in 1680 and 1688, both times by civil authorities. Too little is known
about the case brought in 1688 against the printer Joseph Streater and the
bookseller Benjamin Crayle or Carle to know what the authorities were
after. We do know that the pair was charged with "selling several obscene
and lascivious books," primarily a new translation of *L'Ecole des filles*. This
is an early appearance in English of the adjective *obscene*, still in the process
of being transplanted from French—and a truly pioneering usage of the
term in the domain of print censorship.[64]

The earlier case, however, is far more detailed. It was brought against a
little-known printer-bookseller, John Coxe (a.k.a. John Tartar), on the
grounds that he "with the intention of debauching and corrupting young
men and others of the said King's lieges and subjects, maliciously and
scandalously uttered, published, and offered for sale, a certain most pernicious, wicked and vicious book entitled 'The School of Venus or the
Ladies delight Reduced into Rules of Practice being the Translation of the
French Lescole des filles in Two dialogues'" (cited in Thompson, "Two
Early Editions," 45). In this instance, enough survives to explain why the
authorities intervened. In particular, the indictment provides something
glaringly absent from the French prosecution: it singles out extensive passages as the basis for censorship. The quotations give a clear sense of how
the English censors defined the problem of "pernicious" publications.
They also show that in this case censors made very sensitive readers indeed; they seem to have understood exactly what was innovative in the
novel's definition of obscenity.

Of the fragments cited, Thompson says that "they are by no means the
most erotic passages in the two dialogues" ("Two Early Editions," 45).
True—by today's standards at least. Of the ten passages, however, fully
half are remarkable above all for their flagrant display of four-letter words.
Two others relate to contraception and sex aids. One even exaggerates the
French original's praise of women's sexual good sense: "if Women govern'd
the World and the Church as men do you would soon find they would account ffucking so lawful as it should not be accounted a Misdemeaner"

(46).[65] The remaining two citations are in fact the same passage, merely broken up. This is the only example dangerous in a different way: it can be read as libertine philosophizing (46–47). With this one exception, the secular censors stuck to their bailiwick: the novel was evaluated almost exclusively on secular grounds, and on secular grounds of a new nature, neither political nor libelous. The censors did not, however, take the logical next step, that of determining the nature of the civil offense committed with the work's publication.

The first legal debate ever on obscenity finally took place forty years later and once again in England. At that point, English law at long last gave official recognition to a phenomenon that had been increasingly visible in French law for a full century but that French authorities refused to confront: obscenity's status as a modern censorial category. Obscenity became law in response to the next French obscene novel to find an audience in English translation, *Venus in a Cloister, or the Nun in Her Smock* (often attributed to abbé Jean Barrin). But the way had been prepared for the decision to grant obscenity an independent legal existence by the first little book to give censors nowhere else to look but at sexuality, thereby forcing them to learn to censor an area in which their mission did not originally lie.

3

Two-Letter Words

MOLIÈRE'S *L'ECOLE DES FEMMES*
AND OBSCENITY MADE MODERN

Un mot de deux lettres vous fait peur,
que deviendriez-vous donc s'il y en avait davantage?
—Philippe de La Croix, *La Guerre comique, ou la
Défense de "L'Ecole des femmes"*

Molière is as central to the study of French literature as is Shake-speare to the study of English literature. Also like Shakespeare, Molière was an author in all senses of the term—and the term was very much in evolution—possible in his day. Indeed, from this point of view, one can even argue that Molière was more fully a modern author than Shakespeare. The following pages are above all a reflection on the various ways in which Molière's exceptional authorial status was a product of the combined forces of censorship and obscenity.

I am not claiming that there were no authors before the late seventeenth century, but rather that, in France in the second half of the seventeenth century, the concept of authorship was in full and rapid transition. I will present Molière as the first truly modern author in the French tradition. This means that Molière occupies a unique position in the ranks of major early modern writers: he is at the same time both the most prominent writer in the French tradition and the first modern author in France. Unlike Shakespeare, who is the classic representative of the performed, collaborative writing of the early seventeenth-century stage, Molière is positioned on the modern side of the authorial divide: the plays upon which his reputation is founded are all individual productions and all very much "'written' writing."[1] Unlike Shakespeare—as well as other early modern authors who are assigned leading roles in their national literary traditions, such as Dante and Cervantes—Molière began his career as print author at the precise moment when another kind of modern authorship initially became a reality. He was the first writer to attain truly international status, to achieve the kind of international reputation that only became possible with the spread of print journalism throughout Europe. Molière is also a modern author in that he became increasingly involved with the marketplace. He understood that the book would no longer function as something to be given or exchanged but as a commodity to be bought and sold.[2]

Finally, Molière is the first major author to owe to a significant degree his status to an involvement with censorship. Whereas Shakespeare is credited with having invented many things—the modern individual, for instance—Molière can be credited with a number of inventions essential to modern authorship. In particular, his career confirms Foucault's claim in "What Is an Author?" that the author is a transgressive concept, that authors only truly become authors when their writing is judged transgressive. From this perspective, Molière seems the ultimate modern author. The transgressive plays of his greatest period forced Louis XIV and Colbert finally to make censorship—which, as I have shown, had been slowly and largely ineffectively taking shape for decades—a systematic, bureaucratic institution. And if Molière "invented" censorship, censorship can also be said to have "invented" Molière. As a result of six years of relentless confrontation with that institution, he was transformed from merely an excellent dramatist into the greatest playwright of the French tradition.

Molière's involvement with censorship clearly indicates, moreover, the new role that obscenity would play for modern writers. In all previous instances, when a writer (for example, Ovid, Jean de Meun, and Montaigne) had been censured because his works were considered sexually transgressive, the charge was part of an attempt to undermine his authority, a means of proving that he was unworthy of true authorial status; great authors, or so the argument went, could not be linked to such vulgarity. When Molière became linked to the reinvention of obscenity, however, he used his involvement with dirty words to help found his literary authority. Indeed, Molière's career may teach us that the author of obscene literature was truly the ultimate modern writer.[3] Then, once his display of the scandal of obscenity had attracted the attention of some of the earliest French print journalists, obscenity and censorship combined made Molière the first true precursor of the celebrity author of our own media-obsessed age. His name and his portrait became known all over Europe at the same time as a lurid version of his private life was passed off as his biography. For better and for worse, the modern writer had come of age.

In October 1658, a thirty-six-year-old actor-director who had attracted favorable attention during over a decade touring in the French provinces, arrived in Paris with his company. On October 24 they were invited to the Louvre, where they staged for the king and his court Pierre Corneille's *Nicomède*, which was not well received, and one of the actor's early efforts as a playwright, a now lost one-act farce, *Le Docteur amoureux*, which was. As a result of this partial success, Molière was awarded his first theater in Paris, the Petit-Bourbon, which he shared with another troupe. On November 2 his company played for the first time for the Parisian public; they staged another of their director's early efforts, *L'Etourdi*, to great acclaim.

At this point, Molière was only truly an author in a use of the term never adopted by his native language. In this usage, which existed in Golden Age Spanish, the term *autores* was reserved for the directors of theatrical companies (Chartier, *Publishing Drama*, 61–62). After his arrival in Paris, Molière initially subordinated his other activities to his work for his company. In this, he stands out: no other major French playwright was also the principal actor and the director of a troupe.

When he arrived in Paris, Molière had just begun his transition to a second type of authorship; he was writing, though not yet publishing, the scripts of some of the plays staged by his company. This type of author, as seventeenth-century French dictionaries indicate and as Molière's personal experience would shortly teach him, was becoming obsolete. Henceforth, *author* would be reserved for those who published their works.[4] One reason I describe Molière as fully an author is that—more so than Shakespeare and more so than his greatest French precursor, Corneille, who came on the scene before print culture had fully modified the conditions for authorship—he exploited the new possibilities, from formats to frontispieces, offered by print; he came to understand the advantages, and the disadvantages, of print authorship. Indeed, in this area in particular, Molière is accessible to us as Shakespeare can never be. Whereas we do not fully understand Shakespeare's relation to the marketing of his plays, more information has come down to us about the material conditions of Molière's life as an author than about all the other aspects of his life combined. It is possible, in fact, to document with a precision that would have been the envy of the civil servant in Pepys exactly how Molière marketed his production and how much he made from it.[5]

In one crucial way, Molière the author was like Shakespeare. Their careers were played out on the cusp of the most important modern evolution in authorship: they were patronage artists as well as commercial artists. More than Shakespeare, however, Molière made the transition from the old way (patronage) to the new (commerce). Even the patronage system in which he participated was no longer truly an attempt by a patron to reward financially a writer's fidelity or the importance of his service, but a new type of system, the beginning of state sponsorship of the arts.[6]

In France, both evolutions—in authorship and in patronage—took place together. Molière belonged to the first generation of French writers able (and willing) to sell their manuscripts directly to publishers. Previously, writers used money received as a gift or pension from a wealthy patron to pay part of the printing costs; in return, they received a certain number of copies, which they dedicated to their patrons, with the expectation of additional gratification. Molière arrived on the Parisian scene just as practice was changing. Among the major writers roughly of his generation, Boileau and La Bruyère, for example, did not sell their manuscripts to publishers, whereas Corneille and La Fontaine did.[7] The practice was so new, however, that very few writers indeed managed to get large sums from these sales. Thus, new-style writers such as Corneille still functioned also as traditional patronage artists, dedicating, for instance, prefaces to their works to nobles in return for gratification. The fact that Molière's print income was so substantially offset by the increasingly handsome revenues from his theater gave him the freedom to negotiate print culture in a more thoroughly modern manner.

In addition, his print career took off just as the patronage system in France was entering the modern age. Between late 1662 and early 1664, Louis XIV and Colbert laid the foundation for the first system of systematic state sponsorship of the arts in any European nation. They put into place an official cultural policy that in effect signaled the demise of patronage. In place of the personal bond between patron and writer, the new policy substituted standards—in particular, the quality of the work—to be applied by the king's advisors. Henceforth, those judged worthy of sponsorship were to receive fixed incomes, to be distributed annually.[8]

The new cultural policy has traditionally been portrayed as an attempt to promote France's greatest writers as part of the glorious image of the Sun King's reign. The price of such mutually reflective glory has not, however, been sufficiently stressed. Without control over the book trade, no cultural policy could be properly implemented. And, despite all the laws imposed and reimposed from the 1620s on, this goal had eluded both Richelieu and Mazarin. Thus, at the same time as they debated which writers to sponsor, Louis XIV and Colbert were also deciding on measures—most crucially, the creation of the first official book police anywhere—to achieve that long-desired goal. It was only once their new order was in place that, in the 1670s and 1680s, all the old laws would finally begin to be effectively enforced (Roche, "La Police du livre," 84). It was only then that France truly possessed institutionalized, secular censorship.

To any astute observer of the cultural and political scene such as Molière, three interrelated truths were surely evident: a career in print was increasingly the measure of an author; the financial rewards of such authorship were increasing; censorship—with the complicated relation to literary finances that it entailed—was coming of age. Because Molière began his career after the writers' trials that had made underground classics of the texts they censored, he undoubtedly grasped, in addition, a truth more generally exploited only during the Enlightenment: a censored work had vast commercial appeal. *L'Ecole des femmes*, the play he wrote just as official debate on patronage of the arts was being initiated, inaugurates Molière's six-year-long entanglement with every kind of censorship operative in his day. By the time he had completed his masterpieces, *Le Festin de pierre* (a.k.a. *Dom Juan*) and *Le Tartuffe*, this entanglement with censorship had given definitive shape to his oeuvre—as well as a definitive impetus to the institutionalization of censorship.[9]

※

The years just prior to and just after the inception of Louis XIV's personal reign in 1661 were the last moment in the seventeenth century before the rise of absolutism brought increased centralization and increasingly efficient functioning to the institutions and the bureaucracy upon which the modern French state was founded. This was the final period, for example, before the appointment of Nicolas de La Reynie as Lieutenant General of the Police, with responsibility over the book trade and censorship. La Reynie at long last began the first systematic regulation of those institutions in any European country. The crackdown that led to the creation of the book police began just as the controversy surrounding Molière's *L'Ecole des femmes* dominated the Parisian literary scene. As far as the book trade and its regulation were concerned, the years between *L'Ecole des filles* and *L'Ecole des femmes* were remarkable because, as Martin stresses, everything necessary to guarantee effective state control over the book trade was in place, but—and it's a very big but—somehow the system still could not be made to function. The Parisian print industry continued to be in wild disarray (Febvre and Martin, 377). The authorities were unable to control the book trade even though the Fronde was still recent enough to provide ample cause for concern, even though contemporary events in England were certainly alarming, and even though the crown was faced with a new crisis, one that was often played out in print.[10]

Between 1661 and 1663, Louis XIV and Colbert were putting an end to the spectacular career of Nicolas Fouquet, France's Finance Minister (a role Colbert would take over) and last great private patron of arts and letters (a position the king would assume after institutionalizing it). Until the summer of 1663, they were working up a dossier against Fouquet. The two plays in which Molière staged the drama of obscenity were the product of the last months of 1663, the period just prior to Fouquet's trial. During all this time, the censors were unable to check the flow of pro-Fouquet publications that made public details of the case that the king was trying to keep secret.[11]

During this period, Colbert thought up one measure after another, seeking almost desperately some means of achieving absolute control over what was printed in France and thereby imposing order in a domain that his predecessors had found ungovernable. Thus, he considered the idea of imposing prohibitive taxes on the paper used for printing. He even debated a plan that, if implemented, would have made today's historians of print culture deliriously happy: every print font would have been marked so that the print shop that had produced each book could be established beyond a doubt (Martin, *Livre*, 2:695). Finally, concerned that foreign presses were turning out books in French that were beginning to circulate within France in important numbers, Colbert considered launching what we would call a trade war by prohibiting the sale of all Dutch publications in France.[12]

When these new ideas were judged unworkable, Colbert returned to two familiar means of control (even though neither had as yet proved effective). He tinkered still again with the enforcement of the privilege (Febvre and Martin, 296), and he stepped up his campaign to reduce the number of master printers and print shops in Paris. The brief period between the inception of Louis XIV's personal reign and the beginning of La Reynie's saw the sharpest decline in the entire century: the number of printing houses was cut fully in half, from 72 to 36.[13] Yet, even though the moment at which Colbert would prove that he was the official finally capable of bringing book censorship into the modern age was only a few years away, at this point nothing succeeded in putting an end to the sale of bad books. His policy did, however, have disastrous economic consequences for the French book trade, consequences that would continue to be felt throughout the Enlightenment. Most notably, by formalizing censorship, Colbert guaranteed that controversial printing projects would be carried out beyond French borders. From this point on, a significant percentage of books in French would be printed outside of France. Print historians believe that, because of decisions made at this time, Colbert in fact ensured the eventual domination of the Dutch book trade and, in particular, that many of the great classics of French literature for more than a century were read all over Europe in editions that had not been produced by French printers, but most often by their Dutch counterparts (Febvre and Martin, 298).[14]

Anyone who ran afoul of the system during those years when Colbert was establishing his authority encountered a censorial machine that made up in brutality what it lacked in efficiency. Thus, on September 1, 1662, twenty-three-year-old Claude Le Petit became the first, and the last, writer to be ceremonially and publicly executed because of his publications and by official order of the civil authority in charge of censorship. Le Petit's involvement with clandestine publications was already long—in 1655 he had read proofs for *L'Ecole des filles*. Then, in August 1662, he persuaded his neighbors, sons of the well-known printer, Pierre Rebuffé, to use their father's print shop to run off his latest effort. It was a verse collection whose title advertised its connection to the sexually transgressive poet who had received the first modern writer's trial: *Le Bordel des muses ou les neuf Pucelles putains, caprices satiriques de Théophile le jeune*.[15] During the last fifteen months of his short life, Le Petit had published clandestinely a series of transgressive works. This was just the sort of career the censors were desperate to shut down. Three young men playing a dangerous game gave them a chance to demonstrate their efficiency to Colbert.[16]

The printing was not even finished when officers representing Chancellor Séguier, the government official with primary responsibility over the book trade, descended on the print shop and seized both the manuscript and the sheets that had already been typeset. We have a detailed account of the final episode of Le Petit's life, thanks to three letters addressed to Séguier by Dreux d'Aubray, the officer who presided over the seizure.[17]

The first letter, dated August 23, 1662, starts off "the papers I enclose here are the beginning of a book that deserves to be hidden rather than to appear before you; it must be burned" (148). D'Aubray goes on to explain that they should be able to make the work disappear without leaving a trace: everything at the shop was seized; no copies could have been made public since the print job had not been finished (148). In addition—and those policing the book trade were rarely this lucky—the author "of this abomination" was caught red-handed supervising the printing. What's more, "he has confessed his crime" (148).[18]

So much for the book. The man was made to disappear just as expeditiously. Only two days later, D'Aubray proudly announces that "since it was useless to delay the verdict, the sentence that you will find attached to this letter was handed down this morning" (149–50): "Claude Le Petit was

convicted of the crimes of divine and human lese majesty for having written the book entitled *Le Bordel des muses* . . . and condemned to have his fist
cut off and to be burned alive on the Place de Grève" (150 n. 1). In his last
letter, dated 31 August, D'Aubray is able to inform Séguier that the case is
already closed: "The Claude Le Petit affair has been wrapped up. The
court order has been received to carry out my sentence" (150). The next day,
just over a week after his arrest, this was done.

Anyone aware of how slowly the wheels of justice had turned for the
previous Théophile has to wonder about this rush to judgment. The most
obvious explanation involves Colbert's desire for bureaucratization, which
made censors into civil servants. These immediate precursors of the book
police knew what they were after, and they even knew what to call it. The
Le Petit trial marks the first time that "bad book," destined to become the
official term favored by the eighteenth-century book police, was used to
designate a work the censors are trying to suppress. One of the would-be
printers, Eustache Rebuffé, is "asked why he had printed a bad book"; to
which he "replied that he had been forced to do so out of need" (Lachèvre,
Disciples, xlix). Finally, as d'Aubray repeatedly makes plain, at a time when
the book trade was flagrantly unruly, the affair had been assigned exem-
plary status: "The public needs an example, so we should not delay in any
way. . . . I think that this punishment will check . . . the temerity of our
printers" (149–50).

Quick, efficient proceedings and "bad books": the era of the book police
was clearly dawning. Molière inaugurated his career as a print author, in
the months following the "Le Petit affair," by identifying the problem that
censorship had been trying to isolate since the first Théophile's trial and by
giving it a name: *obscénité*.

Initially, Molière and his company acted a varied repertory. In 1654 in
Lyons, they staged the first of his own plays, *L'Etourdi*. After moving to
Paris in 1658, they staged more and more of his plays—Molière came of
age as an author in the Parisian context. From late 1659 (*Les Précieuses
ridicules*) to Molière's death in early 1673, he produced a steady stream of
hits for his troupe, so much so that, from *L'Ecole des femmes* on, he was its
principal author.

Molière entered print authorship less naturally: many commentators
have noted his reluctance to publish his early plays.[19] Given the atmosphere surrounding print culture around 1660, when Colbert was trying to
make his crackdown effective, Molière's diffidence with respect to this unruly trade seems only logical. Indeed, Molière's transition from stage author to page author appears to have begun in self-defense, to protect his
literary property from the type of unscrupulous printer Colbert wanted to

rein in. In seventeenth-century French theatrical practice, a play belonged to its author until its publication. As long as it remained an oral commodity, he and his company or the company he chose had the exclusive right to stage it and therefore to profit from its box office success. Once it had been published, the play was in the public domain as far as its stage life was concerned; from then on, any company could stage it. Initially, Molière seemed to have been content to negotiate his plays solely as box office commodities; he continued to stage his early plays for years without publishing them.[20] Then, in rough and tumble years for the print industry, unscrupulous editors with idle presses on their hands decided there was money to be made off a rising theatrical star.

The initial casualty was Molière's first major success, *Les Précieuses ridicules*, originally staged on November 18, 1659. At the end of January 1660, while its popularity with audiences was still strong and it was, therefore, early for Molière to think in terms of publication, the play appeared in print in an edition whose title page reads: "*Les Précieuses ridicules.* Comedy. Staged at the Petit-Bourbon Theater." The only thing missing was the name of the play's author, and there was a good reason for this omission. He had not played the customary role in this publication. The privilege, obtained on January 12, 1660, had been requested by a fledgling publisher, Jean Ribou, who had decided simply to short-circuit an author still an innocent in the ways of the book trade. Molière learned about the edition just in time to stop it. To do so, he was obliged to join forces with other editors and to let them bring the play out in great haste—Molière's preface describes the printers tearing the manuscript from his hands in order to rush it into print. This was not the ideal way to begin a career as a published author, as Molière makes clear at the beginning of his preface: "It's a strange thing when people are published in spite of themselves" (*Œuvres complètes*, 1:263).[21]

The shock of learning that his biggest hit to date was about to appear in print without his consent almost taught Molière a lesson. On May 31 he applied for his first privilege, for his earliest play, staged some six years before. He had not learned enough from his recent brush with the pirates of print culture, however. Instead of using the privilege right away, he waited until he was in the process of finally becoming a true print author during the controversy caused by *L'Ecole des femmes*.

Three days before applying for his first privilege, Molière had opened his latest play, *Sganarelle, ou le Cocu imaginaire*. It was a big hit, staged thirty-four consecutive times and kept in repertory for three months. Well before the play had run its course, Ribou struck again, this time with greater cunning. On July 26, 1660, a privilege was issued to someone named the "Sieur de Neuf-Villaine" (a front for Ribou), authorizing him to publish the play, which he proceeded to do in August 1660.[22] The first edition of Molière's second big hit appeared, once again with no author's name on its title page, but this time with a dedication—to Molière from the Sieur de Neuf-Villaine, explaining that "it was time that *we* got into print, and I decided to take on the task" (Molière, *Œuvres complètes*, 1:300; my emphasis).

The secret to what have been called the "surprise privileges" (Thuasne, 7) is explained both by Neuf-Villaine in his dedication and, in more detail, by Molière himself in one of the most extraordinary privileges of all time (for *L'Ecole des maris*), issued on July 9, 1661, by which time the print novice had finally learned the rules of the game. All over Europe in the early modern age, a practice that Shakespeare scholars call "memorial reconstruction" appears to have been common. Thus, some of Molière's earliest works appeared in print in versions based, not on his manuscripts, but on manuscripts established by a person or persons such as the mysterious Sieur de Neuf-Villaine who, after hearing the play performed on a number of occasions, composed a text based on what they had heard. This practice was common at least until the moment I am describing here, when playwrights definitively assumed the mantle of print authorship and began to supervise the publication of their plays. Pirated editions based on memorial reconstruction seem to have been a concern for Molière until shortly after *L'Ecole des femmes;* they were thus undoubtedly one of the principal reasons why he became a consummate print author.[23]

For Molière, fledgling print author and director of a troupe trying to break into the highly competitive world of the Parisian theater, these pirated editions meant an important loss of revenue and of theatrical capital. For those trying to regulate the book trade, they were a red flag signaling another abuse of a regulating device that Colbert was particularly keen to enforce, the privilege. The language of the privilege to *L'Ecole des maris* suggests that this document was drawn up jointly by Molière and someone involved in the war against bad books. The privilege indicates that the pirated editions had not been published without authorization. Those responsible had simply taken out a privilege in the name of the publisher (then standard practice) for a particular play, without naming the play's author. The privilege to *L'Ecole des maris* is thus issued to Molière himself, at the same time as others are "forbidden" to publish the play and as past crimes of print piracy are denounced: "These plays were transcribed by individuals, who had them printed and sold on the basis of letters of privilege that they obtained by surprise [*qu'ils auraient surprises*] from our Lord Chancellor" (Molière, *Œuvres*, 2:350).

As a result of the "surprises" pulled on both Molière and the Chancellor, a new era for the privilege was officially recognized. It began, timidly at first, to take on a function never imagined when it was established. For the first century of its existence, the privilege had been considered either as protecting the state, among the principal arms in its ongoing struggle to know which books were being published and by whom, or protecting the publishers, to whom it granted a monopoly over a given work for a fixed period of time. During this phase, it was all too easy to forget the author's existence: it was then common practice for the Chancellor's office to grant printers a privilege when they submitted a title alone; no one asked to see a manuscript (Martin, "Prééminence," 2:264). Until the period 1640–1660, only in cases of censorship were those in charge of granting the right to publish truly concerned with what seems today an obvious question: Who were the authors of the works being printed?[24]

The privilege created for *L'Ecole des maris* marks early official recognition that authorship could be considered a regulatory principle. This was an important moment in the juridification of writers and writing. Small, if accidental, steps were being taken toward acquiring a protection for writers that would be formalized only at the time of the Revolution, a protection we know as the copyright. Also as a result of this "surprise," Molière understood a new definition of what it meant to be an author: the author as owner of a particular commodity, the standardized and copyable printed text. This definition was recognized before the century's end by Furetière's dictionary: "Royal privileges are granted so that the author may be recompensed for his work." Until the end of his career, Molière would continue to fight for control over the printed version of his plays. And, from this point on, Molière took the important symbolic step of inscribing his author's name—at this point, "J. B. P. Molière"—plainly on the title page of each published edition.[25]

Another obvious lesson to be learned from the piracy of Molière's early plays involves the extent to which he arrived on the French scene at the right moment. Hit plays were desperately sought after by publishers in a time of economic shortage. Molière's initial celebrity also benefited from the contemporary expansion of print culture into less expensive small formats. From the beginning, all his plays, like the classics of modern obscenity, were "little books," books published in the promiscuous duodecimo format.[26] Finally, Molière (along with Racine a few years later) began his print career just as the French language, newly dominant in French printing, was beginning its rise to domination over the European cultural scene—a situation that would make Molière, until the Revolution, probably the best known author in Europe and certainly a more important author internationally than Shakespeare.

For the first time, Molière published *L'Ecole des maris* as soon as its initial popularity had abated; this signals his recognition of the role he would from then on assign print authorship—both as a foundation of his reputation and as a necessary source of revenue.[27] For this was also a moment at which Molière's stage life was in transition. In October 1660 his company was abruptly evicted from its first Parisian home, the Petit-Bourbon Theater, when the decision was suddenly made to demolish it to make room for the Louvre's new colonnade. In exchange, they were promised a better space, one they wouldn't have to share with another troupe, the Palais-Royal theater in which Molière's career would unfold until his death. The new theater, however, could not be made ready until early the next year, so the company was temporarily homeless and without box office income. *L'Ecole des maris,* premiered at the Palais-Royal in June 1661, was Molière's first hit in his new home. (*Dom Garcie de Navarre,* which had opened in February, was the biggest flop of Molière's career; this failure had only made economic matters worse.)

In 1662 Molière began to acquire another kind of professional and financial stability: from May 8 through 14, for the first time, his troupe was in residence at the court (in the château of Saint-Germain)—"This was their consecration," in Couton's words (Molière, *Œuvres complètes,* 1:xlviii). From then on, Molière's association with royal patronage continued unbroken; almost all his plays were staged for the court, and many plays now produced as "straight" theater were originally conceived as an integral part of court festivities. (The acts of *George Dandin,* for example, were originally interwoven with dance interludes.)[28]

In the second half of 1662, Molière finally completed the transition to the page: he at long last had published plays that had been performed years earlier—*L'Etourdi* (staged 1658) left the presses on November 21, 1662, and *Le Dépit amoureux* (staged 1658) was made public three days later. It was as if Molière was taking his last profits from his early work, in preparation for a new start.

That's how it looks in retrospect. One month later, on December 26, *L'Ecole des femmes* opened. This comedy gave Molière his biggest box office success to date; at a time when his company was still struggling to establish itself, the new play turned the tide, ending a difficult period. (After *Psyché,* Molière's lone foray into opera, the genre that was the period's biggest money maker, *L'Ecole des femmes* was the most profitable play of his career.) *L'Ecole des femmes,* the play itself and everything that was part of the enormous controversy that developed in its wake, marked the first time that Molière had truly realized the economic potential of his work.[29] The new play was also Molière's most substantive early work; it has been described as signaling the definitive move in his work away from farce in favor of comedy, as well as the inception of a "new esthetic" for French theater in general (Rey-Flaud, 83).[30] In addition, the play marked a decisive turning point for Molière as author. From this point on he was at least as conscious of the importance of the page, the printed editions of his works, as of that of the stage.

During the winter of 1662–1663, when Molière completed and staged his breakthrough play, anyone with literary aspirations was plotting and scheming. The news was out that Colbert, advised by Jean Chapelain, was drawing up the first list of writers chosen to receive royal pensions; state sponsorship of print culture was about to begin. On March 12, 1663, when the controversy surrounding Molière's play was the talk of the town, and the day before the published version went on sale, the initial recipients received the news. They received their first payments, ceremoniously in pouches embroidered with gold and silk, in June. Molière was on the initial list of thirty-eight writers. When Chapelain recommended him to Colbert, he noted one reservation: "he has a tendency to scurrility" (Molière, *Œuvres complètes*, 1:629).

We'll never know exactly what Chapelain had in mind when he used the neologism *scurrilité*, but he might well have been referring to the sexual double-entendres that had made *L'Ecole des femmes* both such a commercial success and the target of unofficial censorship.[31] With *L'Ecole des femmes*, Molière attained new authorial status at the same time as he became the first person to demonstrate a thorough understanding of the concept that authors and censors together had been elaborating for the past half-century: obscenity. Molière acquired his new status at the same time as he began, surely wittingly, his six-year-long involvement with censorship. It was not the most obvious way of winning royal largesse—except, perhaps, as was the case with Chapelain, when the arbiter was a former royal censor.[32]

The title of Molière's breakthrough play was not necessarily a reference to the original classic of modern obscenity. After all, he was already the author of a *School for Husbands;* if *femmes* is taken to mean "wives," as translators usually do, then the two plays seem to form a matched pair. And yet, while there are obvious resonances between these two plays (in particular, concerning the much older suitor's inability to win out over the younger man, no matter what tricks he resorts to), they are hardly identical twins. For example, the heroine of the earlier play, Isabelle, is anything but an innocent; worldly-wise from the start, she's the opposite of the female lead in *L'Ecole des femmes,* the wildly naïve Agnès. Indeed, Molière's second school play has at least as much in common thematically with the work that, eight years after its publication, was still very much on the French censors' minds. And *femmes* can also be taken to mean "women," making this work a follow-up to *The School for Girls.*

Molière once again turned the story of an uncommonly innocent young woman's awakening to sexuality into a commercial success—which is not to say that the similarities between the two plots go very far; Molière evokes *L'Ecole des filles* only enough to be able to use obscenity to make his play a *succès de scandale.* His initial brush with censorship could be termed, using Pierre Bourdieu's phrase, "career tactics"; he toyed with taboos and provoked controversy in order to obtain the success his still-fledgling company needed. Molière intended, and managed, to stay just this side of the then operative standards for decency. The way he pulled this off proves how completely he had assimilated the lesson of the earlier work's censorship. Those who were responsible for a great deal of the play's success—because of the vehemence with which they called for its suppression—may not have realized it, but what outraged them most in his play were precisely those elements that stayed just short of the line crossed by *L'Ecole des filles.*

Critics have suggested that Molière might have known *L'Ecole des filles.* I'd say that it was impossible that he wasn't familiar with the earlier work. It was, after all, a small world, and a book still very much on the book police's minds could scarcely have been forgotten by so acute an observer of the cultural scene as Molière.[33] The shock of modern obscenity could hardly have been blunted in seven short years and, with the title of his play, Molière signaled to his audience that he was beginning a practice he would continue in all his controversial plays of the 1660s: he forced his contemporaries to confront issues that many of them would clearly have preferred to avoid, forcing them to discover what they did not want to know.

Molière was able to test the limits of the tolerable because, even in the midst of all the confusion regarding the regulation of the French book trade prior to 1667, one area stands out as even grayer than all the rest: the censorship of the stage. In England at the same period, the situation was far more institutionalized. The staging of a play was considered a form of publication; prior to performance, a troupe had to submit a manuscript for approval, which took the form of a license.[34] In France, at least until the scandal created by Molière, staging does not seem to have been viewed as publication. A November 12, 1619, law forbade actors "to stage any play without having shown it to the king's prosecutor, who was then to sign their register" (Delamare, 1:404); the law, however, was evidently never enforced. There is no evidence of any form of theater police or of preperformance screening prior to the problem with Molière.[35]

Indeed, until the opening night of *Le Festin de pierre (Dom Juan)* in February 1665, a playwright could have assumed that anything could be staged—at least once. Even if passages were then suppressed, the play would at least have made a name for itself. Molière was the first French author truly to exploit the commercial value of censorship: his three censored plays brought in as much as five or six other hits.[36] By laying bare all the hypocrisy necessary to create obscenity—that is, to make it into a problem—Molière brought upon himself a year of nonstop censorship. That censorship brought record numbers of spectators to his relatively new theater: the box office receipts for *L'Ecole des femmes* were unheard of at the period.

Upon his initial testing of the limits of what would be tolerated, Molière was censored, not by the state, but by what would later be known as public opinion, by society itself, those without whom, as Molière understood, the taboos decreed by the censors could never take hold. Indeed, the censure of *L'Ecole des femmes* could be seen as confirmation that the new standards for decency, dictated by both the Counter-Reformation Church and the civilizing process, were taking hold. This was no longer a case of one woman (Christine de Pizan) or a small group of writers launching a crusade against an author they esteemed guilty of vulgarity. In this case, a society was attempting to police one of its members.[37]

When Molière opened the printed version of the play by announcing, "I know that for this publication people expect me to add a preface responding to my censors" (*Œuvres complètes*, Couton 1:543), he evoked earlier usage of *censor* as "someone who criticizes another's behavior" (*Dictionnaire de l'Académie Française*, 1694 edition).[38] The form of his response reflects, however, the word's transfer to the policing of print culture. The premier literary critic of the age, Nicolas Boileau, sent Molière his wishes for 1663 in the form of a poem whose title teaches us that, no sooner was it staged than the play had created an outcry: "To M. de Molière on his comedy *L'Ecole des femmes* that people have been attacking" (246).[39] From the beginning, the king showed his support of one of the first state-sponsored authors.[40]

Already in early February, however, Molière's censors began to attack in print. Those involved in this public censorship drama knew from the start that this was a case for print culture, something with the potential to reach an audience far larger than that for the Parisian stage. The format of the first attack is thus particularly appropriate. In early February, Jean Donneau de Visé inaugurated a half-century of almost frenetic presence on the French literary scene by doing what he always did best: beating everyone else to the hottest news of the moment. He obviously delayed his first publication, the three-volume collection *Nouvelles nouvelles,* long enough to insert in the final volume a lengthy account of the dust immediately kicked up by the controversial new play. The insertion proves, first of all, that the fledgling reporter saw that this was a transitional moment for the word featured in his title. To its readers, the title surely announced a type of collection favored by sixteenth-century authors, *nouvelles* in the sense of tales, the ancestor of the modern short story. Volume 1 in fact contains several examples of a kind of short prose fiction that would have been familiar to readers of this genre.[41]

Then, volume 2 suddenly takes the reader up short: the first title, "Les nouvellistes, nouvelle," seems to announce another fictional tale but is in fact about *nouvelles* in what is now the word's dominant meaning, usage that was just beginning to take root in French and that Donneau de Visé would play a crucial role in popularizing. He defines the *nouvellistes* of his title as "men whose profession it is to know everything that's going on in the world, who think they know all the most secret goings-on, and who make all sorts of news public" (2:4). The *nouvelliste,* or newsman, as Donneau de Visé defined him, was a character straight out of Howard Hawkes's *His Girl Friday.* He was the first precursor of today's unsettlingly promiscuous "journalists" busily destroying the last vestiges of a frontier between public and private in their quest for readers.

Donneau de Visé became the newsman incarnate for his age; a few years later, he created the original French precursor of our modern newspapers, *Le Mercure galant,* the first public paper in which there were seemingly no limits to the news the editor would cover.[42] Donneau de Visé initially found his calling the minute that *L'Ecole des femmes* opened. Volume 3 of his compilation includes thirty pages on the new play and its author, pages in which are laid out many of the most significant consequences of the controversy as they would affect Molière. The implications of all this, however, go far beyond the ways in which Molière's life was destined to be changed by these events. Donneau de Visé became a newsman at this time because he understood that the problem of modern obscenity was causing the public to look at writers and writing in a new way and that the new way of looking was attracting a broader audience to the literary scene.

From the moment a newsman got hold of the issue, the rush to judgment was on. On March 13 the original edition of *L'Ecole des femmes* was ready for the spectacular sales that the eight editors who had shared the publication costs were expecting. And Molière had already moved on to the next phase. As Donneau de Visé, predictably, was the first to make public in the *Nouvelles nouvelles* (3:236—was this the first scoop in journalism?), Molière was already at work on his response to his critics, another play, *La Critique de "L'Ecole des femmes."* It is therefore no surprise that, when Donneau de Visé decided to join the ranks of Molière's censors, he presented his attack in the form of a play. Molière got there first: *La Critique de "L'Ecole des femmes"* opened on June 1, barely five months after the play the new play defended.

La Critique teaches us a great deal about what its censors had objected to in *L'Ecole des femmes*. It also provides the first clear indication that Molière had decided on the strategy that, more than any other, would be responsible for the biggest commercial successes of his career. Not only did he refuse to back down in the face of censorship but, on the contrary, in *La Critique's* key scene, Molière gave a name, *obscénité*, to the phenomenon that had made *L'Ecole des femmes* scandalous. He thereby at long last inaugurated the term's official modern existence at the same time as he made clear his understanding of the workings of censorship. His awareness of the importance of print in the equation was also evident: he applied for *La Critique's* privilege almost immediately, on June 10; its published edition left the presses on August 7. By that time Donneau de Visé had gotten into print the first anti-Molière play, *Zélinde, ou la véritable critique de "L'Ecole des femmes" et "La Critique de 'L'Ecole des femmes.'"*[43]

In no time at all, another young author joined the fray. By late September or early October, Molière's rivals at the Hôtel de Bourgogne theater were staging an even more hostile attack, Edme Boursault's *Le Portrait du peintre, ou la Contre-critique de "L'Ecole des femmes,"* which was also—a practice the controversy made into a sort of law—quickly published.[44] By then, Molière was ready with what was to be his last word. In mid-October, *L'Impromptu de Versailles* made its debut in the most august surroundings possible. Louis XIV's court was just beginning its long association with the château at Versailles. Molière's company staged several plays during this, the first of many sojourns there. Among them, *L'Impromptu* was the first of his plays to have its première with the king in the audience. The play is also set at Versailles, as though to advertise Molière's status as an official author. In it, Molière portrays himself as head of the company, as actor—and as author.[45]

At this point, Molière seems to have been trying to put an end to all the commotion, but the emotions he had unleashed were far from spent. In late November one of the period's most experienced newsmen, Charles Robinet, weighed in, allegedly on Molière's side, although in fact his play contains ample criticism, with the publication of *La Panégyrique de "L'Ecole des femmes," ou Conversation comique sur les œuvres de Mr. Molière.*[46] Only a week later, Donneau de Visé attacked once more with *La Réponse à "L'Impromptu de Versailles," ou La Vengeance des marquis.*[47] Neither of these plays appears to have been staged, proof that the controversy had become simultaneously independent of the stage and dependent on print culture's newest audience, the readers of gazettes and the periodical press.

Things were not yet finished, for the controversy spilled over well into a second year. In January another novice playwright, Montfleury, published the last attack on Molière. Only days later, his counterpart at a rival theater, Jean Chevalier, made the controversy central to the plot of his *Les Amours de Calotin.*[48] The appearance in mid-March of Philippe de La Croix's *La Guerre comique, ou la Défense de "L'Ecole des femmes,"* a recapitulation of the controversy's high points, ended the commotion. After some fifteen months, the scandal of *L'Ecole des femmes* had at last lost its ability to provide work for members of a print community fallen on hard times.

That basic fact—the controversy continued just as long as authors and newsmen and publishers could keep it going—explains my decision to include blow-by-blow coverage of its history. The scandal of *L'Ecole des femmes* is a clear sign that a new definition of literary value was becoming accepted: a work was good if people went to see it or if it sold copies. An author's primary objective was, therefore, to do whatever was necessary to attract wide public attention. Already at the controversy's outset, Donneau de Visé, always the first to sense a trend, deplored this new literary reality— even as he sought to take advantage of it. He blamed Molière for having tied literature to the marketplace. Molière defended himself against this charge simply by admitting that it was true. He had a character in *La Critique* sum it up at the end: "[Molière] doesn't care if his plays are attacked, as long as they attract a big audience" (Molière, *Œuvres complètes,* 1:668).[49]

At first glance, it's hard to see why *L'Ecole des femmes* became such a *succès de scandale.* Arnolphe, a rich Parisian bourgeois obsessed with avoiding what he considers the inevitable fate of all husbands, cuckoldry, nevertheless has decided to get married. He feels safe because he selected a young village girl, Agnès, and watched over her upbringing from a very young age with one goal in mind: keeping her absolutely ignorant, "as much of an idiot as possible" (1:1:138). He has just brought her to Paris, where he keeps her locked away. Despite all his efforts, she meets a young man, Horace, who naturally falls madly in love with her. In the end, of course, young love wins out. We discover that the fathers of Agnès and Horace—who, after being separated for years, are suddenly reunited just in time to save the day—had destined them for each other from birth.

The plot seems more a reworking of familiar material than the stuff of scandal.[50] The shock of Molière's particular originality must have been all the greater to a public comfortable in a theatrical context that promised no surprises. By the end of the controversy, the censors had identified several scenes that were widely considered obscene. All the commotion started, however—as Molière surely knew that it would—because of what quickly became known as "the scene of the *the*" (*la scène du 'le'*).

Arnolphe has just learned that, despite all his precautions, Horace has managed to gain access to the house in which Agnès is hidden away. He is frantic to know how far their relations may have progressed. And here's the rub: Agnès is so perfectly innocent that she has no idea of what he's after when he makes the usual linguistic detours that permit speakers to suggest sex without actually saying anything. He is finally forced to get to his point. "Didn't he caress you at all?" "Oh yes! He took me by the hand and by the arm," (2:5:569) replies Agnès, immediately focusing attention on a woman's caressable body parts. "But Agnès, didn't he take you by anything else?" The moment that follows is comic first of all because Molière fractures the alexandrine, the twelve-syllable line in which all high classical drama is written, straining it to the limit—he even divides one line into eight one- and two-syllable exchanges between his two protagonists. In the course of this fractured alexandrine, Arnolphe begins to fear the worst when Agnès admits that Horace did in fact also "take [her by] . . . the . . ." and here, Agnès refuses to go on, for she is certain that Arnolphe "will be furious with her." Five disjointed lines later, "the" finally gets a direct object: "the ribbon that you gave me" (2:5:572–78).[51] By this point, every spectator can guess the words Arnolphe has in mind as the object of *take* that would conclude Agnès's sentence, and *le ruban* (ribbon) evokes phonetically the most obvious candidate: *le téton* (tit) and perhaps also *le con* (cunt).[52]

With the infamous "scene of the *the*"—dissected and reenacted in every one of the defenses, attacks, and counterattacks from late 1662 through early 1664—Molière forced as many of his contemporaries as any author to date had succeeded in reaching to confront what is, in effect, the ur-scene of modern obscenity. In *L'Ecole des filles,* Fanchon's initiation into the joy of sex begins when Suzanne asks whether any of the men who visit her home has ever "touched her in any place?" (187). Not so far, but they've all wanted to do just that, and the first spot they want to put their hands on is her *téton* (187). With that five-letter word, *L'Ecole des filles* reinvented obscenity as the naming of genitalia and sexual characteristics, in particular those of women. From then on, indeed, its protagonists hardly ever stop naming all the "the"s others should take hold of, or have taken hold of, or would like to take hold of.

Molière followed their formula for scandal to the letter, if not always to the word. He won for obscenity its first public airing by turning *the* into a substitute for the terms whose salacious display made *L'Ecole des filles* one of the century's hottest titles. For well over a year, the entire theater and print audience in France repeated his model: everyone continued to say "the," when they really meant "tit," and so forth. "This two-letter word that has caused such a furor, this *the* . . . ," begins Argimont, the lace merchant who is Donneau de Visé's central character in *Zélinde*, when he is interrupted by a lady of quality, Oriane: "You may skip over that"; "Leave that *the* out of it" (Mongrédien, *La Querelle*, 1:30). One of La Croix's characters refuses even to say "the" (*le*): "A two-letter word frightens you, what would happen if it had more [letters]?" asks her interlocutor, to which she, sounding for all the world like the official censors, replies that *the* is "infamous, dreadful, and disgraceful" (Mongrédien, *La Querelle*, 2:237–38).

In *La Critique* Molière returned to the scandal of obscenity. At the exact center of the play (scene 3), Molière gives voice to his most determined censors with the arrival of a new character, Climène. She details the physical effects of obscenity—going over each of the moments when *L'Ecole des femmes*'s comedy is based on the fact that everyone is thinking of the names of female sexual characteristics: one scene "made me sick to my stomach"; whereas during another one, "I thought I would vomit" (Molière, *Œuvres complètes*, 1:647). Climène then attempts to define the obscene: it is "garbage," "filth," that which "alarms one's modesty" and "dirties the imagination." Of the "scene of the *the*" she concludes: "all that dirtiness puts one's eyes out" (1:648–49). The public is blinded by the obscene; it is quite literally what we cannot see or that which we refuse to see—or that which we see only too well and deny.

Then, just as Suzanne taught Fanchon new words, Molière has his characters teach his audience a name for the unsettling new phenomenon. They are discussing—what else?—that omnipresent *the:* "This *the* is supremely insolent," concludes Elise. To which the censor Climène replies, "It has an obscenity which is unbearable" (1:649; see figure 5).[53]

With this sentence, Molière completed the process by which, for a half-century, *obscénité* had been moving toward a foothold in a modern language. Just in time to be useful to the book police who began to exercise their functions four years later, Molière made all seventeenth-century censors a gift of the word they had been seeking in order to pass judgment on

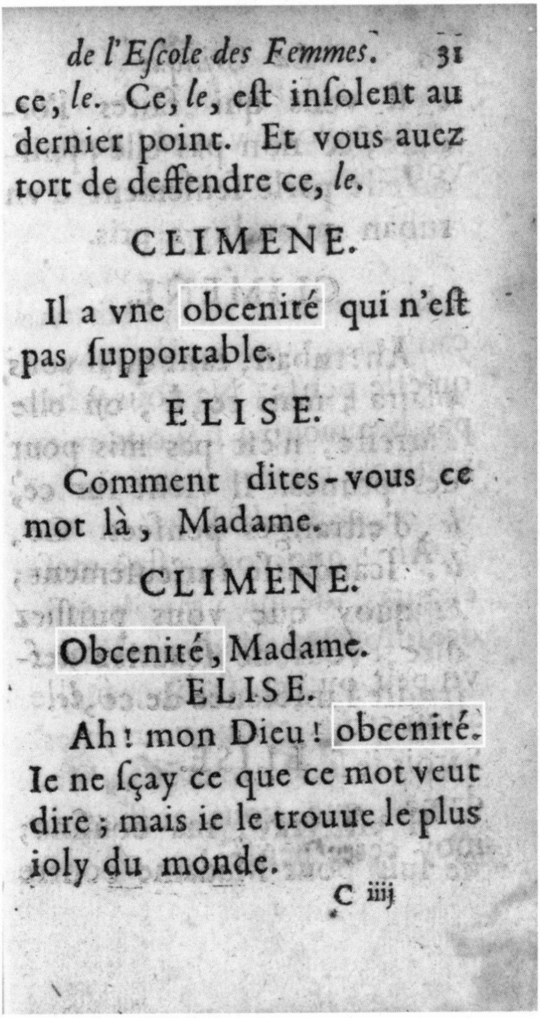

de l'*Efcole des Femmes*.   31
ce, *le*. Ce, *le*, eſt inſolent au
dernier point. Et vous auez
tort de deffendre ce, *le*.

CLIMENE.

Il a vne obcenité qui n'eſt
pas ſupportable.

ELISE.

Comment dites-vous ce
mot là, Madame.

CLIMENE.

Obcenité, Madame.

ELISE.

Ah! mon Dieu! obcenité.
Ie ne ſçay ce que ce mot veut
dire; mais ie le trouue le plus
ioly du monde.

C iiij

FIGURE 5   Molière, *La Critique de "L'Ecole des femmes"* (Paris: Guillaume de Luyne, 1663), page 131 (the first *1* is barely legible). Courtesy of the Bibliothèque Nationale de France, Paris.

a new type of literature. After 150 years during which it was usually only partly understood even by the few who used it, Molière finally brought the vocabulary of the obscene fully into public existence. From this moment on, *obscene* and *obscenity* would begin their relentless invasion of the scene of our modernity. He immediately calls our attention to his innovation by having his characters tell us that this is a neologism: "how do you pronounce that word, Madame?" queries Elise, which gives Climène the chance to repeat: *Obscenity,* and Elise the opportunity to repeat after her: "Oh! My God! Obscenity. I don't know what the word means, but I think it is the prettiest in the world" (1:649–50).

Of Molière's accomplishment, Robinet commented: "[Molière] managed to transform something that many would not countenance in private into a public spectacle" (Mongrédien, *La Querelle,* 1:225). To achieve this goal of bringing obscenity onto both the stage and the page, Molière could follow neither the typographical boldness of *L'Ecole des filles,* nor the bawdy's use of ellipsis. His substitution—inducing the reader to form the names of female genitalia mentally while printing only the most innocuous word— should not be confused, however, with the type of double-entendre obscenity that libertine novels such as Laclos's *Liaisons dangereuses* later made synonymous with sophisticated French humor (the opposite of the *gaulois,* if you will). Molière uses the double-entendre to skewer the very hypocrisy that attracted amateur censors in droves to his plays; in *L'Ecole des femmes* and *La Critique,* every bit as much as in mid-seventeenth-century France, obscenity and the censorship of print culture are inextricably intertwined.[54]

In *La Critique,* Molière presents obscenity as a question of offensiveness—it makes Climène sick—or of indecency—she refers to "the immodesties of [*L'Ecole des femmes*]" (*Œuvres complètes,* 1:658). This view parallels another generally accepted definition, used by D. H. Lawrence in his celebrated defense of *Lady Chatterley's Lover.* In Lawrence's view, which was similar to the notion of "survivals" adopted by anthropologists of his day, obscenities become taboo because they remind a society of an earlier, less-evolved state of culture.[55] This conception is also related to the civilizing process that Norbert Elias has so convincingly documented and, in particular, to the way in which that process succeeded in having culture identified solely with what is most refined and civilized. This redefinition depended upon a "displacement of the threshold of modesty" that dictated, for example, a ban in "polite" society on the naming of primary obscenities (Elias, 187).[56] In France this process was coming into its own in Molière's day; he repeatedly called it to his contemporaries' attention. Here, he does not satirize the reign of all that proclaimed itself not vulgar as he does, for example, in *Le Misanthrope;* just as contemporary conduct manuals were training his audience to do, he completely elides the taboo words.[57] Hence the significance of Molière's choice of setting: *La Critique* marks the first time that he used an aristocratic context for one of his plays and therefore his recognition of the class politics of this view of obscenity.

The problem should not be judged, however, solely on the basis of *La Critique* and the discussion staged there among a group of aristocrats. In his earlier play, Molière shows off obscenity's structure in a setting that is, every bit as much as that of *L'Ecole des filles,* resolutely domestic, middle-class—and ordinary. Note that he does not portray the relation to obscenity of bourgeois citizens of the city as guilty or self-censoring, in the manner of Pepys. Arnolphe is a far cry from the civil servants Elias describes, rising to power at the French court in Colbert's wake and trying to mimic aristocratic ideals (55). Arnolphe's repression of four-letter words has a purely practical goal: it is closer to the taboo dictated by the state's desire to control its subjects' sexuality than to the polite suppressions of "civilized" society.

When Molière has Agnès, another girl next door, set up "the scene of the *the*"—"he took me by the . . ."—when he has a woman pronounce the first modern obscenity to be referred to as such, this female invasion of a traditional male domain reveals an awareness that obscenity was not only threatening because of its potential to shock aristocrats with memories of an earlier, less civilized age. Molière's bourgeois obscene has the potential to take advantage of contemporary print culture's advances in order to corrupt not only the young men specified in the first British law but young women as well. It has a role to play in the self-imagining through which, Anderson argues, the bourgeoisie negotiated its cohesion.

In this respect, Molière's choice of a simple street in front of two houses as the setting for his play takes on new significance.[58] Molière's censors criticized his choice as unbelievable: in *Zélinde,* Donneau de Visé's characters agree that Arnolphe and Chrysalde could never have managed to talk privately in such a spot unless "the plague had hit the city, . . . and its inhabitants were therefore not going out of their houses" (Mongrédien, *La Querelle,* 1:21). This inconsistency was a small price to pay for the street's connotations of completely promiscuous circulation—of people, of conversation, of little books—across class and gender lines.

Roger Herzel describes the play's location in this way: "The action, like that of countless French farces . . . , takes place in a street before two houses, a location that has no particular identity of its own, a no man's land where anything can happen, any character wander on, any encounter can take place" (927). While I agree with much of this, my disagreement first: this is not the generic street of farces, but a street that, like the nature of the play's action, marks a logical step in Molière's progression from the lack of social specificity of the farce toward the domestic comedy of bourgeois life he stages most completely in *Le Tartuffe.* The play's action has hardly begun when Horace, newly returned to the city, obviously Paris, praises it for its "huge population, its superb buildings, its marvelous entertainments" (1:4:289–90), thereby making the audience aware of *L'Ecole des femmes*'s status, along with *L'Ecole des maris,* as the first of Molière's Parisian plays.[59] And he has in mind not just any mythical Paris, furthermore, but the "huge," bustling city of his day. Paris was in rapid expansion: from fewer than four hundred thousand inhabitants at the time of Théophile's trial, it had grown to over six hundred thousand by 1667.

Herzel is right to stress the anything-is-possible, anyone-can-walk-in quality of the street. And if this can be said about the generic street, it was all the more true of the Parisian street in the second half of the seventeenth century—and at no time more so than at the moment just prior to La Reynie's induction as the head of the city's police. Along with the surveillance of the book trade, one of his principal concerns was the regulation of the city's thoroughfares, which were, according to the authorities, far more transgressive than the average contemporary walkways—too noisy, too dark and dirty, too dangerous, in short, a place where Louis's subjects were too prone to contamination, both social and physical. One of the first tasks assigned the capital's new police force was that of cleaning up those streets.[60]

Molière revealed his understanding of obscenity's link to social contamination with the second neologism he coined for *La Critique de "L'Ecole des femmes": s'encanailler,* "to slum it," literally, to frequent the *canaille* or dregs of society. So that the link between the two terms would be unmistakable, he followed the exact scenario he had used to teach his public *obscénité.* Climène the censor concludes her critique of the "shameful" bad taste that causes her contemporaries to rush to see *L'Ecole des femmes* by commenting that "le siècle s'encanaille furieusement" ("our age is slumming it to an appalling extent"; *Œuvres complètes,* 1:660). To which Elise replies, explicitly recalling her reaction to the earlier neologism: "that word is pretty too, *s'encanaille!* Did you invent it, Madame?"[61] With his second gift to the French language, Molière made plain the association of which censors had been aware since Théophile's trial: the obscene was dangerous because it possessed the ability to contaminate across class lines, corrupting the rabble at the same time as it sullied aristocrats by allowing some of the dirt of the slums to rub off on them.

When Molière staged "the scene of the *the*" in a Parisian street, he revealed his awareness that the obscene became a problem for our modernity once its circulation could no longer be controlled. When he chose to evoke this subject and thereby to provoke the first of the encounters with censorship that dominate close to seven years of the ten-year span of his career as a print author, he surely must have calculated that the recognition he could win would be worth the risk.[62]

Molière surely could not have foreseen, however, at least some of the other consequences of his prolonged exposure to the censorial limelight. The positive results first. To begin with, there were the commercial benefits, which far exceeded the considerable take at the box office. As a result of the controversy, Molière became one of the handful of French authors well-known enough to be able to sell their manuscripts: he acquired a marketable reputation. Moreover, in the course of the controversy, Molière may well have succeeded in finally making an author's attempt to take advantage of the market value of his work an accepted fact of literary life. Montfleury portrays one of his characters buying copies of *L'Ecole des femmes* from a female publisher/bookseller—her sex is still another sign of the book trade's evolving economy. The Marquis asks her for Molière's *Impromptu* and is told that "it's not yet printed," to which he replies: "That play is very good; / Molière is a friend of mine; I want him to give it to you, / For money, of course, you understand," and then ends the discussion by telling the bookseller "you would sell a lot of copies, and all over the place" (Molière, *Œuvres complètes*, 2:348–50).[63]

The controversy also made money for another category of individuals trying to make a living from their pens. It marked a significant step toward the launching of newspapers in France. One type of modern print journalism—not the most savory strain, but an inescapable one—was first activated because of the bond the play forged with the obscene: Donneau de Visé and Robinet understood that Molière's chosen road to success was territory a newsman should exploit.[64] These early French newsmen forged a connection between the modern press and modern obscenity in order to tap into the obscene's market value. They thereby initiated another connection that modern journalism has since made obligatory, that between literary obscenity and the laying bare of an author's intimate life.

This connection was first made in seemingly innocent fashion. No sooner did Molière write obscenely than he became a news item—not only the work in which he staged obscenity, but Molière himself. Donneau de Visé's coverage of the controversy began with an extended (ten-page) biography of the author. This was the first time Molière's biography was drawn up; it was among the first times that a living writer's career was charted in print, certainly the first time a writer's biography was so publicly displayed.[65] For the newsman, however, Molière's life had a particular role to play.

In early 1663 Molière was barely forty, and not yet the author of the works today regarded as his masterpieces. Donneau de Visé required a biography as proof of his initial description of Molière as "that famous author" (*Nouvelles nouvelles*, 3:221). He was thereby announcing a basic truth, that newspapers are always inherently about advertising.[66] He was also doing what newsmen have been doing ever since, making Molière famous by declaring that this was already the case—not, of course, because he had Molière's interests at heart, but to become known as someone who recognized talent, every bit as much as those who were, at the same moment, choosing the first state-sponsored writers. In his wake, throughout the controversy, Molière's fame is a given, freely admitted even by his detractors.

This frequent proclaiming of Molière's celebrity had many repercussions, notably one directly related to his new status as a writer able to sell his manuscripts to publishers. The controversy made Molière into an author considered established enough to merit the first edition of his collected works, a two-volume edition at that. Before the end of 1663, Guillaume de Luyne, who had published five of Molière's eight printed plays, brought out *Les Œuvres de Monsieur Molier* [*sic*].[67] The edition was a key step in Molière's acquisition of true—as opposed to journalistically decreed—celebrity status. His first collected works mark the transition from *Molière*'s function as a stage name—of a man who was an actor, the head of a theatrical company, and the composer of plays staged by that company and more recently also published—to *Molière* as an author's name in Foucault's sense of the term: a name that "permits one to group together a certain number of texts, define them, differentiate them from and contrast them to others" ("What Is an Author?" 107). The edition confirms the bond between authorship, obscenity, and censorship. It is still more proof of the accuracy of Foucault's claim that "books really began to have authors" when authors produced transgressive discourse (108).[68] Historically, as Foucault also points out, these developments occurred at the same time as "a system of ownership for texts came into being" (108). Molière's first collected works can be seen as his publishers' last stand, an attempt to grab what they could before the recently consecrated author could take over the rights he was in the process of acquiring to the oeuvre their edition was establishing.

The 1663 edition is what is known as a *recueil factice* or "artificial collection." Collections such as this one are "imitations" or "artificial" because, instead of republishing the various texts they include with consecutive pagination, they simply reprint the plays as already published and arrange them one after the other in volumes. It seems that the edition was another attempt, in the spirit of the thefts via memorial reconstruction of Molière's early plays, to exploit his market value without acknowledging his ownership of his literary property. Because Molière did not this time go on record to protest the venture, some conclude that he knew what was going on.[69]

This first edition of his collected works undoubtedly did not produce extra revenue for Molière. If he did consent to its publication, it was surely because he understood its symbolic importance in the unfolding of his career. Thanks to the controversy, he had accumulated enough name recognition for such a significant publication venture to be considered a worthwhile investment. The collection played an important role in creating an image of Molière as an established author, someone important enough to merit his collected works so early in his career.

It also contributed to the image of Molière as, in the phrase Donneau de Visé chose to open his biography, "someone who is talked about all over Europe" (3:221). Donneau de Visé may have been indulging in another bit of hyperbole to justify his own venture. Nevertheless, various references confirm that, once again as a result of the controversy, Molière was acquiring an audience outside France. The status of French as international cultural language naturally meant an increased presence of foreigners in the Parisian theater audience, spectators who would have brought word of the public censorship home with them (Mongrédien, *La Querelle,* 2:302).[70] Robinet even indicates that the controversy was attracting so much attention that it had become, in and of itself, a tourist destination. Lysandre, one of the participants in his dialogue, is an Englishman who informs the Parisian characters that Molière's plays have been so avidly discussed in London that "even if I hadn't a reason to come to Paris, I think I would have come just to see the play that has caused such a stir in my country" (Mongrédien, *La Querelle,* 1:235). Already in 1663, it appears that Molière was well on his way to becoming perhaps the first truly internationally known author.[71]

In a final ramification of this sudden rise to celebrity, Molière also became the first French author to acquire still another newly invented status symbol: his portrait. For the publication of *L'Ecole des femmes,* Molière took advantage of the increasingly widespread use of frontispieces in "little books." He turned to François Chauveau, the very artist responsible for the ill-fated frontispiece of *L'Ecole des filles.*[72] Chauveau's engraving illustrates a well-known scene, the moment at which Arnolphe, seated, makes a speech to Agnès, who is standing before him, in which he explains the duties of marriage (figure 6). He begins his lecture by instructing her: "Here, look at me here while we are talking" (3:2:677) and ends it when he removes from his pocket what he terms "an important work that will teach you how to become a wife" (3:2:742–43).

Chauveau's engraving illustrates the "here" where Agnès is instructed to look: in a gesture that was apparently from the beginning fixed in the play's staging, Arnolphe uses his index finger to point to his forehead. The image

FIGURE 6   Frontispiece and title page from Molière's *L'Ecole des femmes* (Paris: Louis Billaine, 1663). Frontispiece by François Chauveau. Courtesy of the Bibliothèque Nationale de France, Paris.

stages the structure for modern obscenity that the play confirmed: Agnès's excessively modest dress and defensive body posture seem to be warding off Arnolphe's obscene gaze—indeed, he can be staring only at the part of her body "forgotten" in Roman sexually transgressive poetry and "remembered" in Courbet's *Origine du monde*. Finally, by indicating that the "work" in Arnolphe's pocket is one of those small formats whose portability made them so easy to share with others, it advertises the bond between obscenity and print culture.[73] And, by having a solid bourgeois citizen seated next to his house brandish that book, it evokes the link between the bourgeoisie and print culture.[74]

One thing that Chauveau's frontispiece does not indicate is the identity of the two people it features: they seem, very simply, Arnolphe and Agnès—or rather two middle-class citizens depicted next to the ultimate symbol of the bourgeoisie, its houses. They are representative of the portraits of characters that, from this point on, ornament all the major editions of Molière's plays in that they are remarkable above all for their complete lack of individuality (Jackson, 43). And yet, from the start, Molière's contemporaries did not see it this way. Montfleury has his economically savvy Marquis begin his foray into the world of publishing by asking for Molière's latest. The bookseller offers him *L'Ecole des femmes*. As he accepts the copy, a stage direction reads: "He looks at the first leaf of *L'Ecole des femmes* where Molière is depicted." "Isn't that Molière?" the Marquis queries. The bookseller confirms that it is, and her customer adds, "Yes, that's his portrait" (Mongrédien, *La Querelle,* 2:335).

If we dismiss this exchange as mere padding, we miss the fact that Montfleury is drawing our attention to the concept of the portrait. The bookseller ends the discussion by explaining that "he's preaching a sermon in this scene, / And since he was afraid he wouldn't be taken seriously, he had his portrait painted" (2:335). The bookseller is referring to one meaning the term had acquired in a literary context, a portrait in the sense of an image that guaranteed the authenticity of a text. It is in this way, for example, that Eisenstein explains the growing presence of *individualized* portraits of authors and artists in early modern print culture; once print had begun to make the standardization of texts and images a reality, the desire for individuality developed as a counterforce. Thus, as of the sixteenth century, publishers began to feature portraits of authors as a promotional device.[75]

Molière was the first French author to have benefited fully from the new desire to assign to the best-known authors a visual image by which they could be recognized. We do, of course, have engravings and even occasional painted portraits of earlier literary figures. All these portraits, however, have at most a minimal degree of individuality—one can hardly be certain to have a real sense of what Corneille, for instance, looked like, or even of being able to guess, on the basis of one portrait of the author, that a second portrait, allegedly also of Corneille, represents the same man. With Molière, however, for the first time we note an instance of an author's portrait, in the sense in which Foucault speaks of an author's name. Numerous painted portraits preserve a record of Molière's face during the last decade of his life; once you have seen one of them, you recognize the author in the others, to such an extent that I feel I know what Molière looked like, just as I do with subsequent internationally famous French authors (such as Voltaire and Diderot). For example, figures 7 and 8, portraits by Nicolas Mignard and Charles Coypel, clearly represent the same man.[76]

With this sense of the portrait in mind, let's return to the frontispiece of *L'Ecole des femmes*. Following the lead of Montfleury's Marquis, commen-

FIGURE 7   Nicolas Mignard, *Molière in the Role of César in* La Mort de Pompée (c. 1660). Photograph © Collections de la Comédie Française, Paris.

FIGURE 8   Charles Antoine Coypel. Portrait of Molière. Date uncertain. Photograph © Collections de la Comédie Française, Paris.

tators have always assumed that Molière himself was portrayed there, and not just the character he played. In order to make this assumption, they force themselves to ignore the fact that this image has little in the way of individuality. True, the seated man does have a mustache, as Molière did (although probably not the same kind). Yet, when we compare the image to that of even a fairly crude contemporary painting showing Molière (as opposed to a generic actor) playing Arnolphe (figure 9), we note that, whereas the costume is the same, the face in the frontispiece lacks any sign of true life—and surely Chauveau, the finest artist of the century to turn his hand to book illustration, could have produced more of a likeness, if that had been the task assigned him. Chauveau created another type of portrait, a standardized image perfectly suited to the new, mass-marketed literary product it was to illustrate. Still another consequence of the controversy was to show that Molière's market value now would extend beyond his name: his person, too, was in the process of being commodified.

It is fitting, therefore, that over the centuries the engraving has been thoroughly remodeled to accommodate changing ideas of seventeenth-century style, and yet all the while commentators still continue to identify the image as a portrait of Molière (see, for example, figure 10).[77] The image's long-term fate makes clear just what was at stake when Montfleury's Marquis identified the engraving as a portrait of Molière. As a result of the controversy, Molière may well have become the first writer to experience a side-effect of media exposure all too familiar to any observer of celebrity today—the price of his fame was a certain loss of individuality, and certainly a loss of privacy.

Before we look at how this began, one last comment on the frontispiece to show how hopelessly the invasion of Molière's private life in 1663 has muddled what passes today for his biography. Even such a meticulous scholar as Guibert accepted Montfleury's view of the image: "For the first time since their recent marriage, Molière and Armande Béjart are portrayed together. This is one of the very rare representations, indeed perhaps the only one, of these two individuals. The resemblance is clear, less perhaps in their features than in their attitudes" (1:126). In the original production, however, the role of Agnès was played, not by Armande Béjart, but by Mademoiselle de Brie. Guibert confuses Chauveau's representation of a scene from the original production with a portrait of the man Molière in his private life because, right from the start, that's what commentators have done.

On February 20, 1662, ten months before *L'Ecole des femmes* opened, Jean-Baptiste Poquelin married Armande Béjart. He had just turned forty, while his bride was considerably younger. We don't know Armande's exact

FIGURE 9   Anony-
mous French painting,
*Les Farceurs français et
italiens depuis soixante
ans et plus* (c. 1670).
Detail: *Molière in the
Role of Arnolphe in*
L'Ecole des femmes.
Photograph © Collec-
tions de la Comédie
Française, Paris.

age, though she was about twenty. The difference in their ages, hardly
remarkable by seventeenth-century standards, has been endlessly commented upon by Molière's biographers. In so doing, they are unwittingly
playing into still another aspect of the censorship of *L'Ecole des femmes*.[78]
    While the new husband came from the solid Parisian bourgeoisie he so
often featured in his comedies, Armande's background was less respectable:
she belonged to a family of actors. One of them, her older sister Madeleine
(also Molière's senior by several years), had been influential in his decision
to renounce bourgeois ease in order to take to the stage. She had been a
member of his company from the start, and it is generally agreed that they
had had a long-term liaison. The company's records teach us that the new
bride was soon collecting a share of their profits, which meant that she was
appearing in plays, though we do not know for certain exactly when she
made her debut. (Some say she was on the stage already in Lyons in 1653.
Others say she was in the original cast of *L'Ecole des maris*. Both of these
stories are actively contested.) She appears to have made her Parisian stage
debut in *La Critique de "L'Ecole des femmes,"* in which she inaugurated the
role of Elise who, when Climène first pronounces *obscénité*, explains that

FIGURE 10   Henry (or Hippolyte) Lecomte, *Molière in the Role of Arnolphe in* L'Ecole des femmes *in the Year 1670.* Lithograph by Delpech. Figure 52 in Henry Lecomte, *Costumes de théâtre de 1600 à 1820* (Paris: Delpech, 1824). Private collection, Paris.

she has no idea what it means, but that she finds it "the prettiest word in the world."

The laugh she certainly got for that line must have had added resonance, in view of the cloud thrown over the couple's personal life as soon as the controversy began. It's hard to believe that Molière did not have some inkling that, when he harnessed his star to obscenity and when he did so at that particular time in his life, he would also make himself the object of a particularly scurrilous form of obscene libel. He may well have gotten more than he bargained for.

No sooner had Donneau de Visé ended his biography of Molière in the *Nouvelles nouvelles* than he segued into still more unexplored territory, the scandal sheet, thereby providing a particularly unsavory original definition of what constitutes news. He suggested that *L'Ecole des femmes* was centered on the crisis of an older man obsessed by a much younger woman precisely because Molière was living this drama in real life: "If you want to know why in almost all of his plays [Molière] makes so much fun of cuckolds and portrays jealous men so realistically, it's because he's one of them" (3:235). Mongrédien says of this moment: "For the first time, Molière himself and his private life were attacked" (*La Querelle,* 1:xvii).

It may have been the first time, but it was hardly the last. Even today, critics continue to repeat this evaluation of Molière's marriage and to explain the presence of cuckolds in his theater as an autobiographical commentary. Few bother to point out the decidedly shabby origin of this "biographical" information. Few bother to mention that Molière's fixation on cuckoldry was an obsession he shared with his age; a great deal of contemporary comedy emphasized, every bit as much as Molière's, a figure featured in farce, the cuckold. (The same is true of Roman comedy, and even of Hollywood comedy.) Donneau de Visé's accusations stuck because Molière's censors must somehow have felt that his traffic in the obscene had authorized them to extend the specter of sexual indecency into his private life.[79] And once Molière's censors had started on this route, there was no stopping them. Boursault's *Portrait du peintre* featured a song, "La Chanson de la Coquille," immediately seen as mocking Madeleine Béjart. Only a fragment of this infamous ditty has come down to us, but this is enough to show that it was straight out of the bawdy—it focuses with disgust on the older woman's (Madeleine Béjart was well into her forties at this point) genitalia.[80]

This time, Molière tried to set limits to the newsmen's invasion of his private life. In *L'Impromptu de Versailles,* Molière's character announces that he doesn't mind if other playwrights mock his plays in their own works—"I am happy to help them make a living"—but they have to know when to stop:

> on the condition that they be satisfied with what I am able to grant them with decency. . . . I freely hand over to them my works, my face, my gestures, my words, my intonation, and my style of acting, to do with and to talk about as they like, if they can make a profit from them. . . . But, since I have relinquished all this, they owe me the grace of leaving all the rest to

me and of keeping their hands off the kinds of issues they've been attacking me for in their plays. (scene 5; *Œuvres complètes*, 1:695–96)

This plea bargain, in which the individual just becoming the first modern celebrity author attempted to cut a public deal with the original tabloid journalists, seems to have been the main point of *L'Impromptu*, which ends shortly after these words.[81]

Today, when we know all too well the lengths to which the tabloid press will go to uncover alleged dirty secrets, no one would believe for an instant that Molière could have gotten them to "keep their hands off" his private life. In his *Réponse à "L'Impromptu de Versailles,"* Donneau de Visé practically drooled over the issue of cuckoldry (scene 3; Mongrédien, *La Querelle*, 2:275). And the worst was yet to come. Just as Donneau de Visé's last play was made public and even as his own attack on Molière was being staged, Montfleury took things to the limit. In an approach highly unusual even for an age in which it was not uncommon to see major accusations such as attempted murder brought against apparently respectable people, Montfleury went right to the top and handed the king a formal document accusing Molière of sexual crime. His charges have come down to us in Racine's version of the affair: "He accused him of having married the daughter, after having at one time slept with her mother" (Molière, *Œuvres complètes*, 1:1302).[82] Thus we see the origin of a theory still circulating today, that Armande, far from being Madeleine's sister, was in reality her child, and possibly her child by Molière. Racine added: "But no one listens to Montfleury at court" (Mongrédien, *La Querelle*, 1:xviii). Racine's judgment seems confirmed by the fact that no response to Montfleury's complaint is on record—whereas, on February 28, 1664, the king served as godfather to Molière's son Louis, a gesture surely intended to be seen as equivalent to a public denial of the accusation that his marriage was in some way incestuous.

That the controversy activated when Molière gave a public demonstration of obscenity's functioning ended up this way might be taken for a confirmation of the confusion between libel and obscenity that British law would soon try to undo. In addition, what happened to Molière can be seen as a sign that times were indeed changing as far as societal taboos were concerned. Ultimately, the song "La Chanson de la coquille" was fated to disappear because, even though to many in Boursault's audience it must have been familiar "Gallic" humor, the redrawing of the line between acceptable and unacceptable in matters of sexual decency had left no room for its circulation in polite society. The rumors started by journalists— Molière was unhappy in his choice of a young bride; the marriage was incestuous—remained, however, stubbornly attached to Molière's biography.[83] The newsmen had succeeded, therefore, in creating a portrait of Molière perfectly suited to the frontispiece of *L'Ecole des femmes*.

This portrait of the author of obscene literature is almost diametrically opposed to the contemporary painted portraits that give the viewer the illusion of gaining access to Molière's individuality. In this case, we see what might be thought of as the dark side of commercialization's impact on the individual. At the very moment when Molière's status as hot literary property to be promoted by publishers was becoming an uncontested fact, a (quite possibly imaginary) image of his private life and his sexuality was exposed to public view: Molière's first collected works and Montfleury's incest petition to the king began to circulate within days of each other, full confirmation, if ever any was needed, of the bond between "propriety" in the sense of ownership and in that of decency. Commentators have often concluded that Molière was guilty because he never responded to these charges, but what good would any further airing of the issues have done?

Because he used obscenity to make himself into the first French author able to sell widely on the basis of his name—his new books, his manuscripts, his portraits, his biography, news stories about himself and his associates, even sexual innuendo about his family—Molière learned that the author-commodity would no longer have a right to a private life. Thus, just at the moment when recent histories of private life situate the first intimations of our modern distinctions between public and private, the saga of *L'Ecole des femmes* already makes plain certain conclusions regarding the dangerous erosion of the private because of the ever intensifying public exposure that we might otherwise have believed particular to our own postmodern age. The new kind of portrait Molière then acquired was above all a tribute to the writer's still untapped commercial potential: it was an image that could be mass-marketed; any resemblance to the real man behind the mustache and the stolid, bourgeois hat (porkpie, would we say today?) was purely accidental.

The new portrait was also a fitting monument to the concept of the author that is the long-term legacy of Molière's initial entanglement with censorship. As the controversy began, Molière must have thought that when authors went public—for instance, by putting publication rights in their names or by having their names on the title pages of their printed works—they obtained a type of ownership, a primitive form of copyright, over their production. What he saw all around him, however, were signs of the simultaneous erosion of this new authorial right to property: unscrupulous writers were able to use his name to sell just about anything, while publishers were able to print his works without his legal participation.

The controversy reinforces a lesson learned from the seventeenth century's two obscenity trials: in cases concerning early obscene literature, the state needs an author, for the author is the individual who can be prosecuted.[84] At the same time, however, as authors were in a sense bound to these works through one type of legal mechanism, which eventually resulted in civil obscenity laws, they were in another sense detached from their production by a separate legal mechanism, one in the long run codified as copyright protection. I have in mind here the fact that, since authors of obscene works could never hope to obtain a privilege for them, as soon as these works began to circulate, they were in the public domain; as long as those reproducing them were able to avoid prosecution, they were able to pocket the profits. The author of an obscene work was, therefore, in a real sense not an author at all, for he was incapable of exercising the rights that the new codes governing the book trade were beginning to confer on writers. In Molière's career, and in the history of print culture in general, the status of the author and modern literary obscenity came into existence at the same moment. This intersection between the author as he who holds the copyright (privilege) and he who can be censored or held liable for his work may have been accidental. When he launched obscenity, however, Molière opened a Pandora's box for the modern writer he would incarnate for the French tradition.[85]

Conclusion

BEYOND OBSCENITY?

L'Ecole des femmes was, of course, only Molière's initial involvement with transgressive literature. By the time he won permission to stage *Le Tartuffe*, on February 5, 1669, he was thoroughly schooled in censorship's ways. He had been obliged to rewrite *Le Tartuffe* twice and to withdraw after just fifteen performances the other play often called his masterpiece, *Le Festin de pierre (Dom Juan)*. *Le Festin de pierre (Dom Juan)* was the only major work that would not be published in his lifetime; it was published posthumously solely in a version heavily mutilated by a censorial team led by La Reynie himself. Molière thereby gave the newly created book police the chance to prove its stuff. These were the most complicated—and successful—cases of preperformance and prepublication censorship in seventeenth-century France.

The vocabulary of censorship also came together in Molière's wake. On February 27, 1665—just two weeks after the opening of the most transgressive of Molière's plays, *Le Festin de pierre (Dom Juan)*, and during the period when censors were mutilating it—the king's council passed a ruling specifying measures to be taken "to stop the printing and the sale of bad books." This legislation—reissued in October 1667 (just after *Le Tartuffe*'s second version had been authorized, staged, and once again shut down) and in May 1669 (just after *Le Tartuffe*'s publication)—marks the beginning of the long reign of "bad book" as the official term used to justify the censorship of print culture. This reproachful expression—whenever I read "bad book," I think of someone scolding a naughty child or puppy—was used until the end of the Ancien Régime to squelch all books judged transgressive in political, religious, or sexual terms.[1]

The appearance of "bad books" signaled censorship's definitive secularization: in the 1669 text of the edict, for the first time, the Lieutenant General of the Police is listed as the official in charge of censorship. The division of labor was made clear. Under La Reynie, the Faculty of Theology controlled the censorship only of books for schoolchildren, the Parliament only that of legal texts. In the midst of all this clarity, a gray area remained: the obscene.

True, in Molière's wake, *obscenity* won acceptance in French and from there moved into other modern languages.[2] By 1702, when for the second edition of his *Dictionnaire historique et critique*, Pierre Bayle added the first full-blown discussion of the problem of modern obscenity, he clearly expected his readers to be familiar with the term. From Bayle's exposition, anyone would think that obscenity's odyssey was over, that it had at long last found the place from which it has, periodically over the last three centuries, obliged our modernity to confront issues it would have preferred to avoid. Bayle begins by listing nine different things that can be meant by the phrase "there are obscenities in this book"—which is to admit from the outset that the biggest problem with obscenity is that of knowing just what the censor has in mind when brandishing it (324). The discussion that follows centers on two issues: first, the difficulty for a writer of knowing when he is entering the territory of the obscene, since the frontier defining the decent is constantly being redrawn; second, the question of determining which variants of the obscene are worthy of censorship.[3]

On the first point, Bayle's chief authority is Molière (by then safely enshrined in the pantheon of great French writers, all the scandal he had provoked conveniently forgotten). Bayle explores the logic Molière had satirized in 1663. He explains that, in order to escape prosecution, authors will be forced to banish from their works "an infinite number of words that our language cannot get by without" (335)—for, to those who promote linguistic chastity on the grounds that "any phrase that offends their modesty is an attack on public morality" (340), the sky's the limit on words that can be judged indecent. Then, in a meditation that sums up neatly perhaps the key issue faced by the writers who had forced the French authorities and the Francophone public to recognize the existence of the obscene, he concludes by discussing words that "our fathers"—in particular, Molière—could use, whereas in 1702 Bayle "no longer dares write them out" (346).

Bayle thus deftly recapitulates the dilemma faced by all those who dared to explore the territory of the modern obscene during the initial half-century of its existence: they were not, à la Lenny Bruce, thrusting words in the public's face in order to anesthetize it to their shock value; they were, on the contrary, trying to continue to use words that were being pushed into the official oblivion from which writers such as Lawrence and Bruce would rescue them.

On the second point, Bayle is categoric. A work should fulfill precise conditions in order to become the object of censorship and prosecution: "Its author must present a description of his debauchery, using dirty words; he must be very pleased with himself for this; he must encourage his readers to take the plunge into impurity, which he recommends as the surest way to enjoy life" (324). We might almost think that obscenity's legal future had already arrived, so neatly does Bayle predict the reasoning that, in 1727, would provide the foundation for the first English common-law judgment that the publication of a work was criminally obscene (*Dominus Rex v. Curll*).

Already at this point—although the vocabulary of obscenity had barely begun to infiltrate English and although there was not yet a tradition of original obscene novels in English—the legal status of obscene publications in England was neatly set forth. After decades during which religious and secular censors had simply tried to wield authority over obscene publications, a court of law finally decided to confront the issue of who had authority and on what grounds—with the 1727 trial of the bookseller Edmund Curll because he had printed and marketed a translation of *Vénus dans le cloître*. The case, argued in a civil court, the King's Bench, was remarkably thorough in its consideration of precedent and in its definition of a term whose usage it initiated, "obscene little book." The publication of a work was criminally obscene, the court ruled, when that work "tends to corrupt the morals of the king's subjects and is against the peace of the king," when it "tends to disturb the civil order of society" (Howell, 17:153, 17:159). And, finally, a more original argument: spiritual courts punish verbal offenses; if a similar offense "is reduced to writing, it is a temporal offence" (156). After three days of debate, they came to a unanimous opinion: "this was a temporal offence" (160).

The king's judges decided that they had authority in this case only reluctantly. Witness Lord Fortescue's concern: "I own that this is a great offence; but I know of no law by which we can punish it. Common law is common usage, and where there is no law there can be no transgression" (159). But the justices faced up to the legal dilemma posed by the reinvention of obscenity. The "obscene little books" had become too public, "tending to the corruption of youth" (156); they felt obliged to "create precedent," to "make law" (157), to assign, in short, obscene publications an official place as a criminal offense.

Despite what the justices said (154), this was not the first prosecution of sexually transgressive literature in a temporal court; witness the rulings in lower courts against the booksellers who brought Pepys his "mighty lewd book." *Dominus Rex v. Curll* marks, however, the first time that any temporal court anywhere admitted that, because print had been added to the equation, the authorities had a new problem on their hands. In their decision, along with such familiar terms as "against good morals" (153), a new one appears: *obscene*, used in the phrase "obscene writings" (154), thereby providing, appropriately, a new name for a new offense. That neologism, recently transferred from the native tongue of the "mighty lewd" books, signaled the judicial modernity consciously chosen by the English justices.

Their French counterparts, Bayle's essay makes clear, were not ready for a juridical separation of church and state in matters of obscenity, despite the fact that France had started on this road long before England. The clear division of territory operative under La Reynie had been short-lived: obscene authors, even Bayle concludes, should be punished by both canon law and civil law.[4] This ambivalence lasted all through the eighteenth century. The confusion surrounding the prosecution of sexually transgressive literature, familiar from Théophile's trial, permeates the judgments pronounced against various types of bad books. The refusal to assign a clear status to obscene publications is an origin of the confusion in the Enlightenment category *livres philosophiques*, documented by Robert Darnton (*Forbidden Best-Sellers*). It was as if the failure ever to confront the difference of obscene publications had introduced a fundamental blindness, and a strange obsession, into French law.

Witness the 1770 summing up of the prosecution in a case that, because it helped create and mold public opinion, is now seen as a precursor of the Dreyfus affair. In 1766 the nineteen-year-old Chevalier de La Barre was tried, condemned, and executed on charges of blasphemy and impiety. From the start, the case was related to print culture only because of a detail: the authorities had found in the Chevalier's library a small selection of bad books, ranging from the classic obscene little books to a work with no sexually transgressive content, Voltaire's *Dictionnaire philosophique*. Of these, only Voltaire's work was consistently mentioned during the trial; it was burned along with the Chevalier. How then can we understand the logic behind the presiding magistrate's (Denis-Louis Pasquier) diatribe against the publications that he portrays as united in a conspiracy to bring down Church and state? "Sometimes they are openly hostile to religion. Often, they use obscene and voluptuous stories to corrupt the minds of our youth with these lascivious depictions in order to take advantage of the disorder into which their senses have been thrown to promote impiety. . . . Even women are being initiated into impiety and skepticism. . . . The contagion has penetrated into workshops and even into peasant huts: soon, there will be no faith left, no religion, and no more morality. Our original innocence has been lost" (cited by Claverie, 224–25).

Pasquier's outburst is proof that, a century and a half after a religious censor had tried to get civil authorities to convict Théophile on charges of "impieties, blasphemies, and obscenities," in a case in which obscenity as we now know it was constantly out of place, no progress seems to have been made toward assigning obscenity its proper function. The Chevalier was tried for offenses of a religious nature, most notably of having dese-crated a crucifix. Pasquier's remarks make it sound, however, as if de La Barre had been the first person executed for having *read* obscene works. It is clear that Pasquier knows the principal argument used to justify the civil prosecution of obscene publications: their potential for indiscriminate "contagion" across gender and class lines. And yet, what business did "ob-scene and voluptuous stories" have in this trial? Obscene publications, so long repressed in French legislation, thus returned to the legal theater in curiously displaced fashion. A century and a half after Théophile's trial, the argument that the first secular censors had tried to articulate was in place; it still was not attached to the proper object of prosecution.

1. On July 19, 1791, *obscene* finally appeared in a French law; it forbade the sale of "obscene images" and made no mention of obscene publica-tions.[5]

2. On May 17, 1819, under the Restoration monarchy of Louis XVIII, the law that provided the basis for the censorship of indecent publications during much of the nineteenth century was put on the books. (This was the ordinance cited in 1857 when Baudelaire was condemned for *Les Fleurs du mal* and once again in the same year in the charges against Flaubert for *Madame Bovary*.) The law does not mention obscenity; following the model of the 1629 ordinance, the earliest to include this category and that invoked to prosecute *L'Ecole des filles*, it refers to "offenses against public and religious morality or against good morals."[6]

3. On July 29, 1881, after extensive debate in the Senate, a law combin-ing the two earlier ones was passed; it forbade both "offenses against good morals" in print and the circulation of "obscene images" (Duvergier, 81:301–2).

4. Recent decrees—June 20, 1961; January 31, 1962—designate the con-

demnation of "books that offend good morals" (*outrage aux bonnes mœurs par la voie du livre*).

Under French law, *obscene* and *publications* never have come together.[7]

🦚

In French law, *obscene* appears solely in the policing of visual culture. It is as if the law were able openly to deal only with what had been absent at the time of the vocabulary's reinvention and never with the problem that had prompted both *obscénité*'s creation and the secularization of censorship: the link between obscenity and print. Remember that the most unexpected aspect of obscenity's reinvention is the complete elision of the visual. Not only were there no obscene images in the early obscene little books, but, in France, there was apparently no production of obscene serial imagery before the eighteenth century.[8]

Even then, the visual was slow to catch up. The first painter is imprisoned in the Bastille for sexually transgressive imagery (*figures indécentes*) in 1716 (Funck-Brentano, 184); only in 1732 do arrests step up. That year, an engraver was charged with *estampes obscènes;* by 1734 there are arrests for the production of *gravures obscènes* (254). *Obscene* had begun its association with visual culture in French. Even though, early on, a transfer to the book trade's regulation was attempted—in 1740, a peddler was arrested for selling *livres obscènes* (*Dom B[ougre], portier des Chartreux* is specifically cited) —the term never stuck. The same year, other arrests were made because of books against *bonnes mœurs* or *indécents*.[9]

This repression of print culture in the French prosecution of obscenity may have helped create the idea that the obscene is primarily a problem for visual culture, an impression shared by many today, especially by French speakers. It's easy to see why this would be the case. Shortly after Baudelaire's and Flaubert's prosecutions, Manet's *Olympia* (1865) and Courbet's *Origine du monde* (1866; figure 3 above) could be said to figure the sea change as a result of which images have replaced publications at the center of obscenity's maelstrom. This deviation in obscenity's path began in the voyeuristic fin-de-siècle culture Benjamin describes and has become increasingly prominent in the twentieth century—the example of Mapplethorpe's photography immediately comes to mind. Today, even obscenity's original obsession with four-letter words is acted out on visual terrain, where, inevitably, the terms' ability to scandalize is quickly blunted.

Three and a half centuries after the modern obscene was invented, we may truly have heard it all. After Monicagate and its ostentatious display of verbal obscenity on television, the shock value of words may have disappeared. The press now trumpets the news that the taboo surrounding obscene words will soon no longer exist: first on the big screen, next on the small screen, and soon even on computer screens, an "all-out barrage of four-letter words" has been unleashed.[10]

In obscenity's visual incarnation, the taboo on genitalia is crumbling as well. Editorials deploring the effects of "gross-out" movies and television series focus on scenes that no artist from any prior age would ever have dreamed of seeing in circulation—and in circulation public beyond any earlier age's wildest dreams. The examples are all too familiar: for instance, that of a British television show that "features such stunts as thrusting a see-in-the-dark camera down the trousers of a member of the audience and taking live footage of his penis."[11]

How are we to understand the disappearance of the limits that have separated obscenity from decency since Molière's day? Is the end of these taboos evidence of a general weakening of the civilizing process? Should it encourage us to speculate, along with the theoretician of this notion, Norbert Elias, about the possible existence of a "decivilizing process"?[12] Because obscenity was invented in response to the blurring of class lines by aristocrats anxious to maintain their "civilized" superiority, should we see its demise as proof that we live, finally, in a classless society?

Or should this return of the repressed encourage us to remember factors that our postobscenity age has in common with the last preobscenity epoch? I think here most notably of the fact that, in recent decades, for the first time since the bawdy's demise, we have seen desire, male desire at least, represented not always as an absolute choice between heterosexual and homosexual but as a spectrum—less dogmatic, less definitive.

With this in mind, let's return to the female body parts whose flagrant display was central to the reinvention of obscenity. All through the history of sexually transgressive literature—from antiquity through the bawdy and the obscene to the pornographic—the reader for whom such material is destined has been assumed to be male. Since Théophile's day, that male has been assumed in addition to be heterosexual and to respond only to representations of female genitalia, hence the more and more graphic nature of those representations. Today, those assumptions no longer seem so evident.

The layout of the "Men's Fashion Page" in the *International Herald Tribune* on July 5, 2000, neatly illustrates the new situation. Side-by-side are two articles: "What Do Men Really Want" on the left and, on the right, "Fashion's Walk on the Wild Side," with an overall caption, "Magazines Struggle to Adapt to New Definitions of Masculinity." The left-hand article promotes the message that magazines must now appeal to gay and straight readers alike, that representations based on an absolute choice are passé: "Men now have become so much more androgynous." Those interviewed are scornful of traditional magazines, described as "still harking on about a tired template of leery masculinity"—just the template evident in the right-hand article, which chronicles the use of "pseudo-porn" in men's fashion, in ads featuring men surrounded by actual female porn stars "positioned just short of x-rated." Despite one ad agency's avowed desire to "push the envelope," all these would-be Russ Meyers face the same dilemma, expressed by *Esquire*'s creative director: "It's difficult to define what is porn today, because the boundaries just aren't where they used to be."

And this may be modern obscenity's dead-end: four-letter words have lost their ability to shock—in print or on the air; the display of female genitalia in all forms of visual culture either no longer scandalizes or no longer satisfies the newly broad spectrum of male desire. Can there be obscenity without a generally accepted boundary defining sexual decency? Can obscenity exist in the absence of the rule, in place since *L'Ecole des filles*, dictating the heterosexuality of the public for sexually transgressive representations?[13]

This displacement of obscenity onto the terrain of visual culture may in turn be related to a second displacement, one that in effect signals the end of what I call modern obscenity. Obscenity may well be once again in the process of reinventing itself. *Obscene* and *obscenity*, whose separation from their religious connotations began already in antiquity, seem to be becoming, in our officially irreligious age, the modern equivalent of religious vocabulary: ethical terms. Of late, we have begun to use *obscenity* to designate events or experiences that society refuses to acknowledge as part of its culture; obscenity is thus assigned a key role in the ethical project of forcing society to confront that which it would prefer to shun, in particular, wars and massacres whose bloody violence it would prefer to repress. As a result of the latest reshuffling of the deck, *obscenity* can now designate a sort of public sin of omission. The vocabulary of the obscene could be indicating a new type of civilizing process in the making.

This latest displacement seems to have begun as soon as, with *L'Origine du monde*, Courbet took the quintessential modern tradition of sexually transgressive imagery to the limit. Courbet did not initiate the transfer, but he was active in the events that may have prompted it in France. I have in mind here a shift in visual culture initiated by a medium whose influence was first felt at that moment and most acutely in France: photography. For the first time with the American Civil War—and almost immediately afterward with the 1871 uprising in Paris known as the Commune—great historical events received extensive photographic coverage. For the first time, in particular, civilians were able to confront graphic representations of war dead, coverage that permanently altered public consciousness of war.[14]

At this stage, photographic proof of war's bloody horror was not widely disseminated. Because newspapers were not yet able to print photographs, viewers had to visit the galleries where photographers displayed them. In the twentieth century, photographic coverage has become increasingly immediate, increasingly graphic, and increasingly public. By 1945, for example, Robert Capa documented the final minutes of a G.I.'s life and published the images in *Life* magazine. The aspect of this coverage most manipulated by photographers, editors, and censors, all concerned in various ways with its effect on viewers, was its bloodiness, the violence of its potential impact.[15] No war coverage was both bloodier and more concerned with making as violent an impact as possible than that of the Vietnam War. It seems, therefore, fitting that the earliest usage of *obscenity*'s latest reincarnation may be this 1974 quote: "Vietnam was the most obscene episode of the century."[16]

This, then, is the obscene's newest territory, first invaded just as the visual representation of female genitalia was reaching a limit of its exploitation. At the same time that the pall of obscenity was gradually being removed from the categories of four-letter words and sexuality, the boundary was shifting: obscenity's latest incarnation is related once again to imagery, though of a type that did not exist when the vocabulary was reinvented, the ever more graphic, ever more bloody, and ever more difficult to look at representations of death. From there, *obscenity*'s usage has been extended; it has become a linguistic sentinel, policing the limits of the tolerable in an age of excess—excessive violence, even excessive wealth or profits.[17] This headline from *Newsweek* magazine (August 21, 2000) is virtually self-conscious commentary on *obscenity*'s double semantic drift: "The Dems cancel a Hispanic fund-raiser at the Playboy Mansion. But it's not dirty (legal) pictures that are obscene: it's dirty (legal) money."[18]

Notes

Introduction

1. Here are two examples of this new usage: The *Daily Telegraph* concluded its coverage of the deadly bombing in Omagh with "to those who have had to deal with terrorism in the past, the way in which Gerry Adams and the leaders of Sinn Fein/IRA have been wooed by Tony Blair . . . has seemed obscene" (August 17, 1998). The decision to use the injured Brazilian soccer star Ronaldo in the final against France was labeled "obscene" by the *International Herald Tribune* (July 15, 1998).

2. On the origins of pornography, see the volume edited by Lynn Hunt, especially her introduction. My view of obscenity is parallel to one school of thought on pornography; see Walter Kendrick's argument that there were no works that could be considered pornographic by today's standards before the creation of the word *pornography* in late-eighteenth-century France. Jean-Christophe Abramovici thus characterizes the evolution in the status of the obscene: "At the beginning of the seventeenth century, obscenity is one target of the continuous struggle against impiety and atheism. By the end of the century, it has become an esthetic criterion sufficiently precise to justify, in and of itself, an act of suppression" (*Le livre interdit*, 25). (Unless otherwise specified, all translations from the French are mine.) I agree with Abramovici's sense of the chronology of obscenity's evolution but not with his view of it as a continuous category that simply gained recognition at this time.

3. I am indebted to Elizabeth Eisenstein's discussion of the changing notion of authorship and of the new author-reader relation after the advent of print culture: "The paradoxical implications of making private thoughts public were not fully realized until authors began to address an audience composed of silent and solitary readers. . . . No precedent existed for addressing a large crowd of people who were not gathered together in one place but were scattered in separate dwellings" (230).

4. I will repeat on a number of occasions that anyone speaking of seventeenth-century France can use *mass market* in only a relative sense. Throughout the Ancien Régime, French was the language only of the cultural elite. In his *Histoire de la langue française*, Ferdinand Brunot provides various examples that bring this point home: when, for instance, Louis XIV traveled even a few miles from Paris, the speeches honoring his visits were often in the patois of the region (7:1). Even at the end of the eighteenth century, twelve million French subjects, or half the population, spoke no French and only three million spoke the language correctly (Balibar and Laporte, 31–32). With this situation in mind, it is easier to see why, at the moment of obscenity's reinvention, a print-run of 1,500–2,000 copies would have been considered truly excellent and much smaller ones would have been quite respectable. I describe this market as "mass" for another reason. The 1660s is the first time at which, using less expensive publications and new genres created for modern readers and without classical precedent, the book trade was reaching out to new readerships: in particular, bourgeois readers and women, two groups unlikely to have had a classical education. These readers then became active participants in the literary arena. For information on who was reading in seventeenth-century France—types of

readers, what percentage of the population—where they lived, and what they read, see John Lough (131–35). The information is spotty, but he includes all that has been recovered.

5. I have in mind here Raymond Williams's notion of the "preemergent" phase of culture, during which it is "active and pressing but not yet fully articulated" (126). I am also indebted to Williams's notion of "key words." For another example of the type of analysis I am attempting here, see Kendrick's study of the century between 1755 and 1857 during which the term *pornography* was, in his phrase, "born" (2–3).

6. Because, in seventeenth-century France, knowledge of Roman culture so massively outweighed that of Greek culture, *antiquity* was essentially synonymous with *Rome*. Thus, I will consider solely the Roman context for classical obscenity.

7. The entries for *obscene* and *obscenity* in the *Oxford English Dictionary* (*OED*) both begin by stating that the words entered English "perhaps immediately after F[rench]." The first listed occurrences in English are roughly half a century after the initial French usage. This trajectory, as I will show, is identical to the literary development as a result of which obscene literature in England imitates models created somewhat earlier in France. The only usage I have found that in any way predates the French implantation is from sixteenth-century Italy. In this highly Latinate culture, *obscenus* began to be used again—though as a Latinism. By this, I mean that, even though it is sometimes used in the context of sexually transgressive writing, the awareness is not yet present that a new literary phenomenon was coming into existence, a type of writing that would be characterized by this vocabulary. As Paula Findlen's work shows, *obscenus* was used in the condemnation of books published in Latin in sixteenth-century Italy. Even though in some instances the meaning seems clearly related to modern usage, it is hard to evaluate just how far from its Latin meaning the adjective may have moved. (See Findlen for examples of sixteenth-century Latin texts from Italy in which *obscenus* appears.) In addition, the vocabulary is not used in sexually transgressive texts written in Italian—Antonio Vignali's 1530 *La Cazzaria*, for example. In their *Dizionario Etimologico Italiano*, Carlo Battisti and Giovanni Alessio claim usage as early as the fourteenth century for *osceno*. No other dictionaries provide examples prior to the seventeenth century. Seventeenth-century Italian dictionaries, such as the *Vocabolario degli Accademici della Crusca*, give only minimal entries for the terms, with no examples. It seems that Italian was poised to become the conduit for the vocabulary's entrance into modern languages but that the development stopped short because the conditions for publication and censorship I see as essential to obscenity's reinvention in seventeenth-century France were not present. The fact of the vocabulary's French origin, along with other highly charged terminology positioned at the limit between literature and sexuality (*pornographie, pornographique*), is important for the image of French culture as being somehow inherently sexually dangerous.

8. The *Trésor de la langue française* dictionary presents, as do other sources, as the inaugural appearance of *obscène* in its modern meaning a passage first published in 1534, in *La Bataille fantastique de Rodilardus et de Croacus*, translated by Antoine Milesius from the late-fifteenth-century Latin original of the Italian writer Eliseo Calentius or Calenzio. However, in the example given—*les obscènes ondes* (obscene waves, 35)—*obscene* is clearly still being used in its Latin meaning of "ill-omened." In 1534 the translator did not yet sense that the word was about to move onto a radically new path. In re-creating the early modern trajectories of this vocabulary, I relied on the *Compliment* to Frédéric Godefroy's *Dictionnaire de l'ancienne langue française*, the *Trésor de la langue française*, and the ARTFL (American and French Research on the Treasury of the French Language)

database, originally established to prepare the *Trésor de la langue française* and now updated and administered by the University of Chicago. The Littré and the Robert dictionaries have no information on the pre-nineteenth-century history of the terms.

9. I realize that I'm walking a fine line here, on the one hand describing certain literature as sexually transgressive and on the other saying that this same literature wasn't considered offensive. Whether or not, for example, any of the elite male readers of Roman sexually transgressive literature were actually offended by it, they all surely saw that it was either intended to be offensive or at least toying with the idea that it could offend. I hope that this introduction will make clear that what I see as the key moment in the history of obscenity has nothing to do with its reception by readers, but is the moment at which government officials decide that they will try to stop its circulation. Richlin points out that elegance of form was essential if sexually crude material was to be considered inoffensive, and that this concept still functioned in the Renaissance. Ralph Rosen reminds me that there was probably a good deal of sexually transgressive content in such popular genres as mime and Fescennine (a type of verse featured at weddings and harvest festivals), genres that would not have respected the rule of formal elegance. This material surely enjoyed wider circulation than the Roman sexually transgressive literature familiar to modern readers. Nothing indicates, however, that this material was considered offensive, although audiences probably enjoyed the fact that it was *supposed* to be offensive. Such forms of ephemeral sexually transgressive material are so hard to document, at any period but the present day, that I limit my discussion to works whose circulation was more traditional.

10. So little information about Ovid's persecution has survived that it is now impossible to evaluate the story's accuracy or to understand the disclaimers by Catullus, Pliny, and others concerning their obscene verse. (These disclaimers took the general form of a defense of the author's personal morality—even if he wrote obscene verse, his private respectability was not to be questioned.) On the presence of the obscene in Latin literature, see also J. N. Adams.

11. Before print culture, the theater is the only form that can be thought of as inherently public. It was the only literary tradition that consistently gave classical moralists concern over its potential to corrupt. Such speculation can be traced back at least as far as Plato's concern over the consequences of the theater's ability to make material he found morally offensive public in ways that could not be completely controlled.

12. On the medieval use of what we would call obscenities and on the words used to refer to them, see John Baldwin. Baldwin argues, for example, that such language was the "distinctive mark" of certain vernacular genres, such as the fabliaux (84).

13. I am aware that some scholars would disagree with my position here and would argue that there was a generally recognized and enforced concept of sexually transgressive literature early in the Middle Ages, well before the advent of print culture. They base this view on the existence of scattered passages, such as the moment in *Le Roman de la Rose* when Jean de Meun has his narrator defend himself against critics who might object to his use of "insolent" or "shameless" language (lines 6947 and 6954; *Romance of the Rose*, 133). As in the case of Ovid's alleged persecution, the evidence is inconclusive: it suggests that a charge of literary indecency might have been plausible in thirteenth-century France, but does not prove that critics had actually tried to censure Jean de Meun's language. The fact that Jean de Meun was not blind to the category later known as the obscene is not a confirmation that this awareness was widespread among his contemporaries. By the time the obscene is reinvented, the awareness of this issue is incontrovert-

ibly prevalent. Some might have been surprised that this was the case, but all recognized that standards were changing. To describe the language he presents as transgressive, Jean de Meun has at his disposal only terms such as *baude,* which referred primarily to behavior and had no particular affinity with words or writing (*Roman de la rose,* line 15166; *Romance of the Rose,* 258).

14. In this context, it is surely significant that Christine de Pizan saw the book as an essential measure of authorial status: she established a workshop in which she controlled the preparation of manuscripts of her works for noble patrons. She seems to have been the first author thus to supervise the "publication" of her works in manuscript. She completed her last major work in 1429, on the eve of the Gutenberg revolution.

15. Perhaps because England had invented its own term as soon as the conditions that eventually guaranteed obscenity's reinvention were on the horizon, English speakers only began to use *obscene* once the usage had been reinvented in French. What appears to be the first appearance of *obscene* in its modern context occurs in the charges against those who had printed and sold the 1688 English translation of a French novel I will discuss at length, *L'Ecole des filles.* They were accused of "selling several obscene and lascivious books" (cited by Thomas, 16).

16. Despite the efforts of lexicographers over the past two centuries, *obscene*'s etymology remains completely unknown. See the article by Alain Rey in his *Dictionaire historique de la langue française.* On *obscene*'s missing etymology and the fact that the word cannot be subdivided (i.e., "ob-scenus") in Latin, as many commentators do in order to read new meanings into it, see Jean-Toussaint Desanti (130). Those who create etymologies for the term often do so in order to link the scandal of obscenity to the stage and to subject matter considered inappropriate for the theater. However, etymologies involving the Latin word for stage (*scena* or *scaena*), so favored by recent theoreticians, are all impossible. A particularly spectacular example of the recent involvement of theoreticians with *obscene* that demonstrates its fertile plasticity in their hands is Jean Baudrillard's "What Are You Doing after the Orgy?" See also the other articles in the special issue of *Traverses* devoted to *L'Obscène.* Already in 1947, Havelock Ellis used *obscene* as that which must be kept "off the stage" (175).

17. I will discuss the first cases of censorship in France in the next chapter. When Rabelais's *Pantagruel* was condemned, it was attacked principally on doctrinal grounds, rather than for content that would now be called obscene. The work was censored by a religious authority, the Sorbonne; the verdict was rendered in Latin. The fact that a work condemned on religious grounds was referred to as *obscenus* underscores the confusion that surrounded the vocabulary of the obscene as it survived in Latin; only vernacular usage sets the terminology on its modern course. (Interestingly, the only surviving record of the Sorbonne's condemnation is a 1532 letter by Calvin! I thank Lance Donaldson-Evans for this reference.) See Paul Lapeire on why Rabelais's work was put on the Index (43). There is one other documented sixteenth-century occurrence of *obscène,* in Montaigne's *Essais* (1580): "They wiped their asses . . . with a sponge; that's why *spongia* is an obscene word in Latin" (quoted in Godefroy, *Dictionnaire de l'ancienne langue française*). Montaigne's usage is less modern than Millanges's; he associates *obscene* with words and body parts but with no factors not yet present in Latin obscenity.

18. On the history of *I Modi,* see Bette Talvacchia's fascinating account and also Lynne Lawner's commentary in her edition.

19. See Hunt on how sixteenth-century Italian sexually transgressive material "was

not especially innovative" (28). See David Foxon's discussion of *I Modi* as "on the border-line" between ancient and modern traditions (48).

20. In French, thanks to a printer's desire to avoid prosecution and a poet's personal understanding of nascent societal taboos, *obscene* acquired new life, to signify subject matter that literature should not represent because a culture felt that it violated the boundary that must be maintained around the decent. By the end of the century, the three great early modern dictionaries in French—Richelet's (1680), Furetière's (1690), and the Académie Française's (1694)—all included the term and defined it as "indecent" (Furetière) and "that which offends modesty" (Académie Française). They made it clear through the examples they included that it had a special affinity with words in general and with the literary word in particular.

21. On the bond between print culture and the Reformation, see also Jane O. Newman.

22. For the particulars of the Counter-Reformation policy with regard to the print industry, I am indebted to Dominique Julia's lucid account (238 ff.). Alain Viala provides a chronology of the development of censorial institutions, both in Rome and in France (*La Naissance des institutions*, 360–65).

23. Protestant practice was not uniform on the issue of direct access to the scriptures; Lutheranism did not propose it until the seventeenth century. See Richard Gawthrop and Gerald Strauss.

24. As I will have ample occasion to remark, such screening systems were often decreed but rarely put into effect. The very fact that one had been imagined initiated, however, a new era for print culture. In the early modern book trade, there was an essential distinction between those who made the books (printers, typesetters, binders) and those who sold them. At times, one person played a double role: many printers (*imprimeurs*) had bookshops where they sold their own publications; some booksellers (*libraires*) also functioned as editors because they selected the works they wanted to publish. I will speak of "publishers and printers" or of "printers and booksellers" when I want to include all these categories. Most *libraires* did not own print shops; they commissioned printers for each print job. For more on these categories, see Henri-Jean Martin, *L'Edition parisienne au XVIIe siècle*.

25. After an initial flurry of activity in the sixteenth century, Italy no longer produced sexually transgressive publications. Once obscenity had received its modern form, France was originally the sole center of its production; in the eighteenth century, England gradually became its first rival. As Hunt stresses, "the overwhelming majority of the 1,920 titles" classified as pornographic by the British Library are either French or English; almost none of the titles in other languages were published before 1800 (21). This fact is hardly surprising, when one considers that modern literary obscenity is almost exclusively limited to the novel and also that France and England were the countries in which the modern novel initially was developed. Because of this focus, after the Aretino affair, I will compare the French situation only to that in England.

26. Provincial parliaments were also involved in the struggle for control over the book trade. Because all the books I discuss here were published in Paris, however, I won't discuss their role.

27. Talvacchia contends that images played a particular problem for censors in Renaissance Italy. Only at the century's end was serious attention given to sexually transgressive reproducible images—in 1596 a revised edition of the *Index of Forbidden Books*

included the first prohibition against the printing of such images. Talvacchia explains that some authorities wanted a second index devoted to visual material; she theorizes that the idea failed because, at this point, the censorship of images would have smacked of Protestant iconoclasm and would have been incompatible with Catholicism's defense of images (74).

28. Building on Ginzburg's analysis, Talvacchia describes the sixteenth-century dissemination of erotic prints as having "muddied the prior neat demarcation between the public and the private iconic circuits" (251 n. 4); she characterizes *I Modi* as "the first time that such explicitly sexual subject matter would be released in a serial form, with the potential for a large run and wide distribution" (79).

29. It is notoriously hard to document the existence of such visual material. Nevertheless, I am convinced that, had there been any significant production, it would still be possible to recover at the very least traces of its prosecution. According to Pierre Louÿs, the trial of Théophile de Viau, which I will present as a key moment in the development of both censorship and literary obscenity, was also a watershed in the history of French engraving. Before this point, anatomically correct representations of the body, particularly of the female body, could figure in book illustrations; after the trial, the zones that were about to be contained within the category of the obscene had to be covered with "strategically placed drapes" (cited by Lachèvre, *Procès,* xvi n. 2). (Louÿs was one of the legendary collectors of French erotica both visual and verbal, at a time when this material could still be collected. Thus, he is among the few whose opinion may be considered authoritative in this field about which so many have opinions without ever having seen the objects they allude to. The dispersal of Louÿs's collection was not recorded; scholars still speak of artifacts as having belonged to him, even when their actual whereabouts are unknown.) Thus, literary obscenity took on its modern form unaccompanied by transgressive images. In France, furthermore, it was also unaccompanied by the references to visual culture's powers of seduction that had been so essential to Renaissance Italian material. The cordoning off of literary obscenity from its visual counterpart continued until well into the eighteenth century—even then, seventeenth-century erotic classics were illustrated only with foreign engravings. It was only well into the eighteenth century that France became known for its production of dirty images as well as that of dirty books. Jean Goulemot's study of pornographic fiction may be unintentionally misleading. He says that the sexually transgressive illustrations in the novels he studies are "rare" but fails to mention how late this image-making begins. The earliest example he presents—and it is an engraving produced in Germany—is from 1746 (136). Goulemot cites reports that noted artists—Greuze, for example—produced lewd engravings for private patrons but stresses that almost all the sexually transgressive engravings made in eighteenth-century France were done by "the most mediocre" engravers of the day (142). It seems unlikely that the example of *I Modi* would still have been fresh enough, more than two centuries later, to discourage noted French artists from this domain, but stay away they did. On sexually transgressive reproducible images in eighteenth-century France, see Jean-Pierre Dubost. In his history of the genre, Dubost jumps from *I Modi* to eighteenth-century France. On the voyeurism and the intricate visual currency integral to the sexually transgressive literature of the Italian Renaissance, see Paula Findlen's illuminating essay.

30. The origin of *pornography* is traced to Rétif de la Bretonne's 1769 *Le Pornographe.* As Kendrick notes, the catalogues of Pompeiian artifacts later came to be referred to as "pornography" (11). The word *pornography* first appeared in English in a translation of the German art historian C. O. Müller in a passage in which he describes the existence in an-

tiquity of this type of visual representation. Kendrick gives various examples—including the definition of *pornography* in the 1864 edition of Webster's Dictionary as "licentious painting . . . , examples of which exist in Pompeii" (13)—that illustrate the new primacy suddenly accorded visual culture as the essence of sexually transgressive representations. In the United States the prosecution of material judged obscene has, from the beginning, been carried out almost exclusively against images. By now, obscenity may seem naturally tied to visual culture. The first such prosecution took place in Philadelphia in March 1815, before the country had an obscenity law on the books. The Mayor's Court tried Jesse Sharpless for having exhibited, "for money," a painting pronounced "wicked, scandalous, infamous, and obscene" (Ernst and Schwartz, 12–13). For nearly a century after this, the Customs Censorship Law regulated the shipment by mail and the seizure of many types of obscene images, even daguerreotypes, but did not mention printed matter (21).

31. See, for example, Richlin on the continuity in the definition of primary obscenities in Latin and in contemporary English: the list of terms found in Roman graffiti and literature is virtually identical to that in warnings issued by the U.S. Federal Communications Commission (25). There are, naturally, differences: primary obscenities did not function as expletives in Latin and so presumably did not signify anger, as they do in English today (230 n. 19). In this respect, seventeenth-century French usage remains faithful to Latin.

32. I realize that it is always risky to speak of the bourgeoisie in Ancien Régime France without specifying exactly what one has in mind (bourgeois merchants, the citizens of the city, and so forth). When I refer to the new bourgeois reading public, I am thinking of all the different kinds of nonaristocratic readers who, in the course of the seventeenth century, increasingly became a force to be reckoned with in print culture.

33. Goulemot describes the four categories into which, by the mid-eighteenth century, the book police divided subversive literature: political satires, satires of individuals (only members of the royal family and of the government were important enough to receive the protection of censorship, so this category can be assimilated to the first), atheistic works, and those "against good morals" (23). This last category was the only one not yet recognized when the seventeenth century began. Anne Sauvy comments on "the small number of morally unacceptable works" among the contraband books seized (*livres saisis*) between 1678 and 1701 (11). These instances of censorship tended, however, to be quite spectacular—one case I will present was still active thirty years after it began! See Sauvy's statistics on the types of works censored (11–13).

34. The Edict of Chateaubriant (June 27, 1551) first discussed the author's responsibility for his work and stipulated that each printed book had to bear its author's name. Like so many early censorship laws, however, this one had little initial effect on the book trade.

35. In the literary territory I am discussing, there simply were no female authors. I will therefore make the author "he" to reflect that historical reality.

36. Various examples of the expression's use in a religious context in the 1620s are cited by Sylvie Robic-de Baecque (e.g., 212). Because this was the decade during which the battle between religious and civil authorities for control over censorship was most heated, it is easy to imagine how the transfer could have taken place. The usage was vague, and it remained so, which may well have been part of its appeal. Long after its secular takeover, the expression was still used to designate books suspect for religious reasons. See, for example, Father Louis Habert's 1689 manual for confessors, or the 1685 missive by the Archbishop of Paris, François de Harlay, in which he lists the heretical "bad books" he asks Parliament to suppress (cited by Sauvy, 3). For proof of the expres-

sion's definitive adoption by civil censors by the end of the century, see the quotes from Nicolas Delamare's papers cited by Raymond Birn. See also Daniel Roche's comments on "the imprecision of the vocabulary" of early French censors ("La Censure," 76).

37. In *Les Anormaux*, Foucault reiterates his theory of "the age of repression" and links it to "the formation of capitalist societies" (157). On the basis of the works included by Victorian bibliographers in their catalogues of pornographic literature, Kendrick concludes that "the population of admissible books shows a geometric rise through time; none at all before the sixteenth century, very few then and in the seventeenth, steadily more as the eighteenth century advanced, and an explosion in the nineteenth" (74). An examination of the catalogues of "special collections" of various national libraries leads Hunt to the same conclusion.

38. I realize that I am moving quickly through complicated territory here; I will return to all these points. Note that I am describing only the tradition of sexually transgressive representations; in other literary traditions, that of courtly love for example, the adult woman was the object of desire and her body was evoked as desirable; in such chaste traditions, however, genitalia had no place. In previous controversies over the place of primary obscenities in literature, such as that between Jean de Meun and Christine de Pizan, the male member is the center of attention and female anatomy is not evoked—except, for example, as a rose.

39. Hunt rightly stresses that not all prohibited books sold well (19); the myth remained firmly implanted nonetheless. The best formulation of the desire for censorship is in Diderot's 1763 *Lettre sur le commerce de librairie:* "The more severe the prohibition, the more the book's price goes up. . . . How often booksellers and authors, if they had dared, would have asked police officials: 'Sirs, please, a little judgment condemning me to be whipped?'" (3:108). It was rumored that, by the late seventeenth century, censors sometimes did booksellers a favor and condemned a work so that its price could be raised dramatically (Sauvy, 4). Sauvy even quotes a 1696 article from a periodical that had itself been shut down on several occasions by the censors, advising booksellers to "solicit" censorship as a "sure means of increasing sales" (1). It was widely rumored that La Reynie was willing to arrange this type of publicity for a book (Berkvens-Stevelinck, 54). By all accounts, La Reynie was a far cry from the average censor: Saint-Simon said of him that he "tried to do as little damage and as infrequently as possible" (4:11–12). A cultivated man, he had a huge library, with over 1,500 volumes by the time he founded the book police in 1667 (Saint-Germain, 23). During La Reynie's tenure, it was probably possible to think of a kinder, gentler book police, along the lines of a recent revisionist view of the Spanish Inquisition (see Henry Kamen). J. M. Coetzee discusses the notion that sexually transgressive literature "needs censorship to increase its allure" (26–27).

40. The royal commission began to meet in September 1665 and ended when La Reynie was appointed. On its functioning, see Saint-Germain (25 ff.) and especially Nicole Diament's unpublished dissertation (1 ff.). In the edict that it published at its culmination, the evolution of *police* is evident: the police must "guarantee the public tranquility" and "purge the city of those who might cause disturbances" (Isambert, 18:100); the edict stresses the book police's repressive role (102). Seventeenth-century dictionaries, Furetière's in particular, indicate that *civilisé* and *policé* were virtual synonyms.

41. Roche shows that, from 1660–1669, of the 419 prisoners in the Bastille, 19 percent were from the world of print culture. Of these, 42 percent were print professionals (printers, etc.) and 40 percent were authors ("La Police du livre," 87). The expression "book police" was immediately coined. La Reynie assigned Nicolas Delamare the task of gath-

ering information on any law codes from other societies that applied to the areas over which he had been given authority (Saint-Germain, 37). La Reynie wanted Delamare, in effect, to found a new discipline, police law. Both in his papers, preserved at the Bibliothèque Nationale de France (BNF), and in his *Traité de la police,* Delamare refers to the "book police." During La Reynie's tenure, the number of official censors rose spectacularly. Prior to 1660, there were fewer than ten. By the time French censorship found its first great bureaucrat, Abbé Bignon, in 1699, there were sixty censors (Roche, "La Censure," 83). Then, between 1678 and 1701, Paris knew what Sauvy has termed "the most rigorous censorship at any time during the Ancien Régime" (5), and clandestine publication became virtually impossible.

42. The history of censorship would thus confirm the idea that the true age of French bureaucracy begins in the late seventeenth century. In 1699 Abbé Jean-Paul Bignon was appointed chief censor and immediately initiated methodical record keeping, obliging censors to follow established procedure. A work's title was entered in an official logbook. Next to it were written the author's name, the name of the person requesting permission to publish, the censor's name, and one final word: "rejected" or "approved." The correspondence of eighteenth-century authors also gives accounts of their experiences with the censorship process. On Bignon, see Roche, "La Censure." Roche points out that, in the seventeenth century prior to Bignon's appointment, there are strikingly few records, fewer even than for earlier periods (78). On the book police in the eighteenth century, see Robert Darnton, *The Literary Underground of the Old Regime.*

43. Already on September 10, 1563, Charles IX issued an edict in which *permission* and *privilege* are used interchangeably (Fontanon, 4:375). In all the documents relating to the seventeenth century in the most extensive archive devoted to early modern French print culture, the Anisson-Dupeyron collection at the BNF, I found remarkably few references to the permission. Documents related to censorship in this archive make it clear that, when censors intervened, it was at the stage of the privilege. Edouard Maugis documents cases in the sixteenth century and the early seventeenth century in which only the privilege was mentioned (2:312–13, 2:331). See Alfred Sauman on early usage of the two terms (454–55) and Robert Estivals on the early history of both concepts (34–36). Robert Netz argues persuasively that *permission* really refers to the seal of approval given by the doctors of theology of the Sorbonne and that, once secular censorship began to replace religious screening, the practice of awarding an official document by prepublication censors was abandoned (22–25). (At that point, when the Sorbonne approved a theological work, its permission became known as an "approbation.") I found evidence that this confusion was at least attenuated once Bignon's tenure began in 1699, but Maxime Dury contends that it continued throughout the eighteenth century: "Until the Revolution, documents confuse privilege and permission, with no evident attempt to distinguish in any way between the authorization to publish and the economic monopoly." He also cites numerous examples when *privilege* was used as though it meant *permission* (267–68). For more on the privilege as "an instrument of censorship," see Bernard Barbiche (161–62), Pierre Recht (27), and Claude Colombet (2).

44. On the absence of records, see Estivals (96–98); he cites the 1653 regulation (96). On the registration of privileges, see Viala, *La Naissance de l'écrivain,* chapter 3. On the general lack of prepublication censorship, see Pottinger (56, 63). Jean-Dominique Mellot has found instances when the privilege was considered by official censors as conferring the permission to publish; however, the system of "tacit privileges" he uncovered functioned only in Rouen and only in the early eighteenth century, when Abbé Bignon was

responsible for censorship (9, 596–97). In the seventeenth century, England had a two-stage system that was both remarkably similar to and remarkably different from the French system. The Stationers' Company listed all privileges (the word had the same meaning as in French) in a register. Prior to publication, printers were required to obtain a license or authorization to publish, initially from the Bishop of London, later from one of a small number of authorized officials. In England, both documents were obtained as a matter of course. There has been extensive debate among English book historians as to whether the licensing system functioned as a form of censorship. See Adrian Johns (230). For an excellent overview of the literature on licensing and censorship and a measured view of the question of their relation, see Richard Dutton. On licensing and theater censorship in Elizabethan London, see my chapter 3, n. 34. On the Stationers' notion of a "copy," see Johns, chapter 3.

Chapter 1

1. In 1524 Marcantonio Raimondi, the engraver responsible for the plates that Aretino's sonnets were designed to accompany, was held in the Vatican's prisons. It was said that the Pope himself issued the order for the destruction of the edition of the sonnets and the plates of the engravings. This censorship was also typical of the pre-Théophile era in that it was completely unsystematic: Raimondi simply languished in prison, without anything resembling a trial, until Aretino intervened with ecclesiastical authorities to win his release. No laws had to be invoked—nor were there laws that could have been invoked—to justify the volume's suppression; the Church more or less made up as it went along the rules to be used against publications deemed a menace to religious orthodoxy.

2. In France the two prior cases that most closely resemble modern writers' trials are those of Etienne Dolet and Etienne Durand. Dolet was both a writer and a printer. He was prosecuted less on account of the perceived heretical content of his own works than for the huge quantity of religiously unorthodox books published and distributed by his print shop: he was executed on August 3, 1546 for having stocked forbidden books. Secular authorities were in charge of some of the proceedings against him, but the archbishop of Paris initiated the prosecution. Durand was executed on July 18, 1618, just as Théophile's troubles were about to begin. He was charged with lèse-majesté because he collaborated on a satire of the king, *La Riparographie,* a work that circulated only in manuscript and seems never to have been completed. A secular authority, the king's council, issued the order for his arrest, but he was executed without any type of trial. These two cases indicate that civil authorities were beginning to feel the need to take charge of the prosecution of writers, even those whose work was considered dangerous on religious grounds. Théophile had the misfortune of having his run-ins with the authorities just at the moment when the decision was initially made for the crown clearly to take on the Church for control over censorship.

3. The example of another Italian freethinker, Giulio Vanini, was very much alive during Théophile's run-ins with censorship. In its issue for 1619, the *Mercure français*'s account of Vanini's execution (63–64) is immediately followed by its report of Théophile's first banishment (65). And, lest anyone miss the point, the segue into the next article runs: "since we are on the subject of the punishment of atheists . . ." (65). Vanini was executed by the Parliament of Toulouse on June 9, 1619, a month after Théophile's first banishment. He was executed, however, not as a writer but under the assumed name he had been using while hiding out and on charges of atheism and corruption of young peo-

ple; he had been earning his living as a preceptor and was reported to have taught his young charges more atheism than humanism. *Le Mercure français* is more favorable to Vanini than to Théophile. It was the first French periodical, founded in 1611, and soon became government controlled. It marked the beginning of the public circulation of news, the moment at which news became available to unknown readers. Vanini was a less significant figure on the European scene than Bruno; his influence was, however, particularly important for French freethinkers (see René Pintard).

4. During his trial, Théophile is questioned about his Protestant past and his recent (eighteen months prior to his arrest) conversion to Catholicism. Théophile's conversion may have been a tactical error. As a Protestant, he would have been protected by the Edict of Nantes and some of the material in his poems—what was seen, for example, as his mockery of the Virgin—would not have become an issue. I thank Christian Jouhaud for bringing this to my attention.

5. On Protestantism's invasion of French print culture in the sixteenth century, see Lucien Febvre and Henri-Jean Martin (433 ff.). For an analysis of several spectacular cases of Ancien Régime censorship when religious and secular authorities both intervened, see Roche, "La Censure."

6. Frédéric Lachèvre cites the passage in *Le Procès du poète Théophile de Viau* (xviii). Lachèvre's study is the principal source of information on Théophile's biography and his trial. For a reading of Théophile's work in the context of contemporary freethinking, see my *Libertine Strategies*.

7. The volume is dated 1622 and is thought to have been published by Antoine de Sommaville. The collection's exact history is not clear. Its principal historian to date, Lachèvre, gives a different version of its history in each of his accounts, in *Le Procès du poète Théophile de Viau* and in *Les Recueils collectifs de poésies libres et satyriques publiés depuis 1600 jusqu'à la mort de Théophile (1626)*. Lachèvre contends that the volume was never printed in 1622, but twice in 1623, in April and again in September—though the September printing may have been a second edition rather than a second printing. Antoine Adam, on the other hand, vehemently disagrees with the chronology Lachèvre proposes and argues convincingly that the volume began to circulate at the very end of 1622 (333).

8. When French critics speak of *gauloiserie* or *le gaulois*, they refer to the notion, common currency in a certain vision of French culture, that an important component of the French heritage can be traced to "our ancestors, the Gauls." According to this cultural cliché, the Gauls were a joyful, earthy lot. Witness the definition in Furetière's 1690 dictionary, from the period when the myth appears to have originated—that is, about a half-century after *le gaulois* had ceased to be acceptable—of the Gauls as "hommes gais et aimant joie et liesse" (jubilation). According to the critical line that buys into the myth, *le gaulois* was acceptable for part of the early modern period because its ribald sexuality was consistently so "joyfully" comic. See Abramovici on Théophile's *gauloiserie* (*Le livre interdit*, 25) and Lachèvre on why *le gaulois* would have been tolerated (*Procès*, xxix). While literary critics such as Abramovici and Pia discuss the bawdy's fate in France without offering precise explanations for why it rather suddenly ceased to be tolerated, historians of print culture present quite a different view of the period during which standards changed. According to Bernard Barbiche, for example, the seventeenth century's opening decade was a period of intellectual liberalism "largely because, at that time, the secular surveillance of print culture was exclusively in the hands of the Chancellor [the equivalent of the modern Minister of Justice], a less powerful figure than those who subsequently were responsible for this domain" (367). This explains, according to Barbiche, the

fact that "no important measures were taken in the domain of print culture" early in the century. Pia presents the years of Marie de Médicis's regency as a moment when liberalism continued, whereas, after considering its legal history, Barbiche contends that repression had already begun during this period.

9. The publication history of these *parnasses* and *cabinets satiriques* is complicated and has never been properly studied. Lachèvre's *Les Recueils collectifs* appears to provide the most accurate description, although even limited research shows his bibliography to be far from complete and far from consistently accurate. I consulted collections from several different periods: the early seventeenth century, prior to censorship; at the time when censorship began; after Théophile's trial, when entire collections were sometimes attributed to him. Once it became evident that compilations from these three periods were essentially interchangeable and that they contained many of the same poems, I decided that there was no point in reading every different edition. Because different collections reprint the same poems but in a different order, because no two editions contain the same selection of poems, and because particular editions are often rare—for example, the copy of the 1623 *Cabinet satirique* that I consulted in the Arsenal Library is apparently the only surviving one (Arsenal Réserve 8° BL.9994bis)—I do not provide full references for poems cited. Readers have a good chance of finding the poems I quote in any edition they consult—if not, they will find others in the same vein. Adam shows just how closely the 1622 compilation resembles earlier ones—those published, for example, in 1604, 1614, 1615, and 1617 (335–37). He also feels that it is clear that no one involved in this enterprise was afraid of censorship (338). In these pages, I use *the bawdy* as a synonym for *le gaulois;* I do not intend to imply that the English bawdy shared the fate of its French counterpart with respect to the institution of censorship—although there are so many important similarities in the histories of print culture in England and in France in the seventeenth century that the question should be asked. For more on the English bawdy and why it might have been tolerated, see Donald Thomas's *A Long Time Burning*, chapter 2. Scholars such as Thomas contend that the bawdy began to be censored because it became linked to libel. The same was not true of *le gaulois*, in which the rare satirical elements remain vague and never provoked a response on the part of censors. The adjective *satirical* generally featured in their titles is always spelled *satyrique* to indicate that it refers to the mythological satyr and the figure's legendary lustiness, rather than to satirical intent. On the English bawdy, see also Roger Thompson's *Unfit for Modest Ears*. Thompson stresses that the bawdy developed under the influence of Italian erotic literature; it died out once a French model (what I will describe as the modern obscene) began to replace the Italian one (4–5). The *gaulois*, like the bawdy, was heavily influenced by Italian models; it was, however, as in the case of Théophile's poetry, even more heavily influenced by Latin obscene verse.

10. The title page of the 1622 volume makes, however, no mention of any authors' names, whereas those of previous collections feature, on the title page rather than inside the volume, the names of a number of poets whose verse is included. The actual title page of the 1622 collection is stark in its simplicity: "*Le Parnasse des poètes satiriques.* 1622." On the history of the 1622 *parnasse,* see Jouhaud (*Pouvoirs,* 40–43): "The initiative must have seemed, if not harmless, at least almost risk-free" (40), an assessment with which both Adam and Lachèvre concur.

11. *Cul* is always written out. When it is found in the rhyme position, it is spelled *cu*.

12. I have in mind here the fig leaves actually included by the engravers themselves, rather than the cover-ups overpainted after the fact onto canvases judged too sexually ex-

plicit. The ellipsis may function, in fact, more like another fashion in Renaissance painting, what George Eliot termed those "transparent veils intended to provoke inquisitive glances" (see Leo Steinberg, 154).

13. In *Publishing Drama in Early Modern Europe*, Roger Chartier explains how difficult it is to determine whether responsibility for punctuation should be attributed to printers or to authors. The question of responsibility for punctuation is perhaps even trickier when dealing with transgressive literature, since printers and authors were often equally at risk when it was censored. When discussing the punctuation peculiar to different compilations, I attribute it either to their publishers or their typesetters. In the case of the sonnet by Théophile that played a crucial role in his trial, I assume that he was aware of the new punctuation then being tried out in the printing of bawdy poetry when he composed it.

14. What is particularly unusual about this appearance of the ellipsis is that, within this tradition, it becomes absolutely standardized. After the initial experimentation— with dashes, with periods, repeated two, three, even four times—the formula that subsequently became the official modern sign of something known but not printed in a text became a convention for these volumes. Even the Dutch Elzevier reprints—such as the 1666 Elzevier of the *Cabinet satirique*—faithfully follow this new typographical code. It is not clear exactly when the ellipsis first gained recognition as an official typographical sign in France. It seems likely that it was not before the first half of the eighteenth century; its rise to official status would therefore have been contemporaneous with secular censorship's definitive systematization. The typographical treatises considered authoritative in the mid-seventeenth century—most prominently, Etienne Dolet's *De la Ponctuation de la langue française*, published in 1542, just four years before his execution for printerly transgressions—make no mention of any sign to be used to stand for typographical characters or words that have been suppressed. The ellipsis does not figure in Joseph Moxon's *Mechanick Exercises in the Whole Art of Printing* (1683–84). I thank Bernhard Siegert for sharing with me his as yet unpublished work on the origins of the ellipsis in Germany, where, according to Siegert's fascinating research, the sign comes into existence only in the late eighteenth century, as a post-Enlightenment phenomenon. (It would be interesting to see how the ellipsis's history in German printing relates to that of secular censorship in Germany.) Siegert mentions one example from the period that interests me here of a typographical sign used to indicate an absence. In Descartes's 1637 *Géométrie*, the asterisk was repeated several times to indicate absent or missing terms. Descartes and his printers adopted the typographical code that seems to have been the more obvious choice during the early modern period: for example, the series of asterisks is familiar to readers of early modern fiction from the late seventeenth century on as the typographical replacement for letters suppressed in proper names. Roger Chartier brought to my attention a related early use of a typographical sign to indicate, rather than content that is not included, content that some readers may prefer to skip over. In a preface to the 1579 edition of Laurent Joubert's *Erreurs populaires,* the publisher, S. Millanges, informs readers that they may choose to omit those chapters marked with an asterisk, since they contain "obscene" material. (By "obscene," Millanges referred to primary obscenities; Joubert included them, however, in a medical context, to discuss conception and childbirth, rather than as sexually transgressive content.) The use of what is, in effect, the modern ellipsis in the bawdy compilations is, to my knowledge, unique at that period. Once the bond had been forged between the mark and sexually transgressive literature, however, the ellipsis continued to be exploited in it. See, for example, Goulemot (158) on

the use of ellipses in eighteenth-century erotic novels to suggest an orgasmic progression in the text.

15. The *parnasse* for which Théophile was tried, that of 1622, displays a unique relation to the ellipsis: this is the only collective volume in which the *f* in *foutre* is left out and the ellipsis is used to signal the absence of everything but the word's ending. In principle, this more extended silencing could be seen as a measure taken to ward off censorship. Because any change in a convention may just as readily attract unwanted attention as protect against it, however, whiting out the *f* could also have backfired.

16. "The characters did not wish to take on the most outrageous words, just as long ago the pen of that unfortunate Emperor refused to inscribe on paper and write out an unjust decree that he wanted to sign against St. Basile; similarly, this typeface, feeling uncomfortable under the press, refused to print the most indecent words" (Garasse, 781).

17. The copy in the Bibliothèque Nationale de France (BNF) is in such poor condition that I was unable to obtain a photo of the title page. It appears to have been cropped a bit at the top, probably when the volume was rebound in the nineteenth century. It is clear, however, that the page was never properly centered; the text is often badly centered in this edition.

18. Engravings were expensive to reproduce, so they ran up an edition's cost. The frontispiece to the 1613 *cabinet* is not in the least erotic: it takes the adjective *satyrical* literally and depicts a group of satyrs playing music in a field.

19. Martin situates the statutes in 1617–1618 (*Livre, pouvoirs et société*, 1:54). M. L. Bouchel, the editor of the published edition of the stationers' code, which appeared in 1620, clearly states that they are were ratified and registered on July 9, 1618, thereby confirming Barbiche's version of their history (Bouchel, 1; Barbiche, 369). For my description of this code, I follow Bouchel's text. All commentators are forced to admit that, as usual, we know almost nothing about the way in which this code may or may not have been enforced.

20. Dury pronounces the 1618 statutes the foundation of all early modern legislation governing the book trade (254).

21. Earlier collections habitually include authors' names on their title pages. The publisher's name is often printed as well.

22. I reproduce the exact punctuation used in the 1622 edition. *Sieur* was more or less the equivalent of the more modern *Monsieur*. "Le sieur Théophile" became Théophile's "author's name" in Foucault's sense of the term. In subsequent editions, the beloved woman's name is also spelled "Phillis" and "Philis"—sometimes different spellings appear in the same edition. For the 1622 edition, however, the least likely variant, "Phylis," was chosen. Except for this proper name, I have modernized the French, a practice I will follow throughout. Because this was the first *parnasse* to include poetry by Théophile and the authorities had no other apparent reason for deciding to prosecute this particular compilation, Lachèvre concludes that the censors were going after Théophile in particular, trying to end the activities of a known freethinker who was charismatic enough to be a magnet for like-minded young men. Throughout his volume on Théophile's trial, even though he offers no evidence in support of any of his claims, he insists that the desire to eliminate Théophile was the sole motivation behind the entire enterprise. He even contends that the publishers of the 1622 volume were working in collusion with the authorities, that they included verse by Théophile to help the authorities get their man (see, e.g., *Procès*, 115; and *Recueils*, 52 n. 2). Adam vehemently contests this view (334).

23. I have in mind here both the performance for which Bruce was put on trial for ob-

scenity in 1964 and his testimony at his trial to the effect that, while in the army, he had heard *fuck* four or five times in one sentence—as an adjective, a noun, and a verb. The comparison between Théophile and Lenny Bruce does not end there. Both trials were marked by the same confusion over whether the accused was on trial for obscenity or for offensive religious references. (Recently, in fact, it has been suggested that the confusion was just as profound at Bruce's trial as at Théophile's. In a documentary aired in August 1999, Paul Krassner argues that Bruce's arrest for obscenity was "really a cover for arresting him for blasphemy" [*New York Times*, August 8, 1999].) In the end, while neither man received the harshest sentence possible, both were broken by the trial: neither really resumed his career afterward; both died soon after its conclusion.

24. The story of the possessed woman from Agen is in the third chapter of "Première journée," that of the procession in the fifth chapter. Jacques Prévot's recent edition of writings by *Libertins du XVIIe siècle* makes many of these texts more accessible. Théophile's prose work is often referred to as "Fragments d'une histoire comique"; this title comes from Georges de Scudéry's posthumous edition.

25. These religious censors were not, however, very demanding; they apparently did not bother to examine all of Garasse's huge manuscript (Adam, 345). The principal diatribes against Théophile's sexuality are found in the work's final third. For a reading of *La Doctrine curieuse* that considers the role it played for Garasse and, in particular, the way it made him into an author, see Jouhaud (*Pouvoirs*, 50–75).

26. The date on which the last volumes of an edition left the presses, known as the *achevé d'imprimer*, is included in each volume. While in general these dates can be trusted, it appears that they were on occasion altered by either authors or publishers (see Veyrin-Forrer, "A la recherche des *Précieuses*," 341 n. 15).

27. In view of the link between print culture and the Protestant menace, it is interesting that the Jesuit obsessively compares the freethinkers to Luther—he contends that they, like he, claimed that everyone should have access to the Bible, hardly the type of issue Théophile would have been likely to be concerned about. Many of the sections of Garasse's treatise that seem on the surface most bizarre become comprehensible in this context: he goes on at length about the evils of various topics associated with Protestantism's use of print culture—why women should not be allowed to read the Bible, for instance. Garasse thereby established a fantasmatic link between French freethinkers and foreign Protestants, a suggestion that can hardly have failed to capture the authorities' attention. To my knowledge, there is no evidence that the libertines, who were opposed to all organized religion, had anything to say about any of these issues. The fact that they take on such importance for Garasse confirms the impression that granting more open access to previously restricted material to new literary publics played a central role at the origin of modern censorship.

28. At one point, Garasse does say of the libertines: "In that volume [*Le Parnasse*] they pronounce horrible blasphemies against the vision of beatific love" (780), thereby implying that their sexual audacity represented a threat to religious doctrine. He never returns to this rather ludicrous claim.

29. The conditions for the circulation of the sexually transgressive literature that Garasse describes here are essential to its threat and to its modernity. Prior to this, no literature of this kind had circulated so "democratically," that is, in settings to which access was uncontrolled and uncontrollable.

30. The fact that French bawdy verse makes frequent mention of female sexual characteristics already distinguishes it from Roman obscene poetry, in which female genitalia

appear only rarely and are evoked with disgust. Although a certain disgust with regard to female genitalia is still evident in bawdy poetry—many of *Le Parnasse satirique*'s poems, for example, detail all that is wrong with the "cunts" they mention—the frequent allusion to female sexual organs marks a step toward the invention of the modern obscene. Long after the fact, in 1690, in the examples he chooses to illustrate *obscene* in his *Dictionnaire,* Furetière describes *Le Parnasse satirique* as "full of *obscene* words, of *obscene* verse." He thereby proves that, by the end of the century, the terms used to identify the collection at the time of Théophile's prosecution had been replaced by the vocabulary that the trial helped create. Sexuality, by the way, is not explicitly mentioned in dictionary definitions of *obscene* and *obscenity* prior to the twentieth century.

31. In a moment, I will refer to Foucault's work on the history of sexuality in the ancient world, in which Greek models figure prominently. In order to avoid confusion from the outset, I repeat that, in seventeenth-century France, Greek was almost entirely unknown, whereas poets such as Théophile were excellent Latinists. (Théophile, like many of his generation, composed both poetry and prose in Latin.) The classical literature in which these writers were so thoroughly versed was almost exclusively Latin.

32. The Latinists to whom I showed the Phylis sonnet immediately saw this and said that it was certain that Théophile was trying to create an overtly Latinate ambiance. My informants were particularly sensitive to what they saw as Théophile's proximity to Catullus. Catullus 16, perhaps the most notoriously slippery of his sexually transgressive poems, was evoked as the one Théophile evidently had in mind when writing the poem— and perhaps subsequently when, as I will discuss shortly, he argued in his trial defense that writing about pederasty did not make a pederast of the poet. On Catullus 16 and the obstinate refusal of generations of Latinists to recognize its true sexual subversiveness, a refusal that calls to mind Garasse's almost willful distortions of Théophile, see Richlin (146) and Kendrick (43–44).

33. See Kendrick on the tacitly accepted circulation of bawdy poetry within an elite English audience (55–58).

34. Foucault is speaking here of a Greek model; see also Richlin (e.g., 58) on the continuity of this model for the Roman representation of male desire. The accuracy of Foucault's portrayal of what he termed the history of sexuality in the ancient world has been amply criticized, by Richlin for instance. Nevertheless, what he presents as the Greek model for male desire, based on the refusal of a radical opposition between same-sex love and love for the opposite sex, is confirmed by all recent commentators. See, among others, both Foucault and Richlin on other factors considered essential to the portrayal of the only sexuality that counted in Greece and in Rome, that of the adult male—for example, the essential distinction between active and passive sexuality. In all essential ways, the portrayal of male sexuality in French bawdy poetry conforms to the priapic vision outlined by Richlin.

35. Garasse identifies Phylis as "a prostitute," thereby assimilating the sonnet to the venerable classical tradition of "pornography" in the term's literal sense of writing about whores. More recently, commentators such as Lachèvre have insisted on Phylis's reality in a frantic attempt to prove Théophile's heterosexuality.

36. On the status of the beloved in Roman poetry as "more ideal than real," see Richlin (32–33). When I say that there is no evidence to support Phylis's reality, I do not intend to take sides in the (unfortunately ongoing) debate about Théophile's personal sexual preference. Far too little reliable biographical information has survived to give us any access to the man behind the poems—and we should never forget that Théophile

consistently warned his prosecutors that his literary work should not be taken for autobiography. Finally, Christian Jouhaud reminds me that some of Théophile's erotic poems were written for others—shades of Rostand's nineteenth-century vision of Cyrano de Bergerac—or were used more than once, poetic strategies that refute the idea of a unique and identifiable addressee, a real Phylis. Historical dictionaries contend that *syphilis,* the modern French equivalent of the word Théophile uses, *vérole* (the pox), did not exist before the mid-seventeenth century. However, it is hard to imagine that the poet did not have the new term in mind when he addressed his poem to "Phylis" and spelled the name in this particular manner. Johannes Fabricius's study is the best source of information on both the history and the fantasmatic history of syphilis in early modern Europe. The pan-European syphilitic epidemic began its onslaught in the late fifteenth century; literary references to the disease and anxious commentary on its effects reached their apex in the sixteenth century. There is no evidence of any particular renewal of the syphilitic menace in the early seventeenth century, but the most frightening years were not far in the past. According to Fabricius, as early as 1530, the disease was referred to as "syphilis" and syphilis was known as "the French disease" (xvii).

37. On the particular nature of the sexual degradation Catullus was conveying with that line, see Kendrick (43). Even Garasse knew his Latin poetry well enough to list Théophile's precursors correctly. He uses the traditional justification of *gaulois* literature— it can circulate as long as it is comic—to explain why Latin erotic poetry should not be banned while Théophile's should: "Indecency . . . must be accompanied by a subtlety of wit, as is the case with Terence, with Martial, and Catullus, who slip it in delicately, with great imagination; to recount crudely horrible indecencies, that only Théophile and the authors of the *Parnasse* would do" (782). On the status of anal sex with women in Greek and Latin sexually transgressive poetry, see Richlin (233 n. 13).

38. Garasse is describing the sodomite sonnet and a translation Théophile had completed during his first exile: "[Théophile] realized that there was no better way to compensate for his former crimes than to make the print shop's presses (*les presses de l'Imprimerie*) sweat a bit more decently than he himself formerly sweated as a result of the promiscuousness that he himself flaunts in the first poem of the *Parnasse satirique*" (782).

39. Théophile described his cell in the opening paragraph of his February 1624 pamphlet *Theophilus in carcere.*

40. The authorities called in a series of witnesses who reported not that they themselves had heard Théophile making objectionable statements, but that they knew someone who had described to them having heard Théophile do so—to which the poet consistently replied that hearsay was not grounds for conviction. "The accused said that since the witness didn't know him personally, he could only know what was said about him, in addition to which there were certainly other men named Théophile," was, for example, his comment at the end of his formal confrontation with witness Pierre Galtier on August 18, 1625 (*Procès,* 492). Théophile's most eloquent formulations of the defense that words cannot be seen as criminal actions are found in his "Fragments d'une histoire comique," composed before the trial, although at a time when Théophile was already well aware of the ways in which the censors were using his work against him. See, in particular, the Saba edition (58, 120).

41. In what follows, I will use Garasse's term, *sodomy,* by which he means any sexual activity between men; Théophile himself prefers the term *pederast.* Lachèvre does not reproduce the trial proceedings in a straightforward manner. Each section is broken up with extensive commentary in which he interprets the material he is either about to

present or has just presented, always directed by his idea that the case was a set-up job against the poet—a theory that implies a degree of control over the proceedings that I do not find in them. Until a courageous scholar tackles the difficult task of verifying Lachèvre's work for a new edition of the trial, the only way to get a fresh look at the material is to skip over his commentary and concentrate on the proceedings alone. And it will take a very courageous scholar indeed to tackle this case—as well as someone with extensive training in paleography. I consulted one dossier, the record of Théophile's interrogations between March and June 1624. The dossier had been recently separated from others in the same box; the paper was in good shape (unlike that of many other dossiers from the same period). However, the handwriting was impossible to decipher. I have dealt with many seventeenth-century manuscripts, but have never encountered one even remotely as indecipherable as this. In order to save ink when they recorded trial proceedings, scribes literally did not lift their pens as they moved across the page, thus producing a continuous, unbroken line of writing. In addition, they were writing partly in shorthand. Finally, one of the few people able to decipher these proceedings, Gérard Jubert of the Archives Nationales, informed me that the period of Théophile's trial was known for its particularly impenetrable writing. I worry about Lachèvre's reliability in particular because of his refusal to deal with the issue of homoeroticism. He plays down, to the point of almost effacing it, all talk of this issue in the trial proceedings, because he is convinced that Théophile desired only women. To this end, he is fond of quoting verse and correspondence that indicate the poet's appreciation of female beauty, all the while dismissing similar expressions of interest in men as "excessive sentimental rhetoric and nothing more" (553).

42. The proceedings of Théophile's trial are a rich source of information on contemporary cabaret society. They pinpoint in particular the role these cabarets played in facilitating the circulation of subversive texts across class lines: a number of key prosecution witnesses report having heard the poems they attribute to Théophile recited in taverns; the audiences contained servants and workmen, as well as young bourgeois (see, in particular, *Procès*, 461–62, 468, 479–80). From these descriptions, it would appear that the authorities were correct in believing that this sexually transgressive literature had begun to circulate across class lines. The cabarets named as the scenes of these crimes of literary promiscuity and subversion include such well-known watering holes as the Pomme de Pin, near the Notre Dame bridge (a tavern that already figures in Villon's poetry), Le Berceau, near the Saint-Michel bridge, and the Trois Cuillères, on the rue aux Ours. (Garasse singles out the Pomme de Pin as a particularly dangerous spot, site of innumerable libertine "obscenities.") The cabaret or tavern was a famous Parisian institution in Théophile's day, celebrated, for example, in the anonymous 1628 compilation, *Le Parnasse des muses, ou Recueil des plus belles chansons à danser*. By this time, the cabaret, the first of which appeared in the late Middle Ages, was nearing the end of its reign, soon to be replaced by the café or coffeehouse, a seventeenth-century invention in France. The café took over the tavern's role in facilitating social and literary promiscuity. It also provided a space in which the new luxury goods, just beginning to enter French markets in important quantities during the second half of the seventeenth century, could be displayed to a broad audience. The coffeehouses thus helped spread the new consumerism to which Molière's plays of the 1660s, contemporary with the first flowering of Parisian cafés, testify. The first coffeehouse in Paris was the Café Procope, which opened in 1660. On the early history of English coffeehouses and the threat of social promiscuity associated with them, see John Brewer (34–38).

43. Guibert was technically a bourgeois, since the category was very wide-ranging in the seventeenth century. Butchers, however, were hardly the elite of the bourgeoisie; they had the reputation of being particularly coarse and vulgar—hardly cultivated men. It was surely these connotations that Théophile wanted to evoke. Adam uses Guibert's testimony to show that, since he was not an educated man, the prosecution had been obliged to have him learn his accusations directly from a copy of *Le Parnasse satirique* (385–86). The prosecution's technique reminds us of a basic lesson to be learned from all attempts to suppress sexually transgressive literature: to do so, it is always necessary to give that literature additional public exposure.

44. I am conflating here passages on pages 781 and 782, in which Garasse speaks, first of writing these words, and then of printing them, in each case stressing that only "stable boys" or "beggars" would be capable of such behavior. In each case, the equation that consistently provokes Garasse's anxiety is that between print, sexually transgressive literature, and a nonelite public, with the most dangerous possible audience being that of the lowest station.

45. Lapeire cites archival evidence showing that civil authorities in seventeenth-century Lille were so concerned about the spread of sexually transgressive literature, particularly among working-class youth, that they tried to forbid the sale of *all* new books to this segment of the population (48 n. 1).

46. Adam shows how, even when the sonnet to Phylis is neither recited nor referred to explicitly, words and phrases from the poem infiltrate the testimony of witnesses for the prosecution; he concludes that they must surely have been given the sonnet with instructions to use it to inspire their accusations (373). This theory, which seems more than likely, proves that sexually transgressive literature, and in particular the sonnet made infamous by Garasse's misreading, was the prosecution's central preoccupation.

47. "Faire des vers de sodomie ne rend pas un homme coupable du fait; poète et pédéraste [in the original, "perderastre"] sont deux qualités différentes" (Prévot, 69). The passage is from the *Apologie de Théophile,* written and published in 1624, while Théophile was in prison during the second year of his trial (86). That year, Théophile attempted to plead his case to the outside world in a series of pamphlets probably first published separately and then gathered together in *Recueil de toutes les pièces faites par Théophile depuis sa prise jusqu'à présent* (1624), an in-octavo volume reedited several times before the trial's end. It does not include the *Factum de Théophile présenté à nos seigneurs du parlement,* a true legal document setting out his defense, rather than an attempt at cultivating public opinion. On several occasions, in the *Apologie* and in the other texts he published to plead his case to the outside world, Théophile gives examples to prove that his accusers believed that a poem could only be read literally.

48. Modern commentators concur in their belief that the quality of Théophile's defense obliged the Parliament to acquit him.

49. The print collective responsible for the 1625 *parnasse* obviously decided to take advantage of this relative sense of immunity: in terms of the visual prominence accorded primary obscenities, this was the boldest of all such compilations. The *f* eliminated from *foutre* returns; for the first time ever, *vit* is sometimes written out. (The emphasis remains, however, priapic; *con* is still written "c.") After Théophile's trial, this type of transgressive literature faded from view. From this point on, the entire volume remained identified with the author who had been tried for it, even though he was responsible for so little of it. By the 1660s and Molière's heyday, live authors, or at least those who were unable to defend themselves as forcefully as Théophile had, were punished far more

severely if they dared continue the bawdy tradition. Witness the example of Claude Le Petit, burned at the stake on September 1, 1662, when he was only twenty-four, for having authored a verse collection, *Le Bordel des muses*. On Le Petit's trial, Lachèvre is once again the only source. He calls Le Petit's work "obscene," though seventeenth-century authorities did not. Forty years after Théophile's trial, however, the vocabulary they use to justify censorship had become more varied. True, they did use the same adjectives that had been applied to Théophile's work ("impious," "blasphemous") but, in the language used to condemn Le Petit's work, there is evidence that, the year before Molière thrust the vocabulary of obscenity into a public existence, the authorities were slowly working toward it. They use, for example, the expression *contre les bonnes mœurs* (against good morals), which became a set phrase in subsequent French condemnations of obscene literature; they also favored *infâme* (infamous), the then accepted translation for the Latin *obscenus*. In the forty years that separate the two verdicts, print censorship had begun to come into its own in France.

50. In his sonnet, Théophile could be said to predict this turn away from traditional priapic representations. His depiction of the male member is hardly still another portrait of a mighty phallus. In his sonnet, it is not female genitalia that are disgusting, but the normally all-conquering male member. The clearest example of the self-censorship following Théophile's trial is found in Sorel's *Histoire comique de Francion*, whose original publication was exactly contemporaneous with the edition of the *Parnasse satirique* that brought the censors down on Théophile. When this edition is compared with that published in 1626, shortly after the trial, it is immediately evident that male genitalia, frequently and bluntly named in the original version, are subsequently evoked only by means of circumlocutions—when they are mentioned at all, that is, for Sorel simply deleted many of the references. Sorel's self-censorship in both editions after the trial (1626, 1633) provides eloquent testimony to the impact of Théophile's censorship on the development of the type of sexually transgressive literature intended for above-ground circulation. Sorel deleted many four-letter words and toned down the portrayal of the eponymous main character, Francion, originally a stunning example of the open display of priapic sexuality and subsequently overtly criticized as "perverse" precisely because of the behavior that he had previously incarnated (see, e.g., 380).

Chapter 2

1. Francis Barker's *The Tremulous Private Body* contains a brilliant analysis of the aftershocks of the English civil war. It constitutes a blueprint for the type of study that remains to be done for the same period in France. As a result of the midcentury's political upheaval, in Barker's description, "the older sovereignty of the Elizabethan period was disassembled, and in its place was established a conjunction of novel social spaces and activities, bound together by transformed lines of ideological and physical force, among which new images of the body and its passions were a crucial . . . element" (10). He situates the redefinition of subjectivity within the political context of the rise of the modern state and "the broad process of transition from the feudal to the capitalist mode of production" (11). French historians have traditionally taken a dim view of the Fronde's significance. When the uprising is considered in the context of contemporary events in England, however, the menace of the French unrest to those in power there becomes more apparent. Perhaps because the French unrest did not overturn a monarchy, many of its long-term consequences—economic, in particular, although even in this domain a powerful evolution can be argued for—do not seem as dramatic. In literature, however,

the changes instigated in France ultimately had more revolutionary implications than in England.

2. The same scholar who edited the proceedings of Théophile's trial, Lachèvre, also edited this trial, published in a volume entitled *Le Libertinage au XVIIe siècle: Mélanges*. No scholar since Lachèvre has examined the dossier of *L'Ecole des filles*. Lachèvre gives no indication of where the documents he cites are to be found. The manuscript of these proceedings appears to be definitively lost.

3. The Code Michau of 1629 did not completely eliminate the Sorbonne's participation in the business of censorship. The Doctors of Theology of the Sorbonne could still be called upon to screen religious publications; however, the Chancellery was given control over censorship. This is a moment when the French system's functioning seems to have closely paralleled the English system of licensing. As a point of comparison: whereas a 1643 English ordinance named thirty-three licensers for different subjects (Johns, 239), the 1626 French decree provided for only four reader/censors.

4. Lapeire says that this also marked the first time that *mœurs* appeared in a legal document with the connotation it has had ever since in French law, in which the category of crimes against *bonnes mœurs* includes all sex-related offenses, from rape to adultery to prostitution (43).

5. Chevillier discusses some of the areas in which the new system probably did not function successfully. There was apparently a good deal of confusion, for example, about the procedure to be followed with a work with theological content—did such a work have to be submitted twice? Or could it be submitted only to the Chancellor (406)? He also describes aspects that did become operative and even names a number of the reader/censors who were most frequently called upon. In the decades that followed, there was also controversy among civil authorities over the right to choose the reader/censors. At one point, the king was to name them personally. Then, when the Académie Française was founded in 1634, Richelieu thought that it might have a role at the center of a reorganized system of preventive censorship (see Barbiche, 377). Such squabbling clearly delayed the effective implementation of any system.

6. I borrow the phrase "child of the printed book" from Dickens, *Reformation and Society*, 51. One need only think of the masterpiece of Jansenist propaganda, Pascal's *Lettres provinciales* (1656), to realize how important the use of the vernacular was to Jansenism. The *Lettres provinciales* was also a significant victory over censorship: Pascal naturally chose clandestine publication; the work, which was a huge success, appeared in eighteen opuscules between January 1656 and March 1657.

7. For a reading of the Fronde as dominated by the print industry, see Jouhaud's *Mazarinades: La Fronde des mots*.

8. Martin says of this period: "In all the Ancien Régime, the print industry was probably never freer" ("Une Croissance séculaire," 96).

9. I use the plural for categories (authors, and so forth) for which it has never been learned how many persons were involved; almost all the collaborators seem to have worked as booksellers in the attempted distribution of the text. The proceedings against this work make it abundantly clear that it was, at every stage of its production, a group effort. I realize that it seems strange to speak of a "mass audience" and "mass-marketing" with regard to a work whose initial print-run was apparently only three hundred copies (Lachèvre, *Le Libertinage au XVIIe siècle: Mélanges*, 91). With my choice of terms, I want to convey my sense that those responsible for this publication had decided to make erotic literature available to audiences that would not previously have been aware of its exis-

tence. Everything we know about the work's publication and circulation history demonstrates the success of the publishing collective's marketing strategy. The authorities were so anxious to stop its circulation—and their anxiety could only have resulted from its popularity with new readers—that until the early eighteenth century, the book police were actively involved in its suppression. (See nn. 22 and 23 for more on their efforts.) It seems unlikely that the book was reedited immediately in France. It was, however, republished numerous times in French in numerous cities outside of France. It was also quickly translated into English and Dutch. Indeed, its publication history in English is nearly as complicated as in French. (See n. 23 for what we know about that history.) I give this overview in order to show that the number of copies in any one of these editions is largely irrelevant; the sum total of editions, reeditions, and translations provides the basis for my notion of a mass market. The most likely explanation for the small initial print-run is that those responsible were paying for it; they would have needed to recover their investment before producing additional copies.

10. By the time the authorities bring the situation under control, the number had been reduced by more than half, to thirty-six. To give a point of comparison: in 1662, shortly after the Restoration, when English authorities sought to crack down on the book trade, there were 53 master printers in London. For information on the rise and fall of Parisian printing houses, see Febvre and Martin (296); and Martin, "Une Croissance séculaire" (2:98).

11. As Martin points out, the post-Fronde crisis in the French print industry was compounded by the fact that, all over Europe, print professionals were facing a similar situation: "The Thirty Years' War had left the German market in ruins. Dutch editors, above all the Elzeviers, who had been the traditional intermediaries between France and German-speaking countries, found themselves left with only France. Bad books, forbidden or pirated, circulated more and more widely throughout Europe as the crisis worsened" ("Une Croissance séculaire," 2:96). This crisis in the European print industry can help explain why, even though French censors were very nearly successful in confiscating and destroying the first editions of early obscene works, copies—either printed or manuscript, it's impossible to know—inevitably were smuggled out and immediately reprinted, usually in several editions, all over Europe. The obscene was thus a boon to an industry in crisis. In the case of *L'Ecole des filles,* in particular, we have no choice but to assume that the 1668 edition, the basis for all modern editions, is faithful to the 1655 Parisian original, of which no copy survives.

12. I am not suggesting that this financing proves that they were not the work's authors. On the contrary, in the early modern period some French authors paid for their works to be printed. See, for example, George Hoffmann on the financing of Montaigne's *Essais.*

13. Michel Pastoureau calls Chauveau "the first true artist to devote himself almost entirely to book illustration" (610) and contrasts his work with that of his predecessors, almost always anonymous and without notable talent. The production team's choice of Chauveau reveals their confidence in the project's market potential, as does his decision to take on the job—Chauveau did frontispieces for all the era's best-selling novels.

14. Lachèvre states this for a fact (92). Whenever the trial proceedings offer no evidence to back up his assertions, I will add a note of caution when repeating them. I found no proof of Piot's betrayal.

15. The manuscript, in L'Ange's handwriting, had been well bound in parchment, so

it may not have been the manuscript handed over to the printer. The manuscript confiscated seems to have been intended as a collector's object in its own right.

16. The presiding officer says three times that "we didn't have enough manpower to arrest him and make him a prisoner." Perhaps because he was forced to admit that he was accompanied by at least four others, the officer modifies his story slightly at the end of his account and claims that it was the fact that "several people" had gathered around the house that made them decide "to defer the arrest until they could return with sufficient force" (Lachèvre, *Le Libertinage au XVIIe siècle: Mélanges*, 98). Just as with the initial attempt to arrest Théophile, a modern reader of these documents can only wonder whether the failure to make an arrest should be seen as the result of incompetence or of a desire to allow the alleged author to escape and thereby radically to simplify the ensuing court proceedings.

17. In 1661, when a copy was confiscated at the time of finance minister Nicolas Fouquet's arrest, the book is described as "so impudent and so infamous [the adjective that was the most common translation of the Latin *obscenus*] that we felt obliged to burn it" (cited by Lachèvre, "Les Libertins," 133).

18. The text of all these laws is included in the 1687 compilation of early print laws, *Edit du roi pour le règlement des imprimeurs et libraires de Paris* (89 ff.).

19. "Orthodox Bull: Our most reverend Father Priapus thunders anathemas against all those of either sex who read or listen to these lessons in the art of love, taught in the celebrated *School for Girls*, without ejaculating or being stimulated by either a mental or a bodily convulsion, etc." The fact that the Pope sometimes used bulls to proclaim the condemnation of books whose suppression the Church was seeking surely helps explain the title chosen for the parody. Goulemot cites early texts linking obscene representations to masturbation. Alan Thomas called my attention to the relation between the Bull and postmodern parodies such as that on the copyright page of Dave Eggers's *A Staggering Work of Heartbreaking Genius*.

20. L'Ange had to perform a ritual act of penance, but only in the nearly private setting of a room in the Châtelet, rather than in a public square; he was fined a modest sum, and he was banished from Paris for five years. He took advantage of this time in the country to do more underground printing for someone else who had learned about the usefulness of the press during the civil war. However, the material L'Ange printed for the Duchesse de Montpensier while she was exiled at Saint-Fargeau because of her leading role in the Fronde was destined for circulation only among her intimate friends and was never highly inflammatory, so he had no further run-ins with the law. On the various sentences handed down, see Lachèvre (*Le Libertinage au XVIIe siècle: Mélanges*, 117–20).

21. We know nothing about Millot's fate. Lachèvre claims that he hid out the whole time in Paris and only had it said publicly that he had left the country (*Le Libertinage au XVIIe siècle: Mélanges*, 94). Burning the copies of *L'Ecole des filles* was an unusually wasteful measure; it proves the determination to eliminate the work without leaving a trace. Usually books confiscated by the censors were torn up and, under the supervision of an officer of the courts, thriftily reprocessed into paper to be used for purposes other than printing. See Saint-Germain for a description of the process (169).

22. The archives of the Bastille prove that the case of *L'Ecole des filles* was still very much alive until the end of the century. Even Lachèvre, upon whose authority the attribution to Millot is principally based, admits that his case is founded on very slight evidence (*Le Libertinage au XVIIe siècle: Mélanges*, 93). Naturally, L'Ange was interrogated

repeatedly on the subject of the work's authorship. At first, he attributed it to a certain Comte d'Etelan (101), who was also named by the printer as the person he believed to be the author (105). Eventually, when confronted with the fact that the manuscript was in his handwriting, L'Ange does break down and name the individual with whom he had shared publication costs, Millot (115). Because Millot was still on the lam and therefore in no danger, however, it's hard to take this denunciation seriously. Millot's identity is so uncertain that early commentators constantly spell his name in different ways: one encounters Melot and Helot, among other possibilities.

23. Donald Thomas notes that the work's fame was so great, throughout Europe, that "the title itself was soon enough to make eager buyers part with their money" (12)—so much so that they even bought up a number of frauds, works that simply borrowed the title of the obscene's first modern classic. All studies of obscene, erotic, or pornographic literature begin with an obligatory acknowledgment of *L'Ecole des filles*. It is hardly surprising to find a study of the French tradition, such as Goulemot's, granting pride of place to the work. To see that David Foxon's classic monograph on England opens with an evocation of this French precursor is, however, greater proof of the work's centrality. Foxon notes in particular that "the earliest specific reference I know to a pornographic book is in Pepys's diary" (5); he refers to Pepys's reading of *L'Ecole des filles*. As is the case with all the first classics of erotic literature, there is a great deal of confusion about the early history of this work. No two studies give the same list of alleged seventeenth-century editions (alleged in the sense that, because no copies survive of most of them, we are dealing with hearsay rather than history), translations, and pirated editions. Lachèvre provides the most explicit version (*Le Libertinage au XVIIe siècle: Mélanges*, 124), down to details that cannot possibly be verified since all the copies vanished so long ago. Foxon gives the most reliable discussion of the work's early publication history (33–37). The first edition of which a copy has survived is marked "Fribourg [which may have been Amsterdam]: Roger Bon Temps, 1668"; this is the text on which all modern reeditions are based. ("Fribourg," suggesting the freedom to publish whatever one likes, was obviously used as the cover-up for the city in which the edition was actually printed.) The copy of this edition in the British Library is the sole trace of the work's seventeenth-century history. (The earliest copy in the BNF is from 1798.) Foxon explains that the alleged Dutch translation is a "fraud" (34). In *L'Ecole des filles*'s wake, a tradition of sexually transgressive literature developed in France. Among subsequent seventeenth-century French examples of obscene literature, the most influential were Nicolas Chorier's *L'Académie des dames*, first published in French in 1680 in Grenoble. It was originally published in Latin, some say as early as 1660 (see Pia; Foxon), though the British Library, which owns what may be the only surviving copy of the first edition, lists it as "circa 1665"—in any event, soon after *L'Ecole des filles*. A copy in Latin was sold in Grenoble in 1670 (Martin and Lecocq, 389–90). (The oldest copy in the BNF is in Latin, published in Amsterdam in 1678.) *Vénus dans le cloître, ou la religieuse en chemise*, sometimes attributed to abbé Jean Barrin, was the fledgling genre's next classic; its first edition may have been in 1672, though others say 1682 or 1683. Some still maintain that it appeared only in 1719. (The earliest edition in the BNF is from 1746.) On all these dates, see Goulemot's version (30–31) and Foxon's (38–39, 43), as well as that in the prefaces to all these works in vol. 7 of *Enfer de la Bibliothèque Nationale*, M. Camus, general editor. We owe the fact that we know for certain a good deal about *L'Ecole des filles*'s first edition to the censors and their prosecution of the work. This work continued, long after 1655, to be a particularly sensitive dossier for French censors. In the long list of "works printed without permission or manuscripts that were

seized by order of the king," between 1660 and 1675, the only work the censors were on the lookout for because of its erotic content was *L'Ecole des filles* (Ravaisson-Mollien, 10:304). After the book police seized a manuscript of the work, they note that it had "subsequently been printed in Amsterdam." Later in the century, they also pursued other obscene works, such as Chorier's, but they continued to seize copies of *L'Ecole des filles*. See Birn (617–23) and Sauvy for information on works seized between 1675 and 1709. In 1682 two copies of *L'Ecole des filles* were seized. And in September 1700 the book police made a big haul: inside "a large packet containing tapistry, shipped from Rouen in a postal waggon, addressed to someone named Mr. Delafougère," they came upon ninety-four unbound copies of the Fribourg: Roger Bon Temps edition. (This is the only time the book police specify which edition they seized.) This book raid in 1700 shows that, a half-century after its publication, *L'Ecole des filles* was still eagerly sought after by readers as well as the police.

24. Even in England and even long after that country had acquired its own tradition of literary obscenity, France maintained its reputation as the center of this market. Thus, when in 1857 Lord Campbell was fighting for passage of the Obscene Publications Act, he argued that "bales of publications [written for the single purpose of corrupting the morals of youth] were manufactured in Paris, and imported into this country" (Ernst and Schwartz, 119). According to the commonly held view, obscenity was produced in France and from there invaded other countries.

25. "The area of obscenity in Latin literature seems to have included poetry much more comfortably than it did prose. . . . With the exception of the *Satyricon* and Apuleius' *Metamorphoses*, little Latin prose dealt with sexual material as poetry did" (Richlin, 13).

26. *L'Ecole des filles* may have been Chauveau's next project after *Clélie*. He was also responsible for all the politically charged illustrations in Scudéry's previous novel, *Artamène*, seen by her contemporaries as a barely veiled commentary on the events of the Fronde. Chauveau was among the few book engravers to continue working during the civil war years, when presses were given over to ephemera so quickly produced that there was generally no question of illustrations.

27. On Chorier, see also nn. 23 and 31. Ingrid de Smet and Philip Ford explain that, in the sixteenth century, Latin was considered the language in which sexually transgressive literature could be made public without scandal (x–xi). For contemporary readers, Chorier's decision to write in Latin would have identified his work as a throwback to that earlier practice, as a work for elite readers.

28. Many historians of print culture discuss the end of Latin's reign over the book trade. I find Martin's section in Febvre and Martin, *L'Apparition du livre*, particularly convincing (356–414). On the influence of all these developments on a related one, that of the rise of a national consciousness or nationalism, see the inspired discussion in the first three chapters of Benedict Anderson's *Imagined Communities*.

29. On the proximity between some types of medical discourse published in French and the new obscene literature in the late seventeenth century, see Jean Mainil.

30. Many of the milestones in seventeenth-century print culture were, furthermore, Latin publications: when the Imprimerie royale was founded in 1640, for example, the first work off its presses was in Latin. Martin also discusses this gradual shift in the balance of powers from Latin to French in Febvre and Martin, *L'Apparition du livre* (in particular 480–95). Martin is the first to admit that it is extremely difficult to determine perfectly accurate statistics for publications in France in the sixteenth and seventeenth

centuries for a number of reasons. To begin with, "we only have limited indices, established on the basis of those books that have come down to us, and even this production has not been thoroughly inventoried" ("Classements et conjonctures," 1:443). In addition, Martin's figures are based on the British Library's short-title catalogue, which takes into account only those works in the British national collection. Finally, the statistics he uses calculate all publications on an equal basis, so the publication of a brief royal edict or a pamphlet is equivalent to that of a book. In considering the history of publication in France at this period, one should also remember that works with religious content play a truly overwhelming role: near the beginning of the seventeenth century, such works account for about 30 percent of all publications, whereas, toward the middle of the century, they make up nearly 50 percent of the total production (1:449). The vast percentage of religious publications accounts to a certain extent for Latin's continued importance in the book trade in France, although, as Martin also points out, during the same period the type of work included in the category "religious publications" undergoes a similarly dramatic evolution. Whereas, in the late sixteenth century, one finds mostly treatises and anti-Protestant tracts, by the mid-seventeenth century, there has been a dramatic rise in the publication of such types of works as catechisms and collections of sermons, almost all of which were published in the vernacular. As Martin concludes, these newly important categories of religious publications "indicate the clergy's desire to reach out to the masses" (1:485). To sum up: Martin's statistics should be taken with a grain of salt, as indications of a general trend, rather than as a precise instrument. They do present, nevertheless, an accurate picture of the overall evolution in the book trade in France during the period when modern obscenity was coming into existence.

31. In this context, one additional factor in the shift from Latin to French should be mentioned, the fact that, with the arrival of mass print culture, Latin began to be considered the language in which dangerous knowledge, and dangerous sexual knowledge in particular, could be hidden from the masses. The publication of *L'Ecole des filles* in French signaled a desire to bring that knowledge into the open. See Foxon on "the decent obscurity of the Latin language" (39 n. 2). He believes, for example, that the original publication of Chorier's dialogues in Latin explains why so many copies have survived; Latin obscenity was not prosecuted as fervently as its vernacular counterpart. See Saunders on the 1720 English decision that dangerous subject matter was "concealed from the vulgar in the Latin language, in which language it could not do so much hurt, the learned being better able to judge of it" (438).

32. The costlier earlier projects were intended to be sold off slowly. Febvre and Martin contend that the "monetary shortages" that crippled many business ventures during the second half of the seventeenth century also encouraged editors to turn to more modest projects that could be moved out of storage rapidly. In the late 1650s and the 1660s, laws passed in France reveal a preoccupation, at times bordering on the obsessive, with shortages of gold and silver bullion.

33. Martin, "Une Croissance séculaire" (2:96). The category "small formats" comprises all volumes smaller than in-octavos; principally, in-duodecimo and in-16. Large formats are traditionally associated with erudite readerships; the new, small formats were the preserve of a more worldly public, concerned with less traditional fields of inquiry.

34. The domination of the French language was also facilitated by outside factors that weakened its would-be rivals for Latin's role. From 1620 on, the Thirty Years' War threw the Germanic world into eclipse. And, at the same time, the Counter-Reformation was

also losing steam. (On these factors, see Martin, "Classements et conjonctures," 1:445.) The stage seemed set for a parallel rise to European dominance: that of the French book trade. This takeover, however failed to take place, and the French print industry never became influential outside of France. Part of the problem seems to have been that Colbert's centralization of censorship in the mid-1660s was simply too effective. Many of the measures that he devised to gain control over print practices were so successful that they guaranteed that some of the most profitable publishing ventures in French—the obscene among them—would be carried out outside of France. The fact that France developed the earliest modern censorial machine made money for foreign printers and helped prevent the rise to power of French printing on the coattails of the French language.

35. This explains why, in the creation of a modern vocabulary of obscenity, French usage generated English usage. Among the terms favored by early French censors to justify the suppression of obscene works was *libelle*. See, for example, Lachèvre, *Le Libertinage au XVIIe siècle: Mélanges*, 116, on the use of *libelle* to characterize *L'Ecole des filles*. On the history of *libelle*'s use in French censorship, see Darnton, *Forbidden Best-Sellers*, 198–200. The term seems to have been seen as more or less the equivalent of the soon to be created "bad books." In the late fifteenth century, the term had come to mean "a short work that is satirical or defamatory." (See *Le Robert de la langue française*.) At the beginning of print censorship, in English as well as in French, all dangerous books were termed *libelles*, which was, in the case of obscene works, to confuse the modern obscene with its classical precursor's use of often highly defamatory personal invective. It is never clear that French censors ever grasped the irony of this usage. The classics of obscene literature were all quite literally *libelles*, according to the word's Latin origin: *libellus*, a small book. Their counterparts in England did understand that the newly dangerous small formats had to be distinguished from publications dangerous because they were defamatory. The Law of Obscene Libel, long the basis for print censorship in England, was put into place in 1727. (The impetus for its establishment was a translation of Jean Barrin.) At that time, the Attorney General explained that, when dealing with the censorship of sexually transgressive material, previous judges had misunderstood the term *libel*: henceforth, an "obscene libel" was to be understood as "an obscene little book" (Howell, 157–58).

36. Beginning with *L'Ecole des filles*, all the classics of obscene literature were published in-duodecimo or smaller formats. In contrast, until the end of the seventeenth century, Aretino's dialogues were often published in octavo editions, rather than in the less expensive smaller formats. According to the BNF catalogue, there were a few smaller editions late in the sixteenth century. It is, however, notoriously difficult to obtain information about the first editions of Aretino because so few copies have survived.

37. The earliest English translations were priced from 1 shilling to 3 shillings (Thomas, 20); especially at the bottom end of this scale, this was inexpensive indeed. My informants tell me that a book costing a shilling was bordering on cheap, that anything under 5 shillings was inexpensive, and that really expensive books cost over 1 pound, 20 shillings. We know nothing about the cost of the French seventeenth-century editions of obscene novels, other than the fact of their inexpensive small format.

38. I am not arguing that literature's potential public in midcentury was either huge or especially varied by today's standards. It was, however, undergoing a period of significant expansion. See Geneviève Bollème for statistics on the *Bibliothèque bleue*'s growth. Upper-class readers in far greater numbers were increasingly also accepting the notion, promoted during the second half of the century by the then expanding network of academies

and salons, that every individual should be culturally informed. For some approximation of the number of readers and theatergoers involved, see Viala, *La Naissance de l'écrivain*, especially chapter 4.

39. I base this summary of Foucault's ideas on *Les Anormaux*, but the volumes of his *History of Sexuality* give essentially the same account, though in less succinct fashion. An examination of any of the classic manuals for confessors to which Foucault refers confirms his view of them. Roughly between 1650 and 1750, these manuals were frequently reedited and often expanded as well; virtually any edition contains the type of model for interrogation I describe here. Take, for example, one of the genre's classics, Louis Habert's 1689 *Pratique du sacrement de la pénitence*. Habert devotes a disproportionate amount of his treatise to lust. In the seven deadly sins category, lust gets nineteen pages; others get only eight to nine pages. Lust reappears in several other sections. In his instructions to confessors, Habert explains at length that, in this case, the goal is to learn what the penitent may have done, without—shades of Arnolphe's dilemma in *L'Ecole des femmes*—teaching him or her any new words: The confessor "will use in his interrogations only chaste words . . . because of the danger that, wanting to uncover evil, he might teach it to those who are ignorant of it" (303). Foucault contends that the widening influence of the confession even spread to the criminal justice system, that, at the same time as confessors were being taught to lead penitents through a detailed examination of body parts, magistrates were shifting from outright accusation to repeated interrogation (*History of Sexuality*, 58 ff.). The two earliest modern writers' trials confirm Foucault's model; the prosecution proceeded above all through detailed interrogation.

40. "All the complexity of that particularly Christian problem of confession . . . thereby became limited to one very basic problem, that of a gesture, of the hand, of the relation between the hand and the body, and of this simple question: Are they touching each other?" (*Les Anormaux*, 250).

41. When Foucault discusses the contemporary discursive explosion about sexuality, he clearly did not have women's voices in mind. I am not suggesting that the work's still elusive author might be a woman. Indeed, there is no early tradition of obscene literature by women. The first approximation I know is Madame de Tenain's 1695 *La Religieuse intéressée et amoureuse, avec l'histoire du comte de Clare, nouvelle galante*, a small in-duodecimo that is clearly an inexpensive printing project. It contains an adulterous episode very differently portrayed from those in contemporary novels by women in that there's sex and lots of it. It is, however, chastely described, with no use of primary obscenities. The count speaks, for example, of his mistress's "lovable parts" (70). The novel is noteworthy above all because it marks the first time that erotic prose by women was conceivable. There is no erotic writing by women in Latin (Richlin, 33); in Renaissance France and Italy, women followed the Sapphic model and composed only erotic verse. On the many sexually transgressive texts in which erotic knowledge is imparted in a dialogue between two women, see Peter Cryle (18–21).

42. Female genitalia were clearly the ur-taboo in Roman sexually transgressive literature. Richlin contends, for example, that male genitalia could be obscene but were never considered filthy. Female genitalia were both obscene and filthy; contact with them was shaming (66). In Latin erotic poetry, many parts of the woman's body are described, but "it is as if there were a blank space in the middle of the woman" (47). On the rare occasions when Martial mentions female genitalia, "the context is that of insult" (54). This is the dominant pattern (211). Some vases from antiquity show representations of female genitalia. At the same time, the other object of polymorphous male desire, the boy, is de-

scribed without prohibition. Richlin concludes: "Clearly Latin poets feel an inhibition in describing the sexual areas of women's bodies that they do not feel toward boys" (55). One final remark, on Greek erotic poetry: among the epigrams in the *Palatine Anthology*, "the vivid, explicit epigrams on women include few primary obscenities" (47). This, then, is the model largely followed by all traditions that remained heavily Latinate.

43. This is not to say that, after the invention of modern obscenity, portrayals of female genitalia in the classical mold disappear. See, for example, Birn's description of a manuscript seized by the police in 1702 (602–3). Certainly some pornography—one need think no further than Sade's novels—follows faithfully in this vein.

44. Linda Nochlin recounts the incredible detective work necessary to locate the canvas Courbet painted for the art collector and Turkish ambassador to Saint Petersburg, Khalil Bey. On *L'Origine du monde* and Courbet's use of "extreme foreshortening" to focus in on female genitalia, see Nochlin's entry on the painting in Faunce and Nochlin (176). The definitive taboo related to female genitalia is one that print representations need not confront, one that Courbet's canvas flaunts: pubic hair. On the exclusive focus on female sexual organs in films such as *Emmanuelle*, see Joel Feinberg (134).

45. As far as Pepys was concerned, the new vision of sexual practice was the ultimate turn-on: the print collective had accurately predicted the fantasies of at least one readership it was aiming to attract. Randolf Trumbach discusses the development of pornography in the eighteenth century and speculates on the significance of the veil thrown over male sexuality. Henry Abelove situates the beginning of what he calls the "discourse of modern heterosexuality" in the mid-seventeenth century.

46. I concentrate on the most significant anatomical innovation in *L'Ecole des filles*, the focus on female genitalia. The novel also marks a radical departure from classical precedent in its depiction of male genitalia. In Roman sexually transgressive literature, the male object of male desire is the feminized figure known as the beloved boy (*puer*). The stereotype of male beauty has, therefore, much in common with that of female beauty (Richlin, 33). In *L'Ecole des filles* the male object of desire is no longer a boy but a strapping young man whose physical attributes seem designed to appeal to a female reader. The novel contains no explicit depiction of female same-sex relations. However, the very fact that it presents the basics of female pleasure—where to touch a woman and when—in an exchange between two women could be seen as hinting at this possibility. Modern obscenity first dealt explicitly with lesbianism in the second and third dialogues of Nicolas Chorier's *Satyra sotadica*, possibly published in 1660 and apparently without prosecution, undoubtedly because it appeared in Latin (Foxon, 39). Because those who adapted that novel for an English audience in 1688 feared that the readership that had loved *L'Ecole des filles*'s focus on female sexuality was not ready for an overt portrayal of lesbianism, they removed the two dialogues (Foxon, 41). The translation was prosecuted nevertheless. This same juxtaposition between an obsessively blatant concentration on female genitalia and a sensationalistic depiction of lesbianism was reenacted by Courbet in 1866, when he painted *Le Sommeil* at the same time as *L'Origine du monde* and for the same collector. (On *Le Sommeil*, see Faunce and Nochlin, 175–77.)

47. When the sexually transgressive texts that had previously circulated in print were subjected to censorship, it was always primarily, and often exclusively, because of this satirical or polemical content. For a reading of Aretino's *Ragionamenti* as "far too bitterly polemical to be accused of licentious intent," see Kendrick (61–62). On the use of political satire in sixteenth-century Italian erotic literature in general, see Findlen (26–27).

48. The first English translations respect the novel's egalitarian setting. By 1744, the

two female protagonists have become a married lady and her maid. On Aretino in English translation, see Ian Moulton.

49. Almost all the religious content in the novel is of this kind, details related to daily life in a Catholic country. The Orthodox Bull is among the few moments when the work touches on the kind of religious transgression that often characterizes early modern erotic literature. Nor is the characters' experience of their sexuality mediated by the kind of sophisticated, voyeuristic relation to images, objects, and statues that can be noted in Italian Renaissance works, in which characters are constantly confronted with representations of sexuality. Findlen describes, for example, Nanna in Aretino's *Ragionamenti* as being "moved by images," as "initiated into the pleasures of sex by observing the different images of couples decorating the walls of the monastery and by watching others through various peepholes" (74). She describes various contemporary works in which images and voyeurism abound.

50. We can measure *L'Ecole des filles*'s difference from its Italian precursors in this area, too. Talvacchia points out the innovation of Romano's decision to portray in *I Modi* the sexual exploits of ordinary men and women, rather than those of the pagan gods (4). She stresses, however, that his engravings "owed their conceptual basis as well as their style to antique paradigms" (49). In *L'Ecole des filles* the protagonists are thoroughly ordinary, removed from any classical precedent.

51. I am thinking here of the work's closest precursor, Aretino's *Ragionamenti*. (It was first published in parts, each entitled *Ragionamento della Nanna e della Antonia*.) A century before *L'Ecole des filles*, Aretino had already broken the classical taboo surrounding female genitalia. His erotic scene remains, however, completely unrealistic. By this I mean that his heroines, by virtue of their known, accepted sexual availability, are removed from daily life. This is yet another sign that he was keeping sexually transgressive literature within the boundaries traced for it in antiquity and creating erotica for an elite audience. Aretino's dialogues—generally full of nuns, priests, and monks—also still repeat another configuration destined to disappear from the modern obscene. Their erotic content is shocking in part because, like blasphemy, it is subversive in religious terms. His dialogues, for example, frequently parody ecclesiastical language.

52. See Kendrick on the class politics of the Aretino model (65–66). See Richlin on prostitutes in Roman erotic literature (65).

53. I am quoting from Steinem's "Erotica and Pornography" (36–39). See also Helen Longino's article. On the conformity of Roman sexually transgressive literature with this feminist conception of pornography, see Richlin (65–78). To my knowledge, the first time that this argument (a work should be banned if it can be said to encourage violence against women) was formulated was by Christine de Pizan in her critique of *Le Roman de la Rose;* this was also the first time that a woman had considered the potential impact of such material.

54. John Riddle provides the most detailed history of the literature on contraception. His account of what he terms "the broken trail of learning" (154) is particularly striking. He demonstrates that Renaissance authors knew much less than their classical precursors: "by the fifteenth and sixteenth centuries, few physicians knew about birth control agents, simply because it was not part of their training" (157). So, even though medical writing was "increasingly in the vernacular" (155), the information contained in ancient literature was not passed on in early print culture. (Riddle discusses translations in which the sections on birth control were simply omitted.) Philippe Ariès also describes early print material as "silent" on the subject (466). I found no evidence that any printed text

prior to *L'Ecole des filles* contains a discussion on contraception. On the earliest evidence of the practice of contraception in Europe, see John Boswell, Philippe Ariès, and Etienne Van de Walle.

55. For Foucault's discussion of how these phenomena are interrelated, see part 2 of his *History of Sexuality,* "The Repressive Hypothesis." See also *Les Anormaux* (65).

56. Sections 60 and 61 of the novel (Camus, 262–63) are devoted to contraception. For a convincing analysis of why female characters were traditionally chosen to impart wisdom in these areas, see David Halperin's "Why Is Diotima a Woman?" On the total absence of sexual desire in women in Latin literature, see Richlin (69).

57. Cynical observers of the French scene might remark that it is appropriate that birth control was portrayed as a woman's responsibility at this origin of French commentary on the question. A recent article in *Libération* contrasted the vasectomy's spectacular lack of success in France with the relative acceptance of the procedure in other European countries. Fewer than 1 percent of Frenchmen have undergone a vasectomy, compared with, for example, 16 percent of British men (see John Tagliabue, *International Herald Tribune,* July 11, 2000). According to Lawrence Stone, dildos were first marketed in London only in the 1660s (333–34). This was the decade during which *L'Ecole des filles* was on sale in London. The market for the obscene little book and that for the sex toys it "advertises" thus became evident at the same time.

58. For a reading of the Fronde that stresses the political and military roles played by women, see my *Tender Geographies.* The marquise de Sévigné's letters to her daughter during the years when she was frantic that her child might die in childbirth prove that information on contraception was hard to come by and that what little that did circulate was exchanged with extreme caution, even in manuscript form. Authorities concerned about sexual contamination would surely have been at least as concerned about the public availability of sexually revolutionary information. The novel's best known contemporary reader, Pepys, implicitly links it to contagious disease. In his entry for February 9, 1668, he evokes in succession "doing business," reading *L'Ecole des filles,* and the most devastating "season" for smallpox in recent memory (58).

59. This was undoubtedly one of the copies originally sold to Scarron; his wife was reported to be very close to Fouquet.

60. Bussy's letters to Sévigné are included in Roger Duchêne's edition of her correspondence (3:335). In 1665 he had been exiled after the publication of his *Histoire amoureuse des Gaules,* a work both obscene and libelous, an easily decoded à clef fiction that purported to reveal the sexual foibles of important court ladies, including Sévigné.

61. Rudolph Bell discusses sixteenth-century Italian manuals that directed their advice on children (how to guarantee a male baby, how to raise him, and so forth) to female readers. He speculates that many of their readers were women, though he found no proof of this. These manuals provided no information on birth control. Kendrick discusses the fear of women's access to pornography and the role this played in establishing laws against it in the nineteenth century (26–27).

62. During the trial, Chauveau claimed that he had not known how his engraving would be used; he was released after questioning. His frontispiece is presumed lost along with the original edition. It is generally accepted, however, that the frontispiece to the 1668 edition was inspired by Chauveau's. This is the engraving I reproduce here. This anonymous engraving is far cruder than Chauveau's habitual style; just as is the case with Raimondi's postures, we know this key image only in an inferior version. Ruth Larson also gives a reading of the frontispiece in "Iconography of Feminine Sexual Education."

63. The term *ruelle* was first used to refer to the marquise de Rambouillet's salon because of her practice of receiving her guests while lying in bed and seating them near her. Probably for reasons of legibility, the book portrayed in the frontispiece is a folio rather than a small format. In this context, I repeat the comparison evoked in my introduction. Whereas Aretino's sonnets were designed to accompany sexually transgressive images, and whereas, beginning in the mid-eighteenth century, French obscene literature is accompanied by equally obscene illustrations, the work that inaugurates the modern obscene is illustrated only with this completely nonerotic image. During the entire first century of its existence in France, obscene literature was totally cut off from obscene engravings. A reader unfamiliar with the content of *L'Ecole des filles*, for example, could easily take its frontispiece for the illustration for a volume of seventeenth-century women's writing. All the obscene frontispieces reproduced along with the first obscene novels in recent editions date from much later and were generally produced for foreign editions. For example, we know from the 1744 advertisement for an English translation of *L'Ecole des filles* that it was accompanied by no fewer than twenty-four copper-plate prints "after the manner of Aratine [*sic*]."

64. I have found no instances in which French censors use *obscene* to speak of publications prior to the eighteenth century. The sketchy extant information on the 1688 prosecution is included by Thomas in the introduction to his translation of the novel (15–16). He cites the one passage to which the prosecution is known to have objected; it is hard to tell why this fragment would have been singled out. The 1680 case was prosecuted in the Middlesex County Court, a traveling law court, that is, an assize court presided over by a visiting judge; the 1688 case by Guildhall, the mayor of London's court. Many new print shops sprang up in England during the Interregnum. In 1660 Charles II decided to limit the number of master printers to twenty. *L'Ecole des filles*'s circulation in England began, therefore, in an atmosphere similar to the post-Fronde years of its creation: printers previously busy with politically seditious texts were suddenly out of work.

65. In the French original, women have the hypothetical chance of governing the Church but not the world (202). This is the only example when the English translation strays from the French.

Chapter 3

1. I borrow the phrase "'written' writing" from Francis Barker (50). For Barker, the key divide takes place between Shakespeare, who represents performed writing, and Milton, the figure in the English tradition who first incarnates "'written' writing." When I speak of early modern works as collaborative, I am thinking not only of works produced as a result of a collaboration between writers, but also of those produced by both the author and the print collective that brought his works to the page. With Molière, we can re-create the process as a result of which he took charge of the publication of his plays.

2. Viala contends that the French civil war, the Fronde, was the catalyst that made a new conception of the writer possible: "a decisive modification takes place around 1650." He lists the following factors as essential to the new authorial status, what I am calling modern authorship: the decline in private patronage and the concomitant rise in systematic state sponsorship of writers, the fact that authors became far more likely than before to insist on receiving money (*droits d'auteur*) from publishers for their manuscripts, and the fact that the literary marketplace becomes centered on Paris (*La Naissance de l'écrivain*, 291). We cannot be certain that we know all there is to know about the sales of

manuscripts by writers during the first half of the seventeenth century; the extant contracts between writers and publishers have been more carefully studied for the later decades. However, my case for Molière's authorial status is not based exclusively on the increased importance he placed on the sale of his manuscripts but based rather on the convergence of all the factors I am describing here.

3. Roman authors of obscene literature could be seen as preparing the way for modern authorship, as the most modern of ancient authors. Joseph Farrell's work on the ways in which classical authors portrayed themselves shows that authors associated exclusively with high genres, such as Vergil, described themselves as detached from the materiality of their art: their poems were spoken or sung and the product of divine inspiration rather than human work. On the other hand, writers associated with literary obscenity, such as Catullus and Martial, depicted themselves as writers and evoked the materiality of their craft through references to everything from the ways in which they wrote, to the instruments with which they wrote, to the surfaces on which their work was inscribed. They suggest that obscene literature was somehow more embodied than high genres, that there existed a special link between obscene writing and the author's body.

4. Among seventeenth-century dictionaries, only the most conservative, that of the Académie Française, defines an author as the individual who "composes" a work. Both Richelet and Furetière make it plain that *author* was coming to mean primarily print authors, "an individual who has written a printed book" (Richelet). In Golden Age Spanish, the playwright was known as *poeta* or *ingenio* (Chartier, *Publishing Drama*, 61).

5. In many ways Molière entered the French literary scene at the first moment at which it was possible to become a modern writer. John Lough contrasts, for example, the "humble" position of the patronage playwright with the new possibilities open to stage authors in the second half of the seventeenth century. Because of the proliferation of Parisian theaters during Louis XIV's reign, a playwright could make more and more money from his pen (90–91). Among the first generation of economically successful playwrights, Molière made the most money of all: "in the space of only fifteen years, [Molière] earned some 50,000 *livres* with his pen" (Lough, 96). Jean-Louis Loiselet puts the figure even higher (111). Even though Molière did not live exclusively from his pen, he could have done so. Loiselet's remarkable *De quoi vivait Molière?* assembles all the varied and abundant information on Molière's income during the last fourteen years of his life; others discuss aspects of this issue, but he gives by far the fullest accounting. I have double-checked some of the figures given by different commentators and, predictably, have noted discrepancies. Nothing challenges, however, the big picture—most notably, the fact that Molière used the plays produced while he was running first the Petit-Bourbon and then the Palais-Royal theaters to earn a huge amount of money: a total of 167,645 *livres*, or about 12,000 *livres* a year. This was more than any contemporary author and translated into a very comfortable life indeed (Loiselet, 114). By comparison, Racine earned only 5,000 *livres* a year at the end of his theatrical career, and of this only about 1,200 came from the theater; his income rose to 20,000 *livres* per year at the end of his life (x–xi), when he had given up the theater. In midcentury, a master printer might earn 500 *livres* a year, the secretary of a nobleman 2,000. An author could get by on 1,000 *livres*. The figures also make plain that Molière made less from selling his plays than from marketing them for the stage. Within his company, both he and his wife were paid as actors; he was also paid as playwright. Despite this discrepancy, it is clear that, precisely during the period that interests me here, Molière learned that print was indispensable to his

income in ways we could miss if we considered only the percentage of the total represented by the sale of his manuscripts. For a description of the financial arrangements in Molière's company and of the role of La Grange, who kept the register to which I will often refer, see Loiselet (86). In contrast, Shakespeare's income came principally from his investment in the theatrical company, rather than from his writing. Dryden is generally considered the first English writer to have lived off his earnings; Aphra Behn is widely known as the first Englishwoman to have gained her living from her pen, even though, as Catherine Gallagher stresses, she was far from free of the patronage system (4, 8). So much is known about the finances of his career that it is safe to say that this is among the few areas in which Molière's life is better documented than those of his English contemporaries.

6. All through his career, Molière staged his plays for the king and at court. He was working, however, not at the end of the patronage system but at the beginning of a tradition that still exists in France today, state sponsorship of the arts.

7. Natalie Z. Davis has shown how deeply the gift economy permeated the book trade in sixteenth-century France. (See her chapter "Gifts and Sales.") Molière's generation finally sounded the death knell of that practice and began the transformation of the activity of writing into a sales mode. On the transition from patronage to commerce, see Febvre and Martin (245–47) and Viala (*La Naissance de l'écrivain*, 81). See also Anderson on Luther as the first writer able to have his new books printed solely on the basis of his name and how this fact prepared the way for the situation in seventeenth-century France, where writers were able to sell works directly to publishers, "who bought them as excellent investments in view of their author's market reputations" (39). On precise sums obtained, see below, n. 63. Viala stresses that the sums were growing during the second half of the century (*La Naissance de l'écrivain*, 345). Anderson implies that this was the first time that authors had thus negotiated their production, and I have found no evidence that suggests otherwise. By the late sixteenth century, a few Italian writers did sell manuscripts to publishers—Ann Jones pointed out to me the example of Vecellio and his second book of costumes—but there was no widespread custom among major authors.

8. Orest Ranum compares patronage and state sponsorship (162–63). On the history of this idea in France, see Viala (*La Naissance de l'écrivain*, 81). Viala notes that state sponsorship began just as censorship was reinforced (10). State sponsorship of the arts had been discussed under Louis XIII. Under Louis XIV it became a systematic institution.

9. Molière's title for the play today referred to as *Dom Juan* was *Le Festin de pierre; Dom Juan* is a title invented by those who censored his text when it was finally allowed to be published in 1682. Proof of the acceptance by the book trade of the new literary economy is found in a document from the last quarter of the seventeenth century written to settle a dispute between printers: "Formerly, authors paid publishers part of the cost of printing their works, . . . and even if all were not able to pay, at least no one asked for money. Today, the opposite is true, . . . and we have become so used to it that the art of composition has become in effect a means to earn a living" (BNF Ms.fr.22071, number 177). Proof that Molière's contemporaries saw the three plays for which he was censored as part of the same project is provided by one of the playwright's severest detractors. Using the pseudonym "Rochemont," this latter-day Garasse authored a pamphlet demanding the suppression of *Le Festin de pierre*, in which he described *L'Ecole des femmes* as the first step toward the subsequent plays (Molière, *Le Festin de pierre (Dom Juan)*, 261–62).

10. The contemporary situation in England would have given Louis XIV—who surely followed it closely, since Charles II had spent the Interregnum in France until

1656—much cause for alarm. Charles II had reentered London in May 1660, but already by January 1661 there were uprisings in London.

11. As the record of the imprisonments of writers in the Bastille during these years recorded in Funck-Brentano proves, pro-Fouquet publications were the censors' dominant concern.

12. One of the side effects of the spread of the French language was that typographers competent to handle French-language publications began to be found outside of France. It appears that Colbert would have banned the sale of all Dutch publications if Jean Chapelain had not convinced him that scholars relied heavily on some of these publications and that, if they were banned in France, this would stunt the growth of scholarship (Febvre and Martin, 375).

13. Colbert also ruled that no new master printers would be named and no new presses established, interdictions that were rigorously maintained until 1686. The practice of severely limiting the number of print houses continued until the Revolution (Febvre and Martin, 296–97). A related law first enacted at the same time and for the same purpose forbade the sale of typographic material and fonts to any but licensed master printers and established a register in which all such sales would be noted (Ordinance of May 17, 1663). One of the first tasks assigned La Reynie was that of monitoring the dispersal of all such material when print shops were broken up (Martin, *Livre*, 2:695). In London in the first years of the Restoration, when printers were widely blamed for incitement to rebellion, the crown reduced their number to twenty, at the same moment when their numbers were also limited in France. The number of French printers declined to 23 in 1675, the lowest number in the century. (See Roche, "La Police du livre"; and Martin, "Une Croissance séculaire," 2:96).

14. Molière's involvement with the Dutch book trade starts at just this time, with the publication of the first Elzevier edition of one of his plays, *L'Ecole des femmes*, in 1663. This edition is one proof that this play marked the beginning of Molière's status as an international author. Molière's initial personal brush with the Dutch trade in pirated editions surely taught him a lesson about the fragility of the institution of authorship parallel to that learned by authors of obscene works—his property, like theirs, had passed into the public domain.

15. On Le Petit's arrest and trial, Lachèvre is once again the principal authority. Whenever he lists his sources, I checked seventeenth-century accounts. Lachèvre speculates that the Rebuffé brothers used their father's press in secret (*Disciples*, xlvi). During his interrogations, Le Petit said that he had been given the money to pay for the printing by someone named Chabat, who was to help sell the print-run (l). I have been unable to find any clue concerning the identity of this Chabat.

16. It also helped that Le Petit was of far more modest extraction than most contemporary writers, the son and brother of tailors. (This information is found in the biographical note that prefaces the reedition of his *Paris ridicule* in a 1694 collection, *Le Tableau de la vie et du gouvernement de Messieurs les Cardinaux Richelieu et Mazarin* [236].) No powerful protectors intervened on his behalf.

17. The letters written by d'Aubray were published in 1872 by Philippe Tamizey de Larroque. Only four years later, d'Aubray, too, came to a violent end when he was poisoned by his own daughter, the infamous Marquise de Brinvilliers. She was at the center of the celebrated Affaire des Poisons that spread the fine art of poisoning throughout Parisian high society. According to her trial testimony, she had tried some 25–30 times before succeeding (Ravaisson-Mollien, 4:243). It seems likely, therefore, that at the time

when d'Aubray was strenuously lobbying Séguier for Le Petit's execution, he was already receiving increasingly hefty doses of the potions favored by his century's most celebrated murderess.

18. Le Petit saw himself as a second Théophile, and his contemporaries agreed (Lachèvre, *Disciples*, li). Since the book police succeeded in destroying every trace of *Le Bordel*, it is not clear, however, whether this book was bad in a fashion similar to Théophile's. The work Lachèvre publishes reproduces a German edition allegedly based on a manuscript smuggled out of prison, but it is hard to believe that this is the volume described by Le Petit's contemporaries, François Colletet (Lachèvre, *Disciples*, lii) and Jean Rou (2:314). Le Petit tried to save his co-conspirators: D'Aubray reports that "in order to shield the printer, he says that what has been printed was done in Holland, something which is disproved by the fonts and the paper" (148). In D'Aubray's second letter, written two days later, we learn that Le Petit was soon obliged—the torture applied during seventeenth-century police interrogations was so extreme that it always produced the desired effect—to give them the printers' names (149).

19. See, for example, Chartier on Molière's hesitant passage to print (*Publishing Drama*, 18; *Au bord de la falaise*, 281–83). He discusses reasons why this would have been true, in particular Molière's belief that much was lost in the printed versions of his plays—from elements of staging to tone of voice—and considers ways in which the punctuation of the original editions can be seen as replacing orality. I share Chartier's belief that Molière was partly responsible for the punctuation in the original editions of his plays (282–83). René Bray launched a debate that continues today on whether stage or page was dominant for Molière (34–36).

20. Prior to Molière, seventeenth-century playwrights were often scorned as "mercenary" if they practiced sound financial policy and sold their plays for publication only after their profitable stage runs. David Clarke cites critics—notably Guez de Balzac and Jean Chapelain—who chastised Corneille for his "vulgar interest in the profits his pen could earn him" (10). See, for example, Jean Chapelain's description of plays managed this way: "such is the destiny of venal plays," which become "merchandise to sell" (1:583, 1:695).

21. Molière's run-in with Ribou occurred at the tail end of what Febvre and Martin describe as the heyday of pirated editions in France, the period from 1640–1660 (369–70). They contend that the crisis in the French book trade was so extreme at this time and publishers needed work so badly that publishers were willing to overlook the usual wisdom that it was in their best interest to respect the system of privileges. On Ribou as a "newcomer" to the Parisian book trade and his use of Molière as part of an attempt to establish himself, see Martin ("Prééminence," 264). Because of Molière's decision to fight back, the publication history of *Les Précieuses ridicules* is phenomenally complicated. In the Printers' Community register, the original privilege is in Ribou's name: dated January 12, it was registered on January 18. In the margin, a note adds: "This privilege is null and void." On January 18 another publisher, Guillaume de Luyne, requested a second privilege, presumably with Molière's consent because this time he is at least mentioned as the author of the play (though Molière's name does not appear in the privilege as it is printed in the copies of the first edition published by Luyne). This one was registered the day after Ribou's. Molière continued to fight back: he obtained a court order against Ribou to have all copies of his edition—which had already been printed—seized and destroyed. Curiously, until the play was included in the first collected edition of Molière's works, its title page was never modified to include its author's name, as though it continued to bear

the mark of its initial illegitimacy. Luyne immediately shared his privilege with Charles de Sercy and Claude Barbin, who all printed what appear to be first editions of the play. Luyne, Sercy, and Barbin apparently joined forces and printed their edition/editions in only ten days (January 19–29, 1660; see Martin, "Prééminence," 2:263, on Molière's early brushes with unscrupulous editors). Molière's name appears in the privilege of some of these editions. It is unclear what this means. Most of the privileges I refer to in this chapter are reprinted in Thuasne. Some are also cited in Guibert and in Molière, *Œuvres*. Eugène Despois and Paul Mesnard, the editors of this last collection, give the most reliable accounts of the early publication history of Molière's plays (in this case, 2:42–43). See Veyrin-Forrer, "A la recherche des *Précieuses*," for the best account of the play's complicated publication history. In this privilege, Molière discusses the elements, such as tone of voice, that are lost in the page version.

22. The name is a pseudonym; the person behind it has never been identified. It is written in several different ways, for example, "Villenaine." Apparently, Ribou got around Molière this time by asking for a privilege for a play called *Sganarelle;* Molière took out a privilege for the same play, but he called it *Le Cocu imaginaire* (Martin, "Prééminence," 2:263; Chartier, *Publishing Drama,* 31–32). Molière once again obtained a court order against Ribou; officers were sent to seize copies of the pirated edition. They didn't find many, but they did learn that 1,250 had been printed (Molière, *Œuvres*, 2:150–52).

23. Neuf-Villaine's dedication to Molière and the privilege to *L'Ecole des maris* describe how memorial reconstruction functioned. Memorial reconstruction was apparently common practice in Elizabethan England; it is also familiar to students of Golden Age Spanish drama. Molière's experience proves that it existed in seventeenth-century France, although, because scholars of classical France have not yet begun to look for traces of the phenomenon, it is too soon to estimate how frequently it might have occurred. Not all the pirated editions that cost Molière revenue were based on memorial reconstruction; the problem merits, nevertheless, further investigation. Editions based on memorial reconstruction give us access to something that has otherwise disappeared: the staged version of a play, as opposed to the published version. For an author as fully a man of the theater as Molière was, it is obvious that each play would have been a living thing, changing from performance to performance, rather than the stable text that we now find in modern editions. Editions based on memorial reconstruction contain some elements that Molière did not carry over into the published versions of his plays. See Chartier on memorial reconstruction and on what such a pirated edition adds to our knowledge of *George Dandin (Publishing Drama,* 28–46). The disadvantage of such editions is that, because they were based on oral comprehension alone and generally quickly established, they contain many false readings (generally, they substitute a word or phrase that sounds like what was actually said). Such errors are, however, easily spotted. See the preface to my edition of *Le Festin de pierre (Dom Juan);* in this case, an edition based on a memorial reconstruction is the only source of information on the passages censored when the play was staged.

24. Even in cases of censorship, authors were not necessarily held responsible for their work. Until the seventeenth century, printers were far more likely to be blamed for unorthodox material produced on their presses (see Pottinger, 56).

25. Molière was not the first playwright to obtain privileges in his name; Viala lists early French authors who did so (*La Naissance de l'écrivain,* 95–97). For more on the first privileges granted writers, see Viala's dissertation (*La Naissance des institutions,* 274–78).

He describes 1643–1678 as a "period of conflict" (282), in particular, because authors were "demanding their rights." He rehearses some conflicts between authors and publishers (288–94). Prior to Molière, Corneille alone truly took advantage of the rights that the privilege conferred. For *Cinna*, he even kept the privilege in his name, paid for the printing of the first edition, and only then sold the rights to a Parisian editor. This is but one way in which Corneille was a modern author *avant la lettre;* however, many factors crucial to modern authorial identity were not yet in place in the 1640s, notably, civil censorship and the institutionalized regulation of the book trade. *L'Ecole des maris* is the first play to have Molière's author's name on its title page; the first edition was printed in August 1661. By the time Molière got around, in 1663, to using the privilege he had applied for in 1660 for *L'Etourdi,* his name was printed "J. B. P. MOLIERE," as though the capitals could establish his authorship with greater force. In other words, during the period when *L'Ecole des femmes* occupied center stage in his career, the prominent display of his author's name as a sort of copyright was still a recent practice. During the first years when, in the wake of these pirated editions, Molière's name began to appear in registers, privileges, and on title pages, the spelling varies wildly—we find everything from "Moliers" to "Molieres" to "Molier." Many of these variants are probably due to carelessness, but the widespread instability might also indicate that the actor/writer's stage name was not yet totally familiar to the world of print culture. At first, his author's name is Jean-Baptiste Poquelin Molière. The practice of adding *de* begins in the early 1660s (its appearance in the privilege to *L'Ecole des maris* is an early usage), and is not generalized until later. Raymond Picard considers the practice of adding *de* proof that, because of state sponsorship, writers of this generation had careers previously impossible and were "ennobled" by their talent (65–66). Once he had obtained the privileges to his plays, Molière then signed them over to publishers; this was standard practice. The publisher whose name appears in the privilege often worked in collaboration with other publishers, so that, for a number of the plays, there are several "first" editions (editions that, as far as is known, are identical, all of which appeared at the same time but with different publishers' names on their title pages). As a result, there is often disagreement over which is to be considered the true first edition. Guibert is the best source of information on these editions and on any information that has been gathered by comparing them. See Carla Hesse on the recognition of authorship in French law.

26. The same was not true of the editions of playwrights of the previous generation: Corneille's plays, for example, first appeared occasionally in octavos but generally in far more expensive quartos, which marked them as luxury publications for an elite audience. C. E. J. Caldicott attributes the difference in format and presentation between Corneille's plays and those of Molière to the general decline in the quality of printing in France ("Molière," 8); decreasing quality also meant, however, a cheaper publication accessible to a far broader audience.

27. Much of the scenario that made *L'Ecole des femmes* the hit that moved Molière's career into its definitive phase—the play's Parisian setting, its quick publication, the use of a frontispiece in the first edition, and so forth—was already in place for his first school play. Yet, though it was a big success, the earlier play did not become the megahit Molière needed to change his status. It was only a three-act play, while the French tradition required five acts of all comedies that are to be taken seriously. Above all, however, at the time of *L'Ecole des maris,* Molière had not yet learned to exploit the commercial value of censorship.

28. For a reading of Molière's career as dominated by his role as court writer, see

Caldicott, *La Carrière de Molière*. On the ways in which *George Dandin* might have been interpreted by its different publics, see Chartier, "From Court Festivity to City Spectators."

29. La Grange, one of Molière's lead actors, kept a *Registre*, in which he noted all profits and expenses, making it possible to reconstruct the commerce of Molière's career. On *L'Ecole des femmes*'s opening night, the box office was 1,518 *livres*, the biggest to date. During Molière's lifetime, he made 65,000 *livres* from it, whereas the biggest previous hit, *L'Ecole des maris*, made only 44,000. *Psyché* brought in 77,000 *livres*, but it was more expensive to produce. The only two bigger single-night grosses were for *Le Festin de pierre (Dom Juan)* (2,390) and *Le Tartuffe* (2,890), proving that censorship sold tickets. At the end of each season, the company members split the profits; each actor received a *part* or share, the author two. The *Ecole des femmes* controversy increased profits by nearly 50 percent; the previous year's share was 3,117 *livres*, whereas that year's was 4,534 (La Grange, 53; Loiselet, 124–25). That season turned the Palais-Royal theater into, in Picard's words, "the liveliest and the most popular in Paris" (*Carrière*, 89). It was not, however, the only star in the firmament. The Hôtel de Bourgogne was the "royal troupe"; their pension was twice as large (Loiselet, 105). The Palais-Royal theater held 1,000 spectators, half of whom had only standing room, which cost 1 *livre*, as opposed to the most expensive seats at 5 *livres*. By comparison, in 1669 a copy of *Le Tartuffe*'s second edition sold for one *écu* (three *livres*); this is one of the rare surviving contemporary book prices. (In the April 6, 1669, issue of his newsletter, Robinet tells where to buy the play and gives its price [Rothschild, 3:587].)

30. Bernadette Rey-Flaud contends that the controversy generated by *L'Ecole des femmes* was above all motivated by hostility to what was perceived as Molière's attempt to shift the French comedic tradition onto higher ground with his decision to take on weightier subjects (83). Molière's only prior five-act plays were the two he had published the month before *L'Ecole des femmes*'s opening. One aspect of the "new esthetic" that was commented on by Molière's critics is the fact that his latest play was far less physical than his earlier work. Critics complained that characters did nothing but talk about what they had done and actually did nothing while on stage. Though Molière defended himself against these charges in scene 6 of *La Critique de "L'Ecole des femmes,"* they do have merit. With this play, he was moving French comedy closer to what was already (and would become even more so with the unfolding of Racine's career) the central focus of French tragedy, in which action is almost always described rather than performed. The contemporary novel was evolving in the same way.

31. All seventeenth-century dictionaries and the first edition of Littré's dictionary describe *scurrilité* as rare and link it to the vulgar humor typical of theatrical buffoons, the style for which Molière was primarily known prior to *L'Ecole des femmes*. Chapelain's description of Molière is the earliest example of the word's usage Littré includes.

32. Chapelain was one of the censor/readers most often called upon after the 1629 edict; Colbert's reliance on his judgment when choosing writers for state sponsorship indicates the complicity between censorship and the official cultural policy. Chapelain had also written up the French Academy's official position paper in the 1637 public censorship of Corneille's *Le Cid*, another huge commercial success. He was thus fully aware of censorship's role in making a reputation. In his letters about state sponsorship, Chapelain stressed the necessity of print authorship in the selection process. On the original list of sponsored writers, Molière was down for 1,000 *livres* (his troupe got 4,000 more). This was an impressive amount; even Corneille, with his greatest plays long behind him,

received only 2,000; Racine a mere 600. The royal "gratifications" were not necessarily renewed. Molière remained on the list until his death, whereas about half of the authors originally rewarded were subsequently eliminated. For the early lists of stipends, see vol. 5 of Clément's edition of Colbert's letters. On the jockeying for favor in late 1662, see Racine, *Œuvres*, 1:991, 1:1197; Picard, *La Carrière de Jean Racine*, 62–68. The biggest problem with royal stipends was that, while they looked good on paper, they did not always translate into hard cash. (See, for example, the letter Colbert addressed on June 30, 1662, to a historian explaining that the king had decided to defer payment of the 2,000 *livres* he was down for "because his Majesty needs money at this time," 5:235.)

33. H. G. Hall is among those who believe that Molière must have known *L'Ecole des filles* (89). Larson reads *L'Ecole des filles* as a commentary on the seventeenth-century French tradition of conduct manuals and suggests that, like *L'Ecole des femmes*, it may be seen as a "critique of the period's feminine moral education" ("Sex and Civility," 498). The title *Ecole des filles* was a reasonably popular one in the mid-seventeenth century. In the same year in which Molière staged his play, it was used for an anonymous work published by Louis Chamhoudry. The work deals with many of the same issues as its forbidden precursor, but without a trace of obscenity. In 1666 Montfleury, one of the participants in the controversy over Molière's play, published a play with the same title.

34. During the Elizabethan age, ordinances were passed giving the right to license plays to the mayor of London or an official appointed by him (Chambers, 4:273–76). In general, however, control over the London theaters and anything to be staged at court was in the hands of the Master of the Revels, whose job it was to make certain that no material that could be considered offensive on religious or political grounds was included in plays to be performed before members of the court. His duties were later extended to include the licensing of printed plays. See Tony Tanner on the Master of the Revels as the ur-figure of the censor (4). On the licensing of plays, see Dutton, who contends that the Master of the Revels worked not so much as a censor as he worked with companies to help them be able to bring to the stage "a more free—if discreetly veiled—discussion of 'dangerous matter' than was ever openly admitted" (304).

35. The authors of the various studies concerned with the censorship of the French stage are in complete disagreement as to when the phenomenon began. No one, however, presents any evidence of preperformance censorship prior to the furor created by Molière's plays. The earliest instance I found is cited by Saint-Germain, who notes that it took place, "after *Tartuffe.*" The author censored was Edme Boursault, self-appointed censor of *L'Ecole des femmes*. On October 22, 1668 the Parisian Parliament issued a decree forbidding the performance of a play Boursault had intended to stage at the Marais theater. La Reynie carried out the censorship on the grounds that "actors should not be allowed to evoke notable personages on the stage." Boileau had requested the stop order because he felt that "his person and his works were defamed" by the play (Saint-Germain, 145). Odile Krakovitch claims the first instance of preperformance censorship took place only in 1702, to stop Boindin's *Le Bal d'Auteuil*, and that "the theater police" (*police des théâtres*) was formally organized only in 1706 (15). However, the unit existed well before it was employed in censorship. The earliest evidence I found of its existence is a January 1674 *ordinance pour la police des théâtres*, which discusses the protection of spectators (Colbert, 6:406). This suggests that the theatre police, too, was created in the aftermath of Molière's scandalous plays. It seems likely that it was only in the aftermath of the scandal and the unprecedented success of Molière's three censored plays that performance began to be viewed as publication and, as such, censorable. (This moment coincided neatly with

La Reynie's appointment to direct the Parisian police, the body responsible for control-ling the theater.) The first evidence I found of performance viewed as publication is from a 1664 pamphlet by Abbé Pierre Roullé, *Le Roi glorieux au monde,* calling for the suppres-sion of *Le Tartuffe;* this neo-Garasse contends that Molière used "his diabolical intelli-gence to compose a play that he was about to make public by staging it" (48). The 1619 law Delamare cites was never reissued, unlike others he lists related to the regulation of the-ater audiences.

36. During Molière's entire career, for example, the box office was higher than 2,000 *livres* on only ten occasions: six performance of *Le Tartuffe* and four of *Le Festin de pierre (Dom Juan)* (Loiselet, 65). Both were financial successes, despite the fact that censorship shortened their lifespan in the company's repertory. Economic considerations alone could not have explained Molière's prolonged involvement with transgressive material, but they were surely part of the equation.

37. The power of unofficial censorship in seventeenth-century France should never be underestimated. Colbert's correspondence, for example, contains many references to popular assemblies that attempted to take censorship into their own hands (2:352, 6:32–33).

38. The publication history of *L'Ecole des femmes* proves that Molière had learned how to manage the privilege system. The play opened at the Palais-Royal theater on Decem-ber 26, 1662; its first run was still on when, on February 4, 1663, the privilege was granted to Guillaume de Luyne, who shared the original edition with no fewer than seven other publishers (including, thereby, all the major players except Ribou, whose piracy was cer-tainly too recent for Molière to have forgiven him—although he subsequently published with Ribou again). As Couton points out, such a large-scale collaboration was "abnor-mal: they were clearly hoping to have a bestseller on their hands" (Molière, *Œuvres com-plètes,* 1:529). Couton adds that the same "abnormal" pact among so many publishers was set up again for *La Critique de "L'Ecole des femmes."* This surely proves exceptional sales for the first play. Molière then staged *L'Ecole des femmes* again after the Easter vacation.

39. Boileau uses the verb *fronder,* which has come to mean "to criticize with satire," "to satirize." Three centuries of usage have softened its meaning, but only a decade after the end of the civil war that the verb commemorates, *fronder* surely conveyed a sense of vio-lent hostility.

40. On January 6 the king had already arranged to have the hit play performed for the court at the Louvre; the staging was reported to have been a huge success. (See Loret's account on January 13 in his gazette, a precursor of the first newspapers, which were shortly to burst onto the French scene.)

41. Readers of sixteenth-century French prose fiction would have been reminded, for example, of the *Cent nouvelles nouvelles.* More recently, in 1659, Segrais and Montpensier had produced in collaboration a collection called *Nouvelles françaises,* printed by Jean L'Ange as his next project after *L'Ecole des filles.* In the early 1660s, the modern novel was taking off, partly under the banner of *nouvelle*—Lafayette's *Princesse de Montpensier* (1662) and Scudéry's *Célinte* (1661).

42. The new figure Donneau de Visé incarnated, the journalist who would report anything as long as he found readers, was, predictably, reviled by many. See, for example, Jean de La Bruyère's attack on the man and his paper in *Les Caractères* (83). In the years between Théophile's censorship and Molière's, the French press had developed impres-sively but had still not caught up with developments elsewhere in Europe. Certain cities in Germany and the Low Countries had had newspapers for some time; the first dailies

had begun to appear shortly before 1663. For additional information on early newspapers, see Claude Bellanger (1:137–41).

43. *Zélinde*'s privilege is dated July 15, 1663; its print-run was finished on August 4. In the passage in the *Nouvelles nouvelles* in which he scooped Molière's *Critique*, Donneau de Visé announced that his own play would soon be performed by a rival company, at the Hôtel de Bourgogne theater (2:238). Because, however, no record of an actual staging has come down to us, theater historians now conclude that the play was never performed (Mongrédien, *La Querelle*, 1:8).

44. The privilege for Boursault's play is dated October 30, 1663; its printing was finished on November 17. Boursault, only twenty-five at the time, was already the author of several obscure comedies. He later made a more significant contribution to French letters when he helped develop the epistolary novel.

45. Discussing the troupe's appearance before the court in one of his plays, Molière's character asks, "Is there an author who would not tremble at this test?" (scene 1; Molière, *Œuvres complètes*, 1:677). The play opened in Paris on November 4. Molière evidently believed that it could be understood only in the context of the controversy, for he seldom staged it later in his career and did not publish it. (The play first appeared in the posthumous 1682 edition of his collected works.) *L'Impromptu*, a sort of *Tonight We Improvise* well *avant* Pirandello, was a good match for Versailles, which in 1663 was hardly the grandiose monument we know today. The construction that would transform the modest residence constructed by Louis XIII into the monument to the Sun King's glory had hardly begun; the king was surely improvising every bit as much as Molière. Molière had already staged *L'Ecole des femmes* and *La Critique* for the court several times in 1663, at the Louvre and other residences. The best source of information on the appearances made by his troupe for the king and for high-ranking nobles is Caldicott (*La Carrière de Molière*, 65–85).

46. Robinet had been both a collaborator on the government-controlled periodical, *La Gazette*, and, briefly during the same moment of anarchy in the book trade that had produced the first obscene novel, the editor of his own gazette, originally called *La Muse héroi-comique* (1654–1655) and then *La Muse royale* (1656–1660). His surname proves, by the way, that the authors of *L'Ecole des filles* chose actual bourgeois names. Robinet's play was published on November 30, with a privilege dated October 30; he apparently wrote it early in the fall (Mongrédien, *La Querelle*, 1:164).

47. Donneau de Visé's play was published on December 7; its privilege is dated September 14. In the same volume, the newsman included a "Lettre sur les affaires du théâtre," which repeats the criticisms found in the play.

48. It is said that both of these plays were staged, though neither production has been documented. Montfleury was the son of one of the most famous actors of the day; he wrote for the company at the Hôtel de Bourgogne, while Chevalier wrote for the Marais theater. Montfleury's play was published on January 19, 1664 (privilege January 15), Chevalier's on February 7 (privilege January 30). The final play in the seemingly unending series, by La Croix, probably was not staged. It appeared on March 17 (privilege February 13). La Croix, the last young author to try to take advantage of the scandal of Molière's plays to make a name for himself, failed miserably in his attempt: nothing is known about him other than the fact that he wrote this play.

49. Witness the opening of Donneau de Visé's portrait of Molière in the *Nouvelles nouvelles:* "This author plots to make his plays successful and believes them to be good if

he is successful in attracting a large audience" (3:326). Given the near simultaneity of the newsman's assessment and Molière's self-assessment, it seems safe to conclude that we are dealing here with an accurate evaluation of Molière's position. What was for his critics proof of Molière's lack of serious purpose as an author (you have to be second-rate if you want an audience), seems to have been for Molière a straightforward goal: attack me, criticize me, try to shut me up—but come to see my plays and make others want to see what's causing all the fuss. For a contemporary discussion of whether the fact that a work is selling well is a sign of its quality, see Guéret (35 ff.).

50. Molière's critics commented on his lack of originality. They cited in particular the fact that the plot of the old man trying to keep his young bride perfectly innocent had been used most recently by the same Scarron who marketed copies of *L'Ecole des filles*. (Scarron had in turn borrowed the idea from Maria de Zayas.)

51. For his double-entendre, Molière took advantage of the fact that in French the verb *prendre* (to take) can have as direct objects both "a ribbon" and "my arm" (or whatever bodily part one can think of—*il m'a pris le bras*, etc.). Had it not been for the phrase *prendre le ruban*, I would have translated *prendre* in the first part of their exchange as "touched," since that is closer to the verb's meaning here. Because the precise terms chosen are crucial to my argument, I provide my own translation. In many of the passages I foreground, Molière uses strange syntax, undoubtedly to call attention to the sexual innuendoes.

52. The other scenes considered most scandalous, the description of woman as her husband's soup in which he doesn't like to see other men "wetting their fingers" (2:4:436–39) and the *tarte à la crème* (cream pie) (1:1:98–99), are similarly both comic and obscene because of their evocation of female genitalia.

53. Molière's phrase, *il a une obscénité qui n'est pas supportable*—has a certain syntactic strangeness ("it *has* an obscenity," rather than "there is an obscenity about it"), which could have resulted from uncertainty about the neologism's functioning in actual usage. He might also have been trying to suggest the difference between obscenity as a thing and the quality of that which is obscene. In the original edition of *La Critique*, *obscénité* is consistently misspelled *"obcénité"* (31) (see figure 5). The original edition also features a combination of methods to highlight *obscenity*'s decent stand-in, *the*. The word is in italics (a practice modern editors continue to adopt). It stands out even more because, each time, the word is also raised slightly above the others in the same line. Finally, each of its appearances is punctuated in a manner that is strange, even by seventeenth-century standards: a comma precedes and follows *le* each time it means "the *the*" (30–31). (Modern editors do not include this punctuation.) The original edition of *L'Ecole des femmes* is singled out for its typographical innovativeness; the publisher, Gabriel Quinet, is given full credit (Martin et al., *La Naissance du livre moderne*, 423), but it is hard to believe that Molière had nothing to do with the choices. *Obscenity*'s inaugural moment would thus mark a further step in Molière's acceptance of print authorship: from this point on, the original editions of his plays often featured typographical marks that are in different ways unpronounceable, as though Molière wanted to call attention to the text's existence *as printed text*, to print's ability to mark text in unique ways, and to features of the printed text that would elude the print pirates of memorial reconstruction and could only be appreciated by the solitary reader of the printed text. See, for example, *Le Misanthrope* (78–79) and *Le Tartuffe* (73). In all the publications that sought to capitalize on the controversy, only Montfleury's play picks up on the neologism. His characters merely discuss,

however, how well the actors in the original production of *La Critique* pronounced the new term. Once again, the word appears in italics; this time, it is spelled correctly (original edition [10–11]; Mongrédien, *La Querelle*, [2:337–38]).

54. For the same reason, Molière's practice should not be confused with the elegant double-entendres of such classical precursors as Cicero, who use word play to avoid primary obscenities (Richlin, 18–24). Molière seems to have been toying with the idea that, if the thought police work hard enough, any word can be considered dirty.

55. See Coetzee's discussion of Lawrence's view of obscenity as well as his borrowing from contemporary anthropological thought, which held that "taboos on words with sexual or excretory references are survivals from a less highly evolved stage of European culture" (48–50).

56. To illustrate the fashioning of this taboo, Elias chooses examples from conduct manuals: from the end of the Renaissance on, the sections devoted to bodily functions and the proper way of negotiating them are dramatically reduced. In France this terminology was elided most strikingly during the century following obscenity's reinvention (Elias, 190–91).

57. Even the words evoked by *ruban* testify to the progression Elias documents. Whereas *con* had never been printable, *téton*, still printed as recently as the 1650s (for example, in Scarron's 1653 *Don Japhet d'Arménie*), was pronounced unprintable at the same time as Molière became a print author.

58. Laurent Mahelot's *Mémoire*, a major source of information on the staging of seventeenth-century theater, describes the set as "two houses at the front of the stage, and the rest shows a city square" (119). All Molière's early critics, however, commented on the fact that the play's action takes place *in the street*. At least one other play, Montfleury's *Impromptu de l'Hôtel de Condé*, has a similarly public setting in the arcades of the Palais-Royal, in the shop of a bookseller—Montfleury's choice makes even more evident the link between the promiscuous circulation of the street and that of print culture.

59. The title page identifies the play's setting as "a city square." Some commentators have suggested that Molière could have imagined a provincial city rather than Paris, but Paris had no contemporary rivals in the areas praised by Horace.

60. Louis XIV was the wealthiest sovereign in Europe, and he wanted his capital to testify to this prestige. The 1667 edict establishing the powers of the new police describes in elaborate detail the improvements—the first system of street lighting anywhere, for example—they will carry out to make the streets safe (Isambert, 18:100–103). This program was an obvious success: in 1698, Martin Lister commented on how much better lit Paris was than London; Saint-Germain suggests that Paris began to be called the *ville lumière* because of this reform (77–78). Throughout the original police legislation, laws reforming the streets and laws reforming the book trade are juxtaposed.

61. The noun *canaille* already existed in 1663; Molière's use of the verb marks its initial appearance in French. Once again, he had his finger on his century's linguistic pulse. The word caught on so quickly that it figures in the first edition of Furetière's dictionary as an already accepted term: "to frequent the rabble, the lowest of the low, . . . to frequent people who are worthless" (*gens de néant*, the same term Garasse used to describe the public for Théophile's sodomite sonnet [60]).

62. Molière's critics believed that he had consciously provoked them to attack his play in order to publicize it. See, for example, Donneau de Visé on the "crafty strategy" Molière devised in order to have his play censured (Mongrédien, *La Querelle*, 1:41). He concludes, as do other participants—Chevalier, for instance (Mongrédien, *La Querelle*,

2:367–68, 2:376–77)—that the play's censorship was responsible for its success: "Everyone condemned it, and everyone ran to see it. . . . It succeeded even though no one liked it"; "those who go to see his plays only to censure them and who talk about them all the time are the cause of their success, since their reports compelled others to go to see them" (*Nouvelles nouvelles*, 3:232–33, 3:343). In the preface he added when he published *L'Ecole des femmes*, Molière repeatedly establishes a bond between a work's ability to provoke censorship and its commercial success (*Œuvres complètes*, 1:543–44). Gabriel Guéret immediately understood how censorship had increased *Le Tartuffe*'s success: "It must be admitted that Molière sold this comedy well, and that prohibitions and excommunications were a big help" (49).

63. See n. 20 on the criticism Corneille received because he sold his manuscripts. Robinet eulogizes Molière's ability to commodify his manuscripts: "Up until now, [such plays] were worthless, but he found the secret of making them into the philosopher's stone, and of getting good money for them" (Mongrédien, *La Querelle*, 1:225). The new practice seems to have been winning acceptance, but booksellers had clearly not yet been coerced into paying anything like what manuscripts were actually worth. By having an aristocrat broker the deal with a bourgeois, Montfleury seems to have been indicating that the controversy had helped stamp out opposition to authors' desire to exploit their market value, even among nobles, traditionally portrayed as most hostile to the new economy for literature. On authors' early attempts to sell their manuscripts, see Febvre and Martin (247); on the sums received, see Lough (84–90). Here are a few sales figures: in 1636 Benserade sold *Cléopâtre* for 75 *livres;* in 1637 Rotrou sold four tragedies for 750; in 1669 La Fontaine received 600 for *Psyché*—and Molière 2,000 for *Le Tartuffe*. See Chartier's discussion of how "the new phenomenon of a social status founded solely on the remuneration of writing emerged only with difficulty" (*Order of Books*, 48). On the same phenomenon, see also Robert Darnton, "The Facts of Literary Life in Eighteenth-Century France." The most successful practitioners of less noble genres were able to play by the new economic rules at an earlier date: already in the 1640s and 1650s, Madeleine de Scudéry made a handsome profit from the manuscripts of her novels (Godenne, 11). Martin notes that the move to generalize sales of manuscripts came from playwrights and novelists (*L'Edition parisienne*, 313).

64. The newsman's trade could be profitable indeed. Later in his career, Donneau de Visé earned 12,000 *livres* a year, as much as Molière (Viala, *La Naissance de l'écrivain*, 132). One final category of writer was locked up in important numbers in the Bastille during the Ancien Régime: the *nouvellistes* or newsmen were, as soon as they got onto dangerous ground, actively prosecuted. On the newsmen who were prisoners in the Bastille in the late seventeenth century, see Funck-Brentano.

65. Mongrédien refers to Donneau de Visé's article on Molière as "the earliest publication of any length devoted to Molière" (*La Querelle*, 1:xvii). In French, the word *biographie* did not come into existence until the early eighteenth century; prior to this, the term *vie* was used. The tradition of drawing up biographies for famous authors really began in earnest only in the last years of the seventeenth century. There are scattered earlier lives of famous authors, most notably Claude Binet's *Discours de la vie de Pierre de Ronsard* (1596). Binet's text illustrates perfectly all that separates a "life" from a "biography"; it is almost hagiographic, closer to a saint's "life" than to a writer's. (*Vie* most commonly referred to the lives of saints; some early authors of writers' "lives"—for example, Adrien Baillet, who composed Descartes's in 1691—also authored saints' "lives.") The 1587 edition of *Orlando Furioso* opens with Giovanbattista Pigna's extended "life" of Ariosto;

slightly less hagiographic than similar French efforts, it is still a far cry from what we would consider a biography: Pigna devotes, for example, a long section to Ariosto's body—his wide forehead, for example.

66. Donneau de Visé's major journalistic creation, *Le Mercure galant*, subsequently played a crucial role in having the French press take on a characteristic role: it advertised everything, first of all, itself. From the first issue, it had a header, *Le Mercure* on the left page, *galant* on the right—something no earlier French paper had included. Molière's company also used publicity effectively. In 1662 they budgeted 8 *livres* a day for posters advertising, in red, the play of the day and, in black, the next day's play. The posters informed potential spectators how many people had attended the previous day's performance, how good the play was, and that it was important to arrive early to get good seats (Loiselet, 96–97).

67. It has been suggested that the spelling of Molière's author's name in the title proves how quickly Luyne wanted to get the volumes out and begin cashing in on the rush to celebrity. Just as happened when the first of Molière's plays were published, several editors joined forces and quickly got into the act. In the course of 1664, the same collection was brought out by Charles de Sercy, Gabriel Quinet, and Etienne Loyson. The publishers obviously decided that the privileges originally obtained when the plays were published individually were still valid for this type of compilation, since they did not apply for a new privilege to cover the collection. The absence of official documents makes it impossible to date the edition's print history with precision, although Guibert contends that both volumes were printed in late 1663, even though the second volume is dated 1664 (2:557). It appears that precious few individuals, particularly in this century, have seen any of these editions.

68. For his fifth example of *author,* Furetière includes this meaning: "this *author* was censored." Chartier describes various ways in which, in sixteenth-century France, the author function was developed in relation to censorship (*Order of Books,* 49–51).

69. La Grange says, "M. de Molière received a royal pension, . . . and he printed his thanks to the king in his *Works*"—that is, in a text that opens the first volume of this edition. Because of this, Guibert concludes that "even if [Molière] did not give his formal approval to the project, he did not disapprove of it" (2:556).

70. The fact that François Colletet geared his 1675 guide book, *La Ville de Paris,* specifically to foreign visitors indicates that the vast urban projects of the early part of Louis XIV's reign were attracting a significant wave of tourism. Germain Brice's 1685 *Description nouvelle de la ville de Paris* also targets foreigners who need to know what to see in the city.

71. The newsmen's involvement testifies to the spread of Molière's fame; he was becoming a subject of interest to the provincial and foreign readers who turned to the periodical press for coverage of the Parisian scene. The French language's new status also helped make Molière famous outside of France; companies of French actors were able for the first time to tour outside of France. This practice began just in time to spread Molière's celebrity. His hit plays entered their repertories almost immediately. Witness the example of the next result of Molière's exploitation of censorship, *Le Tartuffe,* first staged in Paris in February 1669. Already by November of the same year Abraham Mitallat's newly created (1668) Comédiens de la Reine de France were touring with it in the Low Countries (Fransen, 123). Saint-Evremond recorded his appreciation of their performance in The Hague in a letter from November 25 (1:206–7). The same troupe was also in Bruxelles on this tour. Molière became internationally known in French before he

acquired a public in translation. He was widely translated, most frequently in English and Dutch. Translations begin to appear with regularity after 1670.

72. Three other frontispieces to Molière plays are sometimes attributed to Chauveau, though they are unsigned, which was not his usual practice (see Jackson, 39). *L'Ecole des maris* was the first of Molière's plays to have a frontispiece; it is among those often attributed to Chauveau. Chauveau subsequently illustrated many of Racine's plays.

73. In the play, the book contains "maxims of marriage"; however, readers of *L'Ecole des femmes* who were also familiar with *L'Ecole des filles* might have made a connection between the books featured in Chauveau's two frontispieces and have seen a relation between the unnamed book in Arnolphe's hand and the copy of *L'Ecole des filles* held up by one of the women, in particular since that little book could have legitimately been described as "an important work that teaches [women] how to become a wife."

74. Febvre and Martin stress that the expansion of the print industry was simultaneous with the rise of a wealthy bourgeoisie—and nowhere was this more true than in France, where the age of great mercantile fortunes occurred later than, for example, in Holland or in England.

75. "Before the fifteenth century, even artists' self-portraits were deprived of individuality. The conditions of scribal culture thus held narcissism in check" (Eisenstein, 233). Then in the sixteenth century "there was a new deliberate promotion by publishers and print dealers of those authors and artists whose works they hoped to sell" (234). Eisenstein's theory of the standardization accomplished by print culture has recently been challenged by Johns (see, e.g., 10–14). Of late, the attention paid to the lack of standardization has taught us a great deal about early printed editions. In the case of the portrait, however, the accuracy of Eisenstein's intuition remains unchallenged; at the same time as authors' works became ever more broadly diffused in editions that their readers believed to be identical, the authors most widely circulated began to be portrayed in increasingly individualized fashion. On sixteenth-century authors' portraits, see Ruth Mortimer. Just to prove once again that there is always classical precedent, Joe Farrell referred me to Ovid's remark about the proliferation of crowned portrait busts (*imagines*) of well-known authors such as himself (*Tristia*, 1:7); there is obviously no way of evaluating the individuality of these *imagines*.

76. The situation concerning Molière's portrait is also exceptional in that so many portraits of him have survived, far more than for any other seventeenth-century author. For a good overview of these portraits, see the catalogue of the *Exposition du IIIe centenaire de la mort de Molière* (Musée des Arts Décoratifs). It is difficult to date these portraits with precision. One of the earliest of the series in which his individuality is plain is probably the portrait by Mignard (figure 7); in it, Molière is shown in the costume he wore when he staged Corneille's 1644 tragedy, *La Mort de Pompée*. La Grange's *Registre* indicates that this was in 1659, so it seems likely that artists began rendering Molière's likeness on canvas about the time that his real celebrity began.

77. Figure 10 is illustration number 52 in a volume from 1824, *Costumes du théâtre de 1600 à 1820* (Lecomte). The lithograph is by Delpech, based on a drawing by Henry Lecomte, who edited the volume. Lecomte entitled the illustration *Molière in the Role of Arnolphe in L'Ecole des femmes in the Year 1670*, as though he were reproducing with great accuracy a precise moment in the history of Molière's involvement with the theater. What he gives us, however, is almost a complete reworking of Molière's costume, a reworking that radically softens and feminizes the original image of Arnolphe. He makes of Molière's well-to-do bourgeois a sort of *petit marquis*, complete with long curls and a

big plume on his hat. Of late, Lecomte's version has been so widely disseminated—in, for example, a 1976 collective volume on Molière in the Hachette Réalités series (Barrault et al., 96) and as a frontispiece to the Classiques Larousse edition of Molière's play—that the silly "portrait" is replacing Molière's face and the equally inappropriate costume is replacing Chauveau's re-creation of Molière's original.

78. On Armande's life, I follow by far the most reliable French biographical dictionary, the *Dictionnaire de biographie française,* edited by J. Balteau et al. There is little agreement about when she was born; the two dates most often proposed are 1640 and 1645, though some argue for 1638, or 1642. If 1645 is the correct year, she would have been seventeen at the time of their marriage, and there would have been a twenty-three-year age difference. If it is 1640, the figures would be twenty-two and eighteen. If 1638, twenty-four and sixteen. If 1642—well, you get the picture. None of these configurations would have seemed at all extraordinary in an age when women often married while they were still young by today's standards and when they often married considerably older men.

79. Richlin discusses the idea that Latin poets of obscenity were "stained by the content of their work" (30); see also Kendrick (31). Commenting on the situation in eighteenth-century England, Brewer argues that "the public's appetite for news, gossip, and scandal about the stage was insatiable, its sense of intimate acquaintance with actors unique. A successful player could only have a public private life" (340). In France by that time, the same would have been true. Molière's life became a subject for scandal to an extent previously unheard of.

80. Donneau de Visé may have authored the song. Boursault did not include it in the published version of his play. On the song, see Molière, *Œuvres complètes* (1:1302, 1:1307). The song was apparently inspired by the fact that, when Molière's comedy *Les Fâcheux* was performed in 1661, it opened on the image of a boulder that turned into a giant shell, which contained a sea nymph reciting the play's prologue. The nymph was played by Madeleine Béjart. Couton speculates that Molière's critics could have "found that the nymph was no longer young enough" (Molière, *Œuvres complètes,* 1:1302).

81. In this discussion (scene 5), Molière specifically refers to Boursault's *Portrait du peintre;* he sets his play prior to Boursault's and thus does not have to mention which "kinds of issues" he has in mind.

82. Racine described the ugly business in a letter from late 1663. See also Mongrédien (*La Querelle,* 1:xvii–xviii) and Mongrédien, *La Vie privée de Molière* (85–88). For a full account of the theory by a proponent, see the entry on Armande Béjart in the *Nouvelle biographie générale.* As Mongrédien points out, not everyone said that Armande was necessarily Molière's daughter by Madeleine—many said that Madeleine had slept around far too much to know who the father was (*La Vie privée de Molière*). Even the accusation of having slept with first mother and then daughter, however, surely left an air of incest about the marriage.

83. Even though "no one listens to Montfleury at court," story lines based on these rumors have become central to what passes for Molière's biography; they have taken over Armande Béjart's biography. For confirmation of this, check the entries on them in any of the French biographical dictionaries or the most recent biography of Molière, by Virginia Scott. In the nearly 350 years since Molière's death, no documents have come to light that can be used to set the rumors to rest. Faced with the lack of evidence, commentators have massively chosen to follow Donneau de Visé and Montfleury. The only detail that I find at all telling is the fact that no birth certificate has been found for Ar-

mande Béjart, which may indicate that there was some problem concerning her parentage that Molière wished to keep out of the public record. However, something far less shocking than incest would surely have been enough to displease a bourgeois family like Molière's.

84. Shortly after the new police force was established, its officers discovered a related need for portraits. When La Reynie was seeking a suspect, he issued "the necessary orders to have the man's portrait sent to all the border crossings" (Saint-Germain, 45). In this case, *portrait* referred to a verbal description sufficiently detailed and individualized to permit officers to make an arrest; they were apparently remarkably effective. For an example of such a portrait, used to arrest someone in the clandestine book trade, see Colbert (6:70).

85. It is in England that the intersection seems most evident. The first English copyright legislation dates from 1709, the first obscenity legislation from 1727. However, in an argument parallel to that made by historians of print culture who argue that obscene works did not effect the contemporary development of censorship, David Saunders contends that, even though "in chronological terms, they almost coincide, . . . the writer as owner of copyright and the writer as the locus of criminal liability . . . stand in no relation to one another" (437). Early English legislation governing obscenity was drawn up in response to the publication of works written by French authors; it would have been particularly easy to overlook issues of authorial protection in the case of foreign authors. Saunders's article is a brilliant demonstration of the complex implications of British obscenity law for the issue of authorial status.

Conclusion

1. The "Arrest du Conseil Privé du 27 février 1665" is quoted in the 1687 *Edit du roi*. When the decree was reissued in 1669, it was also printed up as sheets or handbills that were posted throughout Paris; this "advertisement" surely hastened the implantation of "bad book." On occasion, an equally chiding term, *méchants* (wicked, mean) *livres*, is employed, for example, by La Reynie in a 1670 memorandum to Colbert on Dutch publishers (Ravaisson-Mollien, 219–20). The 1665 decree defined bad books as "against the Catholic faith, his Majesty, and the well-being of his state."

2. *Obscénité* next appeared, ironically, in a 1665 pamphlet by Rochemont calling for the suppression of *Le Festin de pierre (Dom Juan)*—although the author's usage is closer to Garasse than to Molière (267). Indeed, as late as 1660, as Olivier Pot has shown, the Latin *obscenitas* was translated as *infamie* (414). By 1680, however, Primi Visconti uses *paroles obscènes* to mean four-letter words (167). *Obscenity's* definitive implantation seems to have taken place in the century's last two decades. In 1680 Richelet contends that it is still not common usage: "This word, no more than *obscene*, is not generally accepted." In 1694, when Antoine Arnauld uses it in his "Lettre à M. P[errault] au sujet de la 10e satire," he appears to consider that it is still a neologism: "Obscenity, in a manner of speaking . . ." (*pour parler ainsi*). (On Arnauld's use of the term, see Pot [431 n. 61].) By 1690 and 1694, however, neither Furetière nor the Académie Française include any reference to the term's status as a neologism.

3. Bayle added his lengthy (fifty-page) meditation on obscenity, "Eclaircissement sur les obscénités," because, after he published the first edition of his dictionary in 1697, numerous censors (for the most part, religious authorities) had attacked it in print on the grounds that it was obscene.

4. On February 28, 1723—only shortly before the Curll trial—a new code was issued

to govern the French book trade. Titles 14 and 99 ("the commerce of bad books forbidden") show that the vocabulary governing sexually indecent publications had not progressed in any notable way since the previous code, in 1686: "against the purity of morals" is the term featured (Saugrain, 341).

5. Just as was true of all early regulations concerning print culture, the ordinance apparently had little effect; by the following year, Parisian publishers were once again circulating catalogues advertising obscene engravings (Peignot, 152). The complete text of the ordinance is in Duvergier (3:137–38). Peignot discusses the law and its history (152). This "obscene images act" was part of a code issued by the National Assembly to establish a sort of municipal vice squad.

6. "Outrage à la morale publique et religieuse, ou aux bonnes moeurs" (Duvergier, 22:206–7). The judgment against Baudelaire said he was guilty of having used "obscene expressions" (Leclerc, 337). Flaubert was charged with precisely the offenses specified in this ordinance (see Netz, 91; LaCapra, 36). The 1810 penal code was also cited at their trials. The trial of Penguin Books for the publication of *Lady Chatterley's Lover* provides a roughly comparable milestone in English law. Following the model of the Curll case, the publisher was prosecuted under the Obscene Publications Act; the work was always termed "obscene" (Hyde, 1, 53).

7. On the resistance to the use of *obscene* and *obscenity* in the regulation of the book trade in nineteenth- and twentieth-century France, see Bécourt (3–7).

8. Isolated obscene images must have been created in seventeenth-century France for elite collectors. Older traditions of obscene imagery (illuminations in medieval manuscripts, sixteenth-century Italian engravings) surely continued to be in limited circulation. Occasional serial images were produced (illustrations to La Fontaine's *Contes*, for example) that could be considered at least racy. There was, however, no French tradition of obscene printed images parallel to the obscene novels; obscene images were, therefore, not a concern for censorship.

9. Remember Talvacchia's hypothesis that images were not censored in sixteenth-century Italy because this would have smacked of Protestant iconoclasm. By the early eighteenth century, this Counter-Reformation concern might have abated.

10. The authors I cite here, Bill Carter and Lawrie Mifflin, explain what they term the "rapid disappearance of most taste and language restrictions in the U.S. mass media" by arguing that the "public has become desensitized to sexual and scatological material because of mass exposure to news stories like President Bill Clinton's relationship with Monica Lewinsky, with its open discussions of oral sex and cigars as sex toys" (*International Herald Tribune*, July 21, 1999). See also Michael Kelly's assertion that today "nothing is not fit to print, if not in the *Times*, then in some public place" (*International Herald Tribune*, August 8, 1999). The recently released (September 2000) film *The Way of the Gun* opens on a barrage of *fuck* in all its forms so excessive—it is apparently used 120 times in the film's opening sequence—that it seems to signal the end of this taboo. Web site names now feature "the English language's most explicit words" (*International Herald Tribune*, July 22, 1999).

11. George Will, *Washington Post* (June 21, 2000). Carter and Mifflin provide related examples (*International Herald Tribune*, July 21, 1999).

12. On the "decivilizing process," see Elias's *The Germans*, in which, inspired by a meditation on the Holocaust, he contemplates the end of the societal transformation he had traced in his earlier study.

13. Obscenity's contemporary existence is further complicated by the return of its

biggest repressed: female desire. The subject is too vast for this study. Here are two examples of the "complications" I have in mind. Among the currently x-rated ad campaigns are those that feature two women together—since they are attempting to sell *women's* clothing, we may assume that their creators see them as revisions of the use of lesbianism as male turn-on. Then, there is "feminist" porn—notably, the most recent French *succès-de-scandale,* Virginie Despentes's film *Baise-Moi* (Fuck Me). It features real-life porn stars (the self-consciousness of much current sexually transgressive imagery is another sign of obscenity's dysfunction) who, à la Thelma and Louise, take violence into their own hands.

14. Technical limitations forced photographers to focus not on how death occurred in battle but on the mutilated corpses of the war dead. There had been some coverage of the Crimean War, but primarily of buildings and landscapes. Similarly, coverage of the Commune shifts from a record of its destructive effects on Paris to a visual memorial to the twenty-five thousand killed during one bloody week. This photography is an origin of "live" coverage; the events were taking place before the photographers' eyes. In *La Commune photographiée,* Sotteau and Bajac describe anti-*communarde* literature from 1871 in which a female insurgent is characterized as "obscene and ferocious" (44)—as if the violent conflict had immediately caused the term to shift terrain. *Courbet et la Commune* explains the political role played by the artist. On Civil War photography, see Alan Trachtenberg.

15. George Roeder's fascinating study, *The Censored War,* discusses the history of photographic coverage of war and the manipulation of that coverage for propaganda purposes.

16. It is from James Graham's *Bloody Passage;* the *OED* lists it under the vague definition "offensive to the senses, . . . disgusting, repulsive," one of *obscene*'s oldest catch-all categories. I believe that the usage signals a new departure.

17. Obscenity in this new usage is linked to the concept of witnessing, of undoing cultural and historical amnesia with respect to phenomena—most notably, the Holocaust—too long kept out of sight. The vocabulary was used, for example, to describe a recent exhibit of photographs of the lynchings of black men at the Roth Horowitz Gallery in Manhattan (*New York Times,* March 9, 2000). The earliest denunciation of obscene excess noted by the *OED* is from 1974 and refers to oil profits; this is the year of the first Vietnam reference, which suggests a spill-over effect in that period of sweeping moral outrage. This new usage is characteristically Anglo-Saxon; it is at most lightly visible elsewhere. Abramovici says that it has been present in French for the past twenty years and that it is particularly linked to commentary on the Holocaust (*L'Obscénité,* 485–87); the usage, however, is by no means as extensive as in English. Emmanuel Le Roy Ladurie has commented on the recent evolution of *obscene.* He believes that the new usage is strictly political, that it is a manifestation of political correctness: those he calls "hyper-egalitarian" and "superfeminist" condemn as "obscene" all that they consider racist and misogynist. I agree with his view of the time-frame in which this semantic shift has taken place, but disagree with his interpretation of *obscene*'s current connotations. His remarks can be found on the Web site for a writer accused of anti-Semitism, Renaud Camus (http://perso.wanadoo.fr/renaud.camus/). Feinberg notes that *obscene* is shifting onto new terrain in contemporary English, though he does not discuss this usage (97).

18. I also like the phrase a friend reported hearing on National Public Radio in April 2001: "Internet pornography generates obscene profits."

Works Cited

Abelove, Henry. "Some Speculations on the History of 'Sexual Intercourse' During the 'Long Eighteenth Century' in England." In *Nationalisms and Sexualities,* edited by Andrew Parker et al., 335–42. New York: Routledge, 1992.

Abramovici, Jean-Christophe. *Le livre interdit: De Théophile de Viau à Sade.* Paris: Payot, 1996.

———. *L'Obscénité et la pensée française: XVIIe–XVIIIe siècles.* Ph.D. diss., University of Paris X–Nanterre, 1997.

Adam, Antoine. *Théophile de Viau et la libre pensée française en 1620.* Geneva: Droz, 1935.

Adams, J. N. *The Latin Sexual Vocabulary.* Baltimore: Johns Hopkins University Press, 1982.

Anderson, Benedict. *Imagined Communities: Reflections on the Origin and Spread of Nationalism.* London: Verso, 1991.

Anglade, Eugène. *Étude sur la police.* Paris: C. Gérard, 1852.

Ariès, Philippe. "Sur les origines de la contraception en France." *Population* 3 (July–September 1953): 465–72.

Ariosto, Lodovico. *Orlando furioso.* Venice: Vincenzo Valgrisi, 1587.

Baldwin, John. *The Languages of Sex: Five Voices from Northern France around 1200.* Chicago: University of Chicago Press, 1994.

Balibar, Renée, and Dominique Laporte. *Le Français national: Politique et pratiques de la langue nationale sous la Révolution française.* Paris: Hachette, 1974.

Balteau, J., et al., eds. *Dictionnaire de biographie française.* 18 vols. to date. Paris: Letouzey et Ané, 1933–.

Barbiche, Bernard. "Le Régime de l'édition." In Chartier and Martin, 1:367–77.

Barker, Francis. *The Tremulous Private Body: Essays on Subjection.* London: Methuen, 1984.

Barrault, Jean-Louis, et al. *Molière.* Paris: Hachette (Génies et Réalités), 1976.

Barthes, Roland. "Réflexions sur un manuel." In *Œuvres Complètes,* edited by Eric Marty, 2:1241–46. Paris: Editions du Seuil, 1993.

Baudrillard, Jean. "What Are You Doing after the Orgy?" *Traverses* 29 (October 1983): 2–15.

Battisti, Carlo, and Giovanni Alessio. *Dizionario Etimologico Italiano.* Florence: Barbera, 1950–57.

Bayle, Pierre. "Eclaircissement sur les obscénités." *Dictionnaire historique et critique,* 15:324–71. Desoer, 1820.

Bécourt, Daniel. *Livres condamnés, livres interdits: Régime juridique du Livre: Liberté ou censure?* Paris: Cercle de la librairie, 1972.

Bell, Rudolph M. *How to Do It: Guides to Good Living for Renaissance Italians.* Chicago: University of Chicago Press, 1999.

Bellanger, Claude, ed. *Histoire générale de la presse française.* Vol. 1. Paris: Presses Universitaires de France, 1969.

Benjamin, Walter. *The Arcades Project*. Translated by Howard Eiland and Kevin Mc-Laughlin. Cambridge, Mass.: Belknap Press, 1999.

Berkvens-Stevelinck, Christiane. "L'Edition française en Hollande." In Chartier and Martin, 2:316–25.

Binet, Claude. *Discours de la vie de Pierre de Ronsard.* Paris: Gabriel Buon, 1596.

Birn, Raymond. "Les Colporteurs de livres et leur culture à l'aube du siècle des Lumières: Les pornographes du Collège d'Harcourt." *Revue française d'histoire du livre* 11 (October–December 1981): 593–623.

Boileau Despréaux, Nicolas. *Œuvres complètes.* Edited by Françoise Escal. Paris: Gallimard, 1966.

Bollème, Geneviève. *La Bibliothèque Bleue.* Paris: Julliard, 1971.

Boswell, John. *The Kindness of Strangers.* New York: Pantheon Books, 1988.

Bouchel, M. L., ed. *Recueil des statuts et règlements des marchands, libraires, imprimeurs, et relieurs de la ville de Paris.* Paris: François Julliot, 1620.

Bray, René. *Molière, homme de théâtre.* Paris: Mercure de France, 1954.

Brewer, John. *The Pleasures of the Imagination: English Culture in the Eighteenth Century.* New York: Farrar, Straus, Giroux, 1997.

Brice, Germain. *Description nouvelle de la ville de Paris.* Paris: Veuve Audinet, 1685.

Brunot, Ferdinand. *Histoire de la langue française des origines à nos jours.* 13 vols. Paris: Armand Colin, 1966.

Cabinet satyrique, Recueil parfait des vers piquants et gaillards, tirés des secrets cabinets. Paris: Pierre Billaine, 1618.

Caldicott, C. E. J. *La Carrière de Molière: Entre protecteurs et éditeurs.* Amsterdam: Rodopi, 1998.

———. "Molière and His Seventeenth-Century Publishers." *Nottingham French Studies* 33, no. 1 (Spring 1994): 4–11.

Camus, Michel, ed. *Œuvres érotiques du XVIIe siècle.* Vol. 7 of *L'Enfer de la Bibliothèque Nationale.* Paris: Fayard, 1988.

Chambers, E. D. *The Elizabethan Stage.* 4 vols. Oxford: Clarendon Press, 1923.

Chapelain, Jean. *Lettres de Jean Chapelain de l'Académie française.* Paris: Imprimerie nationale, 1880–1883.

Chartier, Roger. *Au bord de la falaise: L'histoire entre certitudes et inquiétude.* Paris: Albin Michel, 1998.

———. "From Court Festivity to City Spectators." In *Forms and Meanings: Texts, Performances, and Audiences from Codex to Computer.* Philadelphia: University of Pennsylvania Press, 1995.

———. *The Order of Books: Readers, Authors, and Libraries in Europe between the Fourteenth and Eighteenth Centuries.* Translated by L. Cochrane. Stanford, Calif.: Stanford University Press, 1994.

———. *Publishing Drama in Early Modern Europe.* London: British Library, 1999.

Chartier, Roger, and Henri-Jean Martin, eds. *Histoire de l'édition française.* 4 vols. Paris: Promodis, 1983–1986.

Chevillier, André. *L'Origine de l'imprimerie de Paris.* Paris: Jean de Laulne, 1694.

Clarke, David R. *Pierre Corneille: Poetics and Political Drama under Louis XIV.* Cambridge: Cambridge University Press, 1992.

Claverie, Elisabeth. "Naissance d'une forme politique: L'Affaire du Chevalier de La Barre." In *Critique et affaires de blasphème à l'époque des Lumières,* edited by Philippe Roussin, 185–265. Paris: Honoré Champion, 1998.

Coetzee, J. M. *Giving Offense: Essays on Censorship.* Chicago: University of Chicago Press, 1996.

Colbert, Jean-Baptiste. *Lettres, instructions, et mémoires de Colbert.* 1868. Edited by Pierre Clément. 8 vols. Lichtenstein: Kraus Reprints, 1979.

Colletet, François. *La Ville de Paris, contenant le nom de ses rues . . . le tout pour l'usage des étrangers.* Paris: A. de Raffe, 1677.

Colletet, Guillaume. *L'Art poétique.* 1658. Edited by P. Jannini. Geneva: Droz, 1965.

Colombet, Claude. *Propriété littéraire et artistique.* Paris: Dalloz, 1976.

La Commune photographiée. Paris: Réunion des musées nationaux, 2000.

Courbet et la Commune. Paris: Réunion des musées nationaux, 2000.

Cryle, Peter. *Geometry in the Boudoir: Configurations of French Erotic Narrative.* Ithaca, N.Y.: Cornell University Press, 1994.

Darnton, Robert. "The Facts of Literary Life in Eighteenth-Century France." In *The Political Culture of the Old Regime,* edited by Keith Michael Baker, 261–91. Oxford: Pergamon Press, 1987.

———. *The Forbidden Best-Sellers of Pre-Revolutionary France.* New York: Norton, 1995.

———. *The Literary Underground of the Old Regime.* Cambridge, Mass.: Harvard University Press, 1982.

Davis, Natalie Zemon. *The Gift in Sixteenth-Century France.* Madison: University of Wisconsin Press, 2000.

DeJean, Joan. "Une Autobiographie en procès: L'affaire Théophile de Viau." *Poétique* 48 (1981): 431–48.

———. *Libertine Strategies: Freedom and the Novel in Seventeenth-Century France.* Columbus: Ohio State University Press, 1981.

———. *Tender Geographies: Women and the Origins of the Novel in France.* New York: Columbia University Press, 1991.

Delamare, Nicolas. *Traité de la police.* 4 vols. Amsterdam: Aux Dépens de la Compagnie, 1719–1738.

Desanti, Jean-Toussaint. "L'Obscène ou les malices du signifiant." *Traverses* 29 (October 1983): 128–34.

Diament, Nicole. *Recherches sur la police parisienne sous Louis XIV à travers Nicolas Delamare.* Ph.D. diss., École de Chartes, 1970.

Dickens, Arthur Godfrey. *Reformation and Society in Sixteenth-Century Europe.* New York: Harcourt Brace Jovanovich, 1955.

Diderot, Denis. *Œuvres.* Edited by Laurent Versini. 5 vols. Paris: Robert Laffont, 1994.

Dolet, Etienne. *La Manière de bien traduire d'une langue en autre. D'avantage. De la ponctuation de la langue française.* Lyon: Etienne Dolet, 1542.

Donneau de Visé, Jean. "Lettre sur les affaires du théâtre." In *Diversités galantes.* Paris: Claude Barbin, 1664.

———. *Nouvelles nouvelles.* 3 vols. Paris: Claude Barbin, 1663.

Dubost, Jean-Pierre. "Notice sur les gravures libertines." In *Romanciers libertins du XVIIIe siècle,* edited by Patrick Wald Lasowski, lxii–xcix. Paris: Gallimard, 2000.

Dury, Maxime. *La Censure: La Prédication silencieuse.* Paris: Publisud, 1995.

Dutton, Richard. "Censorship." In *A New History of Early English Drama,* edited by John D. Cox and David Kastan, 287–304. New York: Columbia University Press, 1997.

Duvergier, Jean Baptiste, et al., eds. *Collection complète des lois, décrets, ordonnances, réglements, et avis du Conseil d'Etat.* Paris: Société du Recueil Sirey, 1831–1836; Paris: Imprimerie de Charles Noblet, 1836–1899.

Edit du roi pour le règlement des imprimeurs et libraires de Paris. Paris: Denis Thierry, 1687.

Eisenstein, Elizabeth. *The Printing Press as an Agent of Change: Communications and Cultural Transformations in Early Modern Europe.* Cambridge: Cambridge University Press, 1979.

Elias, Norbert. *The Civilizing Process.* Translated by Edmund Jephcott. Oxford: Basil Blackwell, 1978.

————. *The Germans: Power Struggles and the Development of Habitus in the Nineteenth and Twentieth Centuries.* New York: Polity Press and Columbia University Press, 1998.

Ellis, Havelock. *Havelock Ellis on Life and Sex: Essays of Love and Virtue.* 1937. Garden City, N.Y.: Garden City Publishing Company, 1947.

Ernst, Morris Leopold, and Alan U. Schwartz. *Censorship: The Search for the Obscene.* New York: Macmillan, 1964.

Estivals, Robert. *La Statistique bibliographique de la France sous la monarchie au XVIIIe siècle.* Paris: Mouton, 1965.

Fabricius, Johannes. *Syphilis in Shakespeare's England.* London: Jessica Kingsley Publishers, 1994.

Farrell, Joseph. "The Ovidian *Corpus:* Poetic Body and Poetic Text." In *Ovidian Transformations: Essays on the Metamorphoses and Its Reception,* edited by P. Hardie, A. Barchiesi, and S. Hinds, 127–41. Cambridge Philological Society suppl. vol. 23. Cambridge: Cambridge Philological Society, 1999.

Faunce, Sarah, and Linda Nochlin. *Courbet Reconsidered.* Brooklyn, N.Y.: Brooklyn Museum, 1988.

Febvre, Lucien, and Henri-Jean Martin. *L'Apparition du livre.* Paris: Albin Michel, 1958.

Feinberg, Joel. *Offense to Others.* Vol. 2 of *The Moral Limits of the Criminal Law.* Oxford: Oxford University Press, 1985.

Findlen, Paula. "Humanism, Politics, and Pornography in Renaissance Italy." In Hunt, 49–108.

Fontanon, Antoine. *Les Edicts et ordonnances des rois de France.* 4 vols. Paris: Jacques du Puys, 1585.

Foucault, Michel. *Les Anormaux: Cours au Collège de France, 1974–1975.* Paris: Gallimard/ Le Seuil, 1999.

————. *History of Sexuality.* Vol. 1. Translated by R. Hurley. New York: Vintage Books, 1980.

————. *L'Usage des plaisirs.* Vol. 2 of *Histoire de la Sexualité.* Paris: Gallimard, 1984.

————. "What Is an Author?" Translated by J. Harari. In *The Foucault Reader,* edited by P. Rabinow, 101–20. New York: Pantheon, 1984.

Foxon, David. *Libertine Literature in England: 1660–1745.* New Hyde Park, N.Y.: University Books, 1965.

Fransen, Jan. *Les Comédiens français en Hollande au XVIIe et XVIIIe siècles.* Paris: Honoré Champion, 1925.

Funck-Brentano, Frantz. *Les Lettres de cachet à Paris, étude suivie d'une liste de prisonniers de la Bastille (1659–1789).* Paris: Imprimerie nationale, 1903.

Gallagher, Catherine. *Nobody's Story: The Vanishing Acts of Women Writers in the Marketplace, 1670–1820.* Berkeley: University of California Press, 1994.

Garasse, François. *La Doctrine curieuse des beaux esprits de ce temps, ou prétendus tels.* Paris: Chappelet, 1623.

Gawthrop, Richard, and Gerald Strauss. "Protestantism and Literacy in Early Modern Germany." *Past and Present* 104 (1984): 31–55.

Ginzburg, Carlo. "Titian, Ovid, and Sixteenth-Century Codes for Erotic Illustration." In *Myths, Emblems, Clues,* translated by John Tedeschi and Anne C. Tedeschi. London: Hutchinson, 1990.

Godenne, René. *Les Romans de Mademoiselle de Scudéry.* Geneva: Droz, 1983.

Goulemot, Jean-Marie. *Ces livres qu'on ne lit que d'une main: Lecture et lecteurs de livres pornographiques au XVIIIe siècle.* Paris: Minerve, 1994.

Graham, James. *Bloody Passage.* London: Macmillan, 1974.

Guéret, Gabriel. *La Promenade de Saint-Cloud.* 1669. Edited by G. Monval. Paris: Libraire des Bibliophiles, 1888.

Guibert, A. J. *Bibliographie des œuvres de Molière publiées au XVIIe siècle.* 2 vols. Paris: Editions du Centre National de la Recherche Scientifique, 1961.

Habert, Louis. *Pratique du sacrement de la pénitence, ou méthode pour l'administrer utilement.* 1689. Paris: Denis Thierry, 1694.

Hall, H. G. *Comedy in Context: Essays on Molière.* Jackson: University Press of Mississippi, 1984.

Halperin, David. "Why Is Diotima a Woman?" In *One Hundred Years of Homosexuality,* 113–51. London: Routledge, 1990.

Herzel, Roger. "The Décor of Molière's Stage: The Testimony of Brissart and Chauveau." *PMLA* 93 (1978): 925–54.

Hesse, Carla. "Enlightenment Epistemology and the Laws of Authorship in Revolutionary France, 1777–1793." *Representations* 30 (Spring 1990): 109–38.

Hoffmann, George. *Montaigne's Career.* Oxford: Clarendon Press, 1998.

Howell, T. B., ed. *A Complete Collection of State Trials.* Vol. 17. London: T. C. Hansard, 1813.

Hunt, Lynn, ed. *The Invention of Pornography: Obscenity and the Origins of Modernity, 1500–1800.* New York: Zone Books, 1993.

Hyde, H. Montgomery. *The "Lady Chatterley's Lover" Trial: Regina v. Penguin Books Limited.* London: Bodley Head, 1990.

Isambert, François-André. *Recueil général des anciennes lois françaises depuis l'an 420 jusqu'à la Révolution de 1789.* Paris: Belin le Prieur, 1821.

Jackson, G. Donald. "Les Frontispices des éditions de Molière parues au XVIIIe siècle: Stéréotypes et expressivité." *Papers on French Seventeenth-Century Literature* 14 (1987): 37–60.

Jean de Meun and Guillaume de Lorris. *The Romance of the Rose.* Translated by Charles Dahlberg. Princeton, N.J.: Princeton University Press, 1971.

———. *Le Roman de la rose.* Edited by Armand Strubel. Paris: Le Livre de Poche, 1992.

Johns, Adrian. *The Nature of the Book: Print and Knowledge in the Making.* Chicago: University of Chicago Press, 1998.

Jouhaud, Christian. *Mazarinades: La Fronde des mots.* Paris: Aubier, 1985.

———. *Les Pouvoirs de la littérature: Histoire d'un paradoxe.* Paris: Gallimard, 2000.

Julia, Dominique. "Reading and the Counter-Reformation." In *A History of Reading in the West,* edited by Giglielmo Cavallo and Roger Chartier, 239–66. London: Polity Press, 1999.

Kamen, Henry. *The Spanish Inquisition: A Historical Revision.* New Haven, Conn.: Yale University Press, 2000.

Kendrick, Walter. *The Secret Museum: Pornography in Modern Culture.* New York: Viking, 1987.

Krakovitch, Odile. *Les Pièces de théâtre soumises à la censure.* Paris: Archives Nationales, 1982.

La Bruyère, Jean de. *Les Caractères, ou les mœurs de ce siècle.* 1688. Edited by Robert Garapon. Paris: Garnier, 1962.

LaCapra, Dominick. *"Madame Bovary" on Trial.* Ithaca, N.Y.: Cornell University Press, 1982.

Lachèvre, Frédéric. *Disciples et successeurs de Théophile: Les œuvres libertines de Claude Le Petit.* Paris: Honoré Champion, 1918.

———. *Le Libertinage au XVIIe siècle: Mélanges.* Paris: Honoré Champion, 1920.

———. "Les Libertins du XVIIe siècle: Claude le Petit." *Revue des livres anciens* 1 (1913): 131–39.

———. *Les Œuvres libertines de Claude Le Petit.* Paris: Capiomont, 1918.

———. *Le Procès du poète Théophile de Viau.* 2 vols. Paris: Honoré Champion, 1909.

———. *Les Recueils collectifs de poésies libres et satyriques publiés depuis 1600 jusqu'à la mort de Théophile (1626).* Paris: Honoré Champion, 1914.

La Grange, sieur de. *Le Registre de la Grange.* Edited by Bret Edward Young and Grace Philputt Young. 2 vols. Paris: Droz, 1947.

Lapeire, Paul. *L'Outrage aux bonnes mœurs par le livre, l'écrit et l'imprimé.* Lille: Douriez-Bataille, 1931.

Larson, Ruth. "The Iconography of Feminine Sexual Education in the Seventeenth Century: Molière, Scarron, Chauveau." *Papers on French Seventeenth-Century Literature,* no. 39 (1993): 499–516.

———. "Sex and Civility in a Seventeenth-Century Dialogue: *L'Escole des filles.*" *Papers on French Seventeenth-Century Literature* 24, no. 47 (1997): 496–512.

Lawner, Lynne, trans. *I modi: The Sixteen Pleasures: An Erotic Album of the Italian Renaissance: Giulio Romano, Marcantonio Raimondi, Pietro Aretino, and Count Jean-Frédéric-Maximilien de Waldeck.* Evanston, Ill.: Northwestern University Press, 1988.

Lawrence, D. H. *Lady Chatterley's Lover and A Propos of "Lady Chatterley's Lover."* Edited by Michael Squires. Cambridge: Cambridge University Press, 1993.

Leclerc, Yvan. *Crimes écrits: La littérature en procès au XIXe siècle.* Paris: Plon, 1991.

Lecomte, Henry. *Costumes de théâtre de 1600 à 1820.* Paris: Delpech, 1824.

Lederer, Laura, ed. *Women on Pornography.* New York: William Morrow, 1980.

Le Maire, Nicolas. *Le sanctuaire fermé aux profanes, ou la Bible défendue au vulgaire, divisé en trois parties, par M. Le Maire.* Paris: S. et G. Cramoisy, 1651.

Loiselet, Jean-Louis. *De quoi vivait Molière?* Paris: Deux-Rives, 1950.

Longino, Helen E. "Pornography, Oppression, and Freedom: A Closer Look." In Lederer, 40–54.

Loret, Jean. *La Muze historique.* Edited by Ch.-L. Livet. 4 vols. Paris: P. Jannet, 1857–1878.

Lough, John. *Writer and Public in France from the Middle Ages to the Present Day.* Oxford: Clarendon Press, 1978.

Mahelot, Laurent. *Le Mémoire de Mahelot.* Edited by H. C. Lancaster. Paris: Honoré Champion, 1920.

Mainil, Jean. *Dans les règles du plaisir: Théorie de la différence dans le discours obscène romanesque et médical de l'Ancien Régime.* Paris: Kimé, 1996.

Martin, Henri-Jean. "Classements et conjonctures." In Chartier and Martin, 1:429-457.

———. "Une Croissance séculaire." In Chartier and Martin, 2:95-103.

———. *L'Edition parisienne au XVIIe siècle.* Paris: A. Colin, 1952.

———. *Livre, pouvoirs et société au XVIIe siècle (1598-1701).* 2 vols. Geneva: Droz, 1969.

———. "La Prééminence de la librairie parisienne." In Chartier and Martin, 2:263-81.

Martin, Henri-Jean, Jean-Marc Chatelain, Isabelle Diu, Aude Le Dividich, and Laurent Pinon, eds. *La Naissance du livre moderne (XIVe-XVIIe siècles).* Paris: Editions du Cercle de la Librairie, 2000.

Martin, Henri-Jean, and Anne-Marie Lecocq. *Les Registres du libraire Nicolas (1645-1668): Livres et lecteurs à Grenoble.* 2 vols. Geneva: Droz, 1977.

Maugis, Edouard. *Histoire du parlement de Paris.* 2 vols. Paris: Auguste Picard, 1914.

Mellot, Jean-Dominique. *L'Edition rouennaise et ses marchés (vers 1600-vers 1730): Dynamisme provincial et centralisme parisien.* Paris: Ecole des Chartes, 1998.

Le Mercure français, ou Suite de l'histoire de notre temps. Vol. 5. Paris: Etienne Richer, 1619.

Millanges, Simon. "Au Lecteur." Preface to *Erreurs populaires,* 2d ed., by Laurent Joubert. Bordeaux: S. Millanges, 1579.

[Millot, Michel.] *L'Ecole des filles.* In *Œuvres érotiques du XVIIe siècle,* vol. 7 of *L'Enfer de la Bibliothèque Nationale,* edited by Michel Camus. Paris: Fayard, 1988.

———. *The School of Venus.* Translated by Donald Thomas. New York: New American Library, 1971.

Molière, Jean-Baptiste Poquelin. *La Critique de "L'Ecole des femmes."* Paris: G. de Luyne, 1663.

———. *L'Ecole des femmes.* Edited by Gérard Sablayrolles. Paris: Librairie Larousse/ Nouveaux Classiques Larousse, 1965.

———. *Le Festin de pierre (Dom Juan).* Edited by J. DeJean. Geneva: Droz, 1999.

———. *Le Misanthrope.* Paris: Jean Ribou, 1667.

———. *Œuvres complètes.* Edited by Georges Couton. Bibliothèque de la Pléiade. 2 vols. Paris: Gallimard, 1971.

———. *Œuvres.* Edited by Eugène Despois and Paul Mesnard. 11 vols. Paris: Hachette, 1873-1929.

———. *Le Tartuffe.* Paris: Jean Ribou, 1669.

Mongrédien, Georges, ed. *La Querelle de "L'Ecole des femmes."* 2 vols. Paris: Nizet, 1971.

———, ed. *Recueil des textes et des documents du XVIIe siècle relatifs à Molière.* 2 vols. Paris: Editions du CNRS, 1965.

Montfleury, A. J. *L'Impromptu de l'Hôtel de Condé.* Paris: N. Pepingué, 1664.

Mortimer, Ruth. *A Portrait of the Author in Sixteenth-Century France: A Paper Presented on the Occasion of the Fiftieth Anniversary of the Hanes Foundation for the Study of the Origin and Development of the Book.* Chapel Hill, N.C.: Hanes Foundation, 1980.

Moulton, Ian. "Crafty Whores: The Moralizing of Aretino's Dialogues." *Critical Survey* 12, no. 2 (2000): 88-105.

Moxon, Joseph. *Mechanick Exercises on the Whole Art of Printing.* 1683-84. 2d ed. Edited by Herbert Davis and Harry Carter. New York: Dover Publications, 1978.

Musée des Arts Décoratifs. *Exposition du IIIe centenaire de la mort de Molière.* Paris: Hemmerlé, Petit et Cie, 1973.

Netz, Robert. *Histoire de la censure dans l'édition.* Paris: Presses Universitaires de France, 1998.

Newman, Jane O. "The Word Made Print: Luther's 1522 New Testament in an Age of Mechanical Reproduction." *Representations* 11 (1985): 95-133.

Nochlin, Linda. "Courbet's *L'Origine du monde:* The Origin Without an Original." *October* 87 (1986): 76–86.

Ovid. *Tristia.* Translated by Arthur Leslie Wheeler. Cambridge, Mass.: Harvard University Press, 1924.

Le Parnasse des muses, ou Recueil des plus belles chansons à danser. Paris: Charles Hulpeau, 1628.

Parnasse satyrique. Paris: 1668.

Pastoreau, Michel. "L'Illustration du livre: Comprendre ou rêver?" In Chartier and Martin, 1:602–28.

Peignot, Gabriel. *Essai historique sur la liberté d'écrire chez les anciens et chez les modernes.* 1832. Geneva: Slatkine Reprints, 1970.

Pepys, Samuel. *The Diary of Samuel Pepys.* Edited by Robert Latham and William Matthews. Berkeley: University of California Press, 1976.

Pia, Pascal. *Les Livres de l'enfer: Bibliographie critique des ouvrages érotiques dans leurs différentes éditions du XVIe siècle à nos jours.* 2 vols. Paris: Coulet et Faure, 1978.

Picard, Raymond. *La Carrière de Jean Racine.* Paris: Gallimard, 1956.

Pigna, Giovanbattista, ed. *Orlando furioso,* by Lodovico Ariosto. Venice: Vincenzo Valgrisi, 1587.

Pintard, René. *Le libertinage érudit dans la première moitié du XVIIe siècle.* Paris: Boivin, 1943.

Poldo d'Albenas, Jean. *Discours historial de l'antique et illustre cité de Nîmes.* Lyon: Guillaume Roville, 1559.

Pot, Olivier. "La Question de l'obscenité à l'âge classique." *XVIIe siècle* 43 (October—December 1991): 403–36.

Pottinger, David T. *The French Book Trade in the Ancien Regime, 1500–1791.* Cambridge, Mass.: Harvard University Press, 1958.

Prévot, Jacques, ed. *Libertins du XVIIe siècle.* Paris: Gallimard, 1998.

Racine, Jean. *Œuvres.* Edited by Raymond Picard. Paris: Gallimard, 1964.

Ranum, Orest. *Artisans of Glory.* Chapel Hill: University of North Carolina Press, 1980.

Ravaisson-Mollien, François. *Archives de la Bastille: Documents inédits.* Paris: Lauriel, Durand et Pedone, 1883.

Recht, Pierre. *Le Droit d'auteur, une nouvelle forme de propriété.* Paris: L. G. D. J., 1969.

Recueil de toutes les pièces faites par Théophile, depuis sa prise jusqu'à présent. N.p.: n.p., 1624.

Réponses aux observations touchant "Le Festin de pierre" de Monsieur de Molière. Paris: Gabriel Guinet, 1665.

Rey, Alain. *Dictionnaire historique de la langue française.* Paris: Dictionnaires Le Robert, 1998.

Rey-Flaud, Bernadette. *Molière et la farce.* Geneva: Droz, 1996.

Richlin, Amy. *The Garden of Priapus: Sexuality and Aggression in Roman Humor.* New York: Oxford University Press, 1992.

Riddle, John M. *Contraception and Abortion from the Ancient World to the Renaissance.* Cambridge, Mass.: Harvard University Press, 1992.

Robic-de Baecque, Sylvie. *Le Salut par l'excès: Jean-Pierre Camus, 1584–1652, la poétique d'un évêque romancier.* Paris: Champion, 1999.

Roche, Daniel. "La Censure." In Chartier and Martin, 2:76–83.

———. "La Police du livre." In Chartier and Martin, 2:84–91.

[Rochemont, sieur de.] *Observations sur une comédie de Molière intitulée "Le Festin de pierre."* 1665. In Molière, *Le Festin de pierre,* 262–80.

Roeder, George H., Jr. *The Censored War: American Visual Experience during World War II.* New Haven, Conn.: Yale University Press, 1993.

Rothschild, James de, ed. *Les Continuateurs de Loret (1665–1689).* 5 vols. Paris: Morgand et Fatout, 1881.

Rou, Jean. *Mémoires.* Edited by F. Waddington. 2 vols. Paris: Agence Centrale de la Société de l'histoire du protestantisme français, 1857.

Roullé, Abbé Pierre. *Le Roi Glorieux au monde, ou Louis XIV le plus glorieux de tous les rois du monde.* N.p.: n.p., 1664.

Sabatié, Léon. *La Censure.* Paris: A. Pedone, 1908.

Saint-Evremond, Charles de Marquetel de Saint Renis. *Lettres.* Edited by René Ternois. 2 vols. Paris: Marcel Didier, 1967.

Saint-Germain, Jacques. *La Reynie et la police au grand siècle.* Paris: Hachette, 1962.

Saint-Simon, Louis de Rouvroy, duc de. *Mémoires.* Edited by Arthur de Boislisle. Paris: Hachette, 1902.

Saugrain, Claude Marin. *Code de la librairie et de l'imprimerie.* Paris: Aux Dépens de la Communauté, 1724.

Sauman, Alfred. "Press, Pulpit, and Censorship in France before Richelieu." *Proceedings of the American Philosophical Society* 120, no. 6 (1976): 439–63.

Saunders, David. "Copyright, Obscenity, and Literary History." *ELH* 57 (1990): 431–44.

Sauvy, Anne. *Livres saisis à Paris entre 1678 et 1701.* The Hague: Martinus Nijhoff, 1972.

Scott, Virginia. *Molière: A Theatrical Life.* Cambridge: Cambridge University Press, 2000.

Sévigné, Marie de Rabutin Chantal, Marquise de. *Correspondance.* Edited by Roger Duchêne. 3 vols. Paris: Gallimard, 1972.

Siegert, Bernhard. "Omission Marks." Unpublished essay, 1999.

Smet, Ingrid de, and Philip J. Ford, eds. *Eros et Priapus: Erotisme et obscénité dans la littérature néo-latine.* Geneva: Droz, 1997.

Sorel, Charles. *L'Histoire comique de Francion.* 1623–1633. Edited by Yves Giraud. Paris: Garnier-Flammarion, 1979.

Sotteau, Stéphanie, and Quentin Bajac. "Eugène Appert, les premiers photomontages politiques." In *La Commune photographiée,* 40–48. Paris: Réunion des musées nationaux, 2000.

Steinberg, Leo. *The Sexuality of Christ in Renaissance Art and in Modern Oblivion.* 2d ed. Chicago: University of Chicago Press, 1996.

Steinem, Gloria. "Erotica and Pornography: A Clear and Present Difference." In Lederer, 35–39.

Stone, Lawrence. *The Family, Sex, and Marriage in England, 1500–1800.* Abr. ed. New York: Harper and Row, 1979.

Le Tableau de la vie et du gouvernement de Messieurs les Cardinaux Richelieu et Mazarin. Cologne: Pierre Manteau, 1694.

Talvacchia, Bette. *Taking Positions: On the Erotic in Renaissance Culture.* Princeton, N.J.: Princeton University Press, 1999.

Tamizey de Larroque, Philippe. "Trois lettres inédites relatives à Claude Le Petit." *Bulletin du bouquiniste* 29 (1872): 147–51.

Tanner, Tony. "Licence and Licencing: To the Presse or to the Spunge." *Journal of the History of Ideas* 38 (January–March 1977): 3–18.

[Tenain, Madame de.] *La Religieuse intéressée et amoureuse avec l'histoire du comte de Clare, nouvelle galante.* Cologne: chez ***, 1695.

Thomas, Donald. *A Long Time Burning: The History of Literary Censorship in England.* London: Routledge and Kegan Paul, 1969.

Thompson, Roger. "Two Early Editions of Restoration Erotica." *The Library: A Quarterly Journal of Bibliography* 32, no. 1 (March 1977): 45–48.

———. *Unfit for Modest Ears: A Study of Pornographic, Obscene, and Bawdy Works Written and Published in England in the Second Half of the Seventeenth Century.* London: MacMillan, 1979.

Thuasne, Louis. *Les privilèges des éditions originales de Molière.* Paris: Henri Leclerc, 1924.

Trachtenberg, Alan. *Reading American Photographs.* New York: Hill and Wang, 1989.

Trumbach, Randolph. "Erotic Fantasy and Male Libertinism in Enlightenment England." In Hunt, 253–82.

Van de Walle, Etienne. "Motivation and Technology in the Decline of French Fertility." In *Family and Sexuality in French History,* edited by R. Wheaton and T. Hareven, 35–78. Philadelphia: University of Pennsylvania Press, 1980.

Veyrin-Forrer, Jeanne. "A la recherche des *Précieuses.*" In *La Lettre et le texte: Trente années de recherche sur l'histoire du livre.* Collection de l'Ecole Normale Supérieure de Jeunes Filles, no. 34 (1987): 339–66.

Viala, Alain. *La Naissance de l'écrivain: sociologie de la littérature à l'âge classique.* Paris: Editions de Minuit, 1985.

———. *La Naissance des institutions de la vie littéraire en France au XVIIe siècle (1643–1665).* Ph.D. diss., Université de Lille-III, 1982.

Viau, Théophile de. "Fragments d'une histoire comique." In *Prose, 1623–1624,* edited by Guido Saba. Turin: Bottega d'Erasmo, 1965.

Visconti, Primi. *Mémoires sur la cour de Louis XIV, 1673–1681.* Edited by Jean-François Solmon. Paris: Perrin, 1988.

Wickham, Glynne. *Early English Stages: 1300 to 1660.* 2 vols. London: Routledge and Kegan Paul; New York: Columbia University Press, 1959.

Williams, Raymond. *Marxism and Literature.* Oxford: Oxford University Press, 1977.

Index

Abelove, Henry, 159n. 45
Abramovici, Jean-Christophe, 131n. 2, 141–42n. 8, 181n. 17
Académie Française, 151n. 5, 169–70n. 32
achevé d'imprimer, 145n. 26
Adam, Antoine, 141n. 7, 142n. 9, 144n. 22, 149nn. 43, 46
Adams, J. N., 133n. 10
advertisement, 4, 180–81n. 13; of books, 169n. 29; and newspapers, 108, 176n. 66; of sex aids, 161n. 57; of sexually transgressive literature, 58; of the theater, 176n. 66
Affaire des Poisons, L', 165–66n. 17
aid, sex, 77, 82, 161n. 57
Albenas, Jean Poldo d', 9
Anderson, Benedict, 81, 155n. 28, 164n. 7
androgyny, 128–29
Ange, Jean L', 62, 64, 77, 152–53n. 15, 153n. 20; as printer, 171n. 41
antiquity: censorship in, 3, 6; image of desire in, 20; obscene images in, 136–37n. 30; synonymous with Rome in seventeenth-century France, 132n. 6, 146n. 31
Aretino, Pietro, 9–10, 29, 58, 75–76, 135n. 25, 140n. 1, 157n. 36, 159n. 47, 159–60n. 48, 160n. 49, 162n. 63; class politics of, 160n. 51; religious parody in, 160n. 51
Ariès, Philippe, 160–61n. 54
Ariosto, Ludovico, his life drawn up, 175–76n. 65
Arnauld, Antoine, 179n. 2
ARTFL database, 132n. 8
Aubray, Dreux d', 90–91, 165–66n. 17, 166n. 18
authenticity, of a work, 112
authors: collaborative, 84, 162n. 1; commercial, 163–64n. 5, 164n. 7, 172–73n. 49, 174–75n. 62, 175n. 63; as commodities, 120; created by censorship, 65, 85, 109, 176n. 68, 179n. 85; creation of modern, 53, 84–85, 109; female, 137n. 35; in Golden Age Spanish, 86; held responsible for their works, 17, 27, 52–53, 65, 137n. 34, 149–50n. 49, 153n. 16; income, 110; individual, 84; as individuals who can be prosecuted for obscene publications, 121, 179n. 85; in Italy, 164n. 7; and newspapers,

85, 99, 110, 118; of obscene literature, 65, 120, 133n. 10; obtaining privileges in their own name, 167–68n. 25; patronage, 85–86, 163–64n. 5, 164nn. 7–8; paying for the publication of their works, 152n. 11, 162–63n. 2; print, 85–86, 163n. 4; in the public domain, 165n. 14, 179n. 85; relation to readers, 131n. 3; and the sales of their manuscripts, 62, 86–87, 94, 101, 107–8, 163–64n. 5, 164nn. 7, 9, 166n. 20, 175n. 63; state-sponsored, 96, 98, 169–70n. 32. *See also* life, private; Molière, Jean-Baptiste Poquelin de
authorship: economics of, 86, 108, 174–75n. 62, 175n. 63; modern, 10, 17, 84–85, 162–63n. 2; recognition of, 17; as regulatory principle for print culture, 65; relation to censorship, 26–27, 53, 65, 85, 108–9, 176n. 68, 179n. 85. *See also* status, authorial

Baillet, Adrien, 175–76n. 65
Bakhtin, Mikhail, 6, 75
Baldwin, John, 133n. 12
Balibar, Renée, 131–32n. 4
Balzac, Guez de, 166n. 20
Barbiche, Bernard, 139n. 43, 141–42n. 8, 144n. 19, 151n. 5
Barbin, Claude, 166–67n. 21
Barker, Francis, 150–51n. 1, 162n. 1
Barrin, Abbé Jean, 83, 124, 154n. 23, 157n. 35
Barthes, Roland, 23
Bastille, the: archives of, 24, 153–54n. 22; prisoners in, 22, 65, 127, 138n. 41, 165n. 11, 175n. 64
Baudelaire, Charles, 3, 52; his trial, 30, 126–27, 180n. 6
Baudrillard, Jean, 134n. 16
bawdy, 8, 145–46n. 30; first prosecution of, 43, 59; relation to *obscene*, 8, 128; why tolerated, 39
Bayle, Pierre, 123–24; and the definition of modern obscenity, 123, 125, 179n. 3
Bécourt, Daniel, 180n. 7
Behn, Aphra, 163–64n. 5
Béjart, Armande, 115–17, 119, 178nn. 78, 82, 178–79n. 83

Béjart, Madeleine, 118–19, 178nn. 80, 82
Bell, Rudolph, 161n. 61
Bellanger, Claude, 171–72n. 42
Benjamin, Walter, 4–5, 127
Berkvens-Stevelinck, Christiane, 138n. 39
Bible, the: direct access to, 11, 135n. 23, 145n. 27; forbidden to women and nonaristocratic males, 12, 16; in translation, 11
Bibliothèque bleue, 157–58n. 38
Bignon, Abbé Jean-Paul, 138–39n. 41, 139nn. 42–43
Binet, Claude, 175–76n. 65
biography: history of the term, 175–76n. 65; Molière's, 108–10, 118, 120, 178n. 78
Birn, Raymond, 137–38n. 36, 154–55n. 23, 159n. 43
birthrate, fear of a declining, 54
blasphemy, relation to obscene publications, 43, 50–51, 125–26, 144–45n. 23, 145n. 28, 149–50n. 49
body, the: of authors of obscene literature, 163n. 3; in confessors' manuals, 158n. 39; parts of, 42–43, 48–49, 53, 71, 102, 111, 128–29, 134n. 17, 138n. 38; portrayal of orifices, 42–43; portrayal of the sexualized, 20, 71, 128–29, 158n. 39. *See also* genitalia
Boileau, Nicolas, 87, 98, 170–71n. 35, 171n. 39
Bollème, Geneviève, 157–58n. 38
book police, 103, 122; creation of the expression, 138–39n. 41; development of, 2, 13, 23, 87–88. *See also* La Reynie, Nicolas de; police
books: "bad," 18, 89, 91, 122, 179n. 1; as commodities, 85; formats, 3, 68–69; "obscene little," 124; price of, 69, 169n. 29; and publication projects, 3; small, 69, 94, 111, 177n. 73; as threat to public morality, 17. *See also* editions; paper
booksellers: dishonest dealings with authors, 26–27, 33, 92–94, 109–10, 121, 166–67n. 21, 167n. 22; function of in France, 135n. 24; held responsible by censors, 17, 53, 125; portrayed in literature, 112, 174n. 58; reluctant to pay for authors' manuscripts, 175n. 63. *See also* printers
Boswell, John, 160–61n. 54
Bouchel, M. L., 144n. 19
Bourdieu, Pierre, 97
bourgeoisie, the: definitions of, in Ancien Régime France, 137n. 32, 149n. 43; literary genres designed to appeal to, 80–81; and mercantile fortunes, 177n. 74; in Molière's theater, 106; and print culture, 81, 111, 177n. 74; readers of obscene works, 51, 79–80; re-

lation to modern literary obscenity, 75, 81, 106, 111; symbols of, 111. *See also* Anderson, Benedict
Boursault, Edme, 100, 118, 172n. 44, 178nn. 80–81; his play censored, 170–71n. 35
Bray, René, 166n. 19
Brewer, John, 148n. 42, 178n. 79
Brice, Germain, 176n. 70
Brinvilliers, Marie-Madeleine d'Aubray, Marquise de, 165–66n. 17
Bruce, Lenny, 35, 41, 124, 144–45n. 23
Bruno, Giordano, 30, 140–41n. 3
Brunot, Ferdinand, 131–32n. 4
bureaucracy, in France, 139n. 42
Bussy, Roger de Rabutin, Comte de, 161n. 60

cabarets: associated with freethinkers, 45, 51–52; information on, in seventeenth-century Paris, 148n. 42
cabinets satiriques, 35, 142n. 9, 143n. 14
cafés, 70, 148n. 42; and social promiscuity, 148n. 42. *See also* cabarets
Caldicott, C. E. J., 168n. 26, 168–69n. 28, 172n. 45
Calentius, Eliseo, 132n. 8
Camus, Michel, 154n. 23
Camus, Renaud, 181n. 17
Capa, Robert, 130
Cato ("Censorius," Marcus Porcius), 9
Catullus, Gaius Valerius, 47–48, 52, 133n. 10; as model for Théophile, 146n. 32, 147n. 37, 163n. 3
celebrity: authors', 85, 94, 108–10; and newspaper coverage, 108–10. *See also* status, authorial
censors: English, 82–83, 151n. 3; first secular, in France, 18, 40, 59–60, 96, 169–70n. 32; numbers of, in France, 138–39n. 41, 151n. 3; private, 171n. 37
censorship: and authorial status, 21, 85, 108–9, 169–70n. 32, 176n. 68; bureaucratic, 16, 85, 156–57n. 34; categories for, in Ancien Régime France, 137n. 33; considering plays as publications, 170–71n. 35; creation of state-sponsored, 16, 32, 87, 141–42n. 8; developed in relation to obscene publications, 23, 39, 82–83, 179n. 85; ecclesiastical, 9–12, 29, 32, 140n. 1, 145n. 25; enforcement of, 25–26; in England, 82–83, 119, 124–25, 139–40n. 44, 157n. 35, 162n. 64, 170n. 34, 179n. 85; and French culture, 27, 85, 87; French legal history of, 24, 38, 126–27; French secularization of, 10, 23, 32, 39–40, 59–60, 123, 141–

42n. 8; French vocabulary of, 18, 40, 60, 63, 103–4, 122–23, 126–27, 137–38n. 36, 149–50n. 49, 151n. 4, 153n. 17, 157n. 35, 162n. 64, 179n. 1, 179–80n. 4, 180nn. 6–7; in Italy, 8, 159n. 47; of journalists, 165n. 11; modern, 30–31, 58, 85, 87; of obscene images, 126–27, 180nn. 8–9; of obscene publications, 12, 16, 126–27, 153nn. 21–22, 162n. 64; of political publications, 16, 140n. 2, 159n. 47; preperformance, 170–71n. 35; prepublication, 139nn. 43–44; relation to print culture, 2, 4, 21, 87; of religious publications, 16, 151n. 5; self-, 18–19, 150n. 50; selling books, 4, 21, 85, 87, 107, 138n. 39, 171n. 36, 174–75n. 62, 175n. 63; of the stage, 97–98, 122, 170n. 34, 170–71n. 35; struggle between secular and religious authorities for control over, 40, 43; 59–60, 124–25, 140n. 2, 141n. 5; unofficial, 171n. 37; of words, 2, 127–28, 144n. 15. *See also Ecole des filles, L'; Parnasse des poètes satiriques, Le;* Viau, Théophile de
censure, societal, 98
Cervantes, Miguel de, 85
Chancellery: archives of, 24; as censoring authority in France, 13, 26, 60, 94, 141–42n. 8, 151nn. 3, 5
Chapelain, Jean, 96, 165n. 12, 166n. 20, 169n. 31, 169–70n. 32
Charles II, 164–65n. 10
Chartier, Roger, 86, 143nn. 13–14, 163n. 4, 176n. 67; on memorial reconstruction, 167n. 23; on Molière, 166n. 19, 167n. 22, 168–69n. 28; on the new literary economy, 175n. 63
Châtelet, the, 153n. 20; as censoring authority, 63
Chaucer, Geoffrey, 18
Chauveau, François, 62, 67, 80–81, 110–11, 152n. 13, 155n. 26, 161–62n. 62, 177nn. 72–73. *See also* frontispieces
Chevalier, Jean, 101, 172n. 48, 174–75n. 62
Chevillier, André, 24, 26, 40, 59, 151n. 5
Chorier, Nicolas, 67, 154n. 23, 155n. 27, 156n. 31, 159nn. 45–46
Cicero, Marcus Tullius, 174n. 54
circulation, literary: in antiquity, 7, 147n. 37; of images, 128; and obscenity's reinvention, 7, 37, 78–80; uncontrolled, 4, 51, 58, 69, 99, 128, 145n. 29, 148n. 42, 149n. 44. *See also* publics, for literature; readers; *s'encanailler*
civilisé, 138n. 40
civilization: and the civilizing process, 19, 39, 105, 128–29; and the decivilizing process, 180n. 12. *See also* Elias, Norbert

Clarke, David, 166n. 20
class, and obscenity, 107, 126, 128
Clinton, William, 2, 180n. 10
Coetzee, J. M., 138n. 39, 174n. 55
Colbert, Jean-Baptiste: and control over print culture, 89, 156–57n. 34, 165n. 12, 171n. 37, 179n. 84; reforms initiated by, 22, 85, 87, 165n. 13; and state sponsorship of the arts, 87, 169–70n. 32
Colletet, François, 166n. 18, 176n. 70
Colletet, Guillaume, 10, 13, 43, 72
Commune, the, and photography, 129–30, 181n. 14
Community of Printers, Publishers, and Binders, Parisian, 26, 38; statutes, 38, 64, 144nn. 19–20
confession: and the incitement to discourse on sexuality, 71; manuals for, 71, 158n. 39; and "touchings," 158n. 40. *See also* Habert, Father Louis; lust
consumerism, in seventeenth-century France, 148n. 42
contamination, threat of social: linked to print culture, 45, 49, 51–52, 126; linked to venereal disease, 45, 48–49; Molière's understanding of, 107. *See also s'encanailler*
contraception, 17, 161n. 61; early evidence on, 76–77, 161n. 56; in France today, 161n. 57; history of the literature on, 160–61n. 54; women's role in, 77, 161n. 58
copyright, 93, 120–21, 167–68n. 25; English legislation concerning, 179n. 85
Corneille, Pierre, 86–87, 112, 167–68n. 25; controversy over *Le Cid,* 169–70n. 32; formats in which his plays published, 168n. 26; and the sale of his manuscripts, 166n. 20
corruption, threat of social: and cabarets, 45, 148n. 42; and print culture, 45, 49, 107, 124, 126
Council of Trent, and ecclesiastical censorship, 11–12
Counter-Reformation, 11; and the imposition of new sexual norms, 16, 19, 71, 98; and the print industry, 135n. 22
Courbet, Gustave, 73, 127, 129, 159nn. 44, 46
Couton, Georges, 95, 171n. 38, 178n. 80
Coxe, John, 82
Coypel, Charles, 112, 114
Critique de "L'Ecole des femmes," La (Molière), 100; aristocratic setting, 105; and Armande Béjart, 116; and *obscénité,* 100, 103–5, 117; use of punctuation in, 173–74n. 53
Cryle, Peter, 158–59n. 42

cuckoldry, 101, 118–19

culture, print. *See* print culture

culture, visual, 14–15, 136n. 29; censorship of, 136–37n. 30, 180nn. 8–9; and Italian sexually transgressive literature, 160n. 49; and the new definition of obscenity, 129–30, 162n. 63; regulation of, 126–27. *See also* images

Curll, Edmund, 114–15, 124–25

Dante Alighieri, 85

Darnton, Robert, 125, 139n. 42, 157n. 35, 175n. 63

Davis, Natalie Z., 164n. 7

death, representation of: linked to obscenity, 129–30; and photography, 181n. 14

decency, new standards for, 18–19, 30, 32, 46, 52, 54, 98, 119, 127–29, 135n. 20; linked to representations of sexuality, 55, 128–29. *See also* Counter-Reformation

DeJean, Joan, 141n. 6, 161n. 58

Delamare, Nicolas, 98, 137–38n. 36, 138–39n. 41, 170–71n. 35; and the creation of police law, 138–39n. 41

democratization, of knowledge, 22

demography, 49, 54; origins of, 76

Desanti, Jean-Toussaint, 134n. 16

Descartes, René, 143n. 14

desire: new vision of, 54–55; portrayal of female, 20, 180–81n. 13; portrayal of male, 20, 46–48, 55, 74, 128–29, 146n. 34. *See also* heterosexuality; homosexuality

Despois, Eugène, and Paul Mesnard, edition of Molière, 166–67n. 21

Diament, Nicole, 138n. 40

Dickens, Arthur, 11, 151n. 6

dictionaries: French historical, 132–33n. 8, 169n. 31; seventeenth-century French, 14, 98, 135n. 20, 138n. 40, 141n. 8, 163n. 4, 169n. 31. *See also* Furetière, Antoine; Richelet, Pierre

Dictionnaire de l'Académie Française, 98

Diderot, Denis, on censorship, 138n. 39

dildos, first marketed, 161n. 57. *See also* aid, sex

disease: contagious, 161n. 58; venereal, 45–46, 48–49

Dolet, Etienne, 53, 140n. 2; on punctuation, 143n. 14

Donaldson-Evans, Lance, 134n. 17

Donneau de Visé, Jean, 99, 110, 171–72n. 42; attacks on Molière, 100–101, 103, 106, 108, 119, 172nn. 43, 47, 174–75n. 62; biography of Molière, 108–10, 118, 172–73n. 49, 175n. 64, 178nn. 80–81, 178–79n. 83; income, 175n. 64;

as newsman, 176n. 66. *See also* newsmen; newspapers; tabloids

droits d'auteur, 162–63n. 2. *See also* authors, paid for the publication of their works

drunkenness, as libertine offense, 51

Dryden, John, 163–64n. 5

Dubost, Jean-Pierre, 136n. 29

Durand, Etienne, 140n. 2

Dury, Maxime, 139n. 43, 144n. 20

Dutton, Richard, 139–40n. 44, 170n. 34

Duvergier, Jean Baptiste, 180nn. 5–6

Ecole des femmes, L' (Molière): controversy surrounding, 19, 98–103, 172nn. 43–48; definition of a work's success, 174–75n. 62; definition of obscenity, 106; and *L'Ecole des filles*, 97, 102–3, 177n. 73; and female genitalia, 102–3, 111, 173n. 51–52; frontispiece, 111–13, 118, 120, 177n. 73; plot of, 104–5, 173n. 50; publication history, 171n. 38; and "the scene of the *the*," 102–3, 107, 173n. 51; set in a street, 106–7

Ecole des filles, L': authorship of, 62, 65, 151–52n. 9, 153–54n. 22; bourgeois setting of, 75, 77, 160nn. 49–50; censorship of, 63–66, 151–52n. 9, 153nn. 16, 20–21, 154n. 23, 162n. 64; and *L'Ecole des femmes*, 97; in England, 134n. 15, 151–52n. 9, 157n. 37, 159n. 46, 159–60n. 48, 161n. 57, 162nn. 63–65; as first work of modern obscenity, 27, 63, 72, 75, 154n. 23; focus on female genitalia in, 72–74, 76, 159n. 46; foreign editions of, 66, 69, 78, 82–83, 154–55n. 23; and the Fronde, 61, 77; history of its editions, 152n. 11, 154n. 23; manuscripts of, 152–53n. 15, 154–55n. 23; marketing of, 61; mutual sexual pleasure in, 76; names in, 172n. 46; new portrayal of female sexuality in, 72–73, 77, 159n. 46; as novel, 57, 66–67, 70; and Orthodox Bull, 153n. 19, 160n. 49; plot of, 70; publication format of, 157n. 36; readers, 153n. 17; related to confessors' manuals, 71; secularization of obscenity in, 77; tailored for bourgeois readers, 81; in translation, 159n. 46, 159–60n. 48; trial proceedings, 151n. 2

Edit du roi pour le règlement des imprimeurs et libraires de Paris, 153n. 18

editions: less expensive, 37; of Molière's works, 109–10

education, classical. *See* readers, elite male

Eisenstein, Elizabeth, 112, 131n. 3, 177n. 75

Elias, Norbert, 19, 39, 105, 128, 174nn. 56–57, 180n. 12

Eliot, George, 142–43n. 12
ellipsis, 15, 35–36, 42, 48, 142–43n. 12, 143n. 14, 144n. 15
Ellis, Havelock, 134n. 16
Elzivier, editions, 37, 143n. 14, 152n. 11, 165n. 14
England: censorship in, 139–40n. 44, 151n. 3; censorship of obscene publications in, 12, 82–83, 124–25, 155n. 24, 156n. 31, 157n. 35, 179n. 85; censorship of the stage in, 97; numbers of master printers in, 165n. 13; and obscenity law, 14, 69, 82, 155n. 24, 179n. 85; production of pornography in, 57, 66; regulation of print culture in, 56–57, 152n. 10. *See also* war, English civil
engravings: cost of, in publications, 144n. 18; obscene, 180nn. 5, 8; and sexually transgressive literature, 144n. 18. *See also* frontispieces
erotica, French, visual, 136n. 29
Estivals, Robert, 139n. 43
ethics. See *obscenity,* relation to ethical issues

Fabricius, Johannes, 49, 146–47n. 36
farce, 116, 118, 169n. 31
Farrell, Joseph, 163n. 3, 177n. 75
Febvre, Lucien, with Henri-Jean Martin, 141n. 5, 152n. 10, 156n. 32, 164n. 7, 165n. 12, 175n. 63, 177n. 74
Feinberg, Joel, 159n. 44, 181n. 17
Findlen, Paula, 132n. 7, 136n. 29, 159n. 47, 160n. 49
Flaubert, Gustave, 3; trial, 30, 126–27, 180n. 6
fonts, print, 147n. 38, 165n. 13; marking, to aid censorship, 89
Ford, Philip, 155n. 27
formats, publication: large, 68, 168n. 26; less expensive, 131–32n. 4, 156n. 32, 157n. 36, 168n. 26; small, 3, 68–69, 94, 111, 124, 156n. 33, 157n. 36
Foucault, Michel: on the author's function, 26–27, 65, 85, 109, 112; on the history of sexuality, 19, 48, 76, 146nn. 31, 34, 158n. 39; and the incitement to discourse, 20, 71, 76, 158n. 41; on the repression of discourse on sexuality, 138n. 37, 161n. 55
Fouquet, Nicolas, 78, 89, 153n. 17, 161n. 59, 165n. 11
Foxon, David, 57, 134–35n. 19, 154n. 23, 156n. 31, 159n. 46
France: censorship in, 16, 40–43, 97; circulation of images in, 14; ecclesiastical censorship in, 12, 29, 32; failure to dominate the European print industry, 156–57n. 34; as multiconfessional country, 11; and the pro-
duction of obscene images, 14; and the production of obscene literature, 2, 5, 14, 67, 155n. 24; state sponsorship of the arts in, 86–87; and style, 5
freethinking, in France, 43–44, 51, 140–41n. 3, 145n. 27
French language: as international cultural language, 94–95, 110, 156–57n. 34, 176–77n. 71; as language of the cultural elite, 131–32n. 4; plays staged outside of France in, 176–77n. 71; printing outside of France in, 165n. 12
Fronde, the, 56–57, 60, 153n. 20, 161n. 58; effects on literature, 58, 150–51n. 1, 155n. 26, 162–63n. 2; and print culture, 57, 61, 77, 88, 151n. 7
fronder, 171n. 39
frontispieces: engravers of, 152n. 13; first obscene, 162n. 63; Molière's, 110–11, 115, 120, 177nn. 72–73; in sexually transgressive books, 37, 62, 80–81, 144n. 18, 161–62n. 61, 162n. 63. *See also* Chauveau, François
Funck-Bretano, Frantz, 165n. 11, 175n. 64
Furetière, Antoine, dictionary, 141n. 8, 145–46n. 30, 163n. 4, 174n. 61, 176n. 68. *See also* dictionaries, seventeenth-century French

Gallagher, Catherine, 163–64n. 5
Garasse, Father François: fear of social promiscuity, 148n. 42, 149n. 44; and four-letter words, 36; on Latin sexually transgressive poetry, 147n. 37; and *obscénité,* 13, 45; on print culture's threat, 147n. 38; on sodomy, 147–48n. 41; and Théophile's prosecution, 44, 48–49, 52, 145nn. 25, 27, 149n. 46
gaulois, le, 33, 37, 55, 119, 142n. 9; defined, 141n. 8; tolerated, 37
Gawthrop, Richard, 135n. 23
genitalia: female, 20, 47, 54, 71–74, 76, 102, 105, 111, 118, 128–29, 138n. 38, 145–46n. 30, 150n. 50, 158n. 41, 158–59n. 42, 173n. 52; male, 34, 47, 54, 128, 130, 150n. 50; presence in obscene images of, 127–28, 136n. 29, 159nn. 44, 46; presence in obscene literature of, 53, 72–73, 159nn. 43, 45
genres, new literary: creation of more domestic and interior, 57, 66–67, 80–81; intended for readers without classical training, 131–32n. 4. *See also* novel, the modern
Ginzburg, Carlo, 14, 136n. 28
Godefroy, Frédéric, 132n. 8, 134n. 17
Godenne, René, 175n. 63
Goulemot, Jean, 136n. 29, 137n. 33, 143n. 14, 153n. 19, 154n. 23

Graham, James, 181n. 16
Guéret, Gabriel, 172–73n. 49, 174–75n. 62
Guibert, A. J., 115, 166–67n. 21, 167–68n. 25, 176nn. 67, 69
Guibert, Pierre, 51–52, 149n. 43

Habert, Father Louis, 71, 137–38n. 36, 158n. 39
hair, pubic, representations of, 159n. 44
Hall, H. G., 170n. 33
Halperin, David, 161n. 56
heretics, execution of, 31
Herzel, Roger, 106–7
Hesse, Carla, 167–68n. 25
heterosexuality: imposition of, 46, 54, 77, 129, 146–47n. 36, 159n. 45; and readerships, 128–29. *See also* sexuality
Hoffmann, George, 152n. 12
homoeroticism, 46, 74; fear of, 147–48n. 41; prosecution of representations of, 46, 54
homosexuality, 47, 52, 74; female, 159n. 46, 180–81n. 13; origins of term, 4. *See also* sexuality
Hôtel de Bourgogne, theater, 100, 169n. 29, 172nn. 43, 48
Hunt, Lynn, 131n. 2, 134–35n. 19, 135n. 25, 138nn. 37, 39
Hyde, H. Montgomery, 180n. 6

images: and Catholicism, 135–36n. 27, 180n. 9; censorship of, 126–27, 180nn. 8–9; circulation of, 14, 136n. 29; "dirty," 136n. 29; and literary obscenity in France, 136n. 29, 160n. 49, 162n. 63; obscene, 14, 126–27, 129–30, 135–36n. 27, 136n. 29, 180nn. 5, 8–10; and print culture, 14, 127–28; and Protestantism, 135–36n. 27; serially reproducible, 135–36n. 27, 136nn. 28–29, 180n. 8. *See also* frontispieces; Pompeii
I Modi, 9–10, 14, 134n. 18, 134–35n. 19, 136n. 28; portrays ordinary men and women, 160n. 50
Imprimerie Royale, L', 155–56n. 30
Impromptu de Versailles, L' (Molière), 100, 118–19, 172n. 45
incest, rumors of, 119–20, 178n. 82, 178–79n. 83. *See also* Molière, private life invaded
Index of Forbidden Books: and censorship, 31; first edition of, 11; in France, 31; and images, 135–36n. 27
individuality: loss of, 115; of portraits, 112, 115
Inquisition, the, 30, 138n. 39
interiority, in literature, 57, 80–81
Isambert, François-André, 138n. 40
Italy: censorship in, 8–9, 14; circulation of images in Renaissance, 14, 135–36n. 27, 136n. 29; obscene literature in, 8, 134–35n. 19, 135n. 25, 136n. 29

Jansenism, and print culture, 60, 62
Jean de Meun, 8, 85, 133n. 13, 138n. 38
Johns, Adrian, 139–40n. 44, 177n. 75
Jones, Ann, 164n. 7
Joubert, Laurent, 9
Jouhaud, Christian, 141n. 4, 142n. 10, 145n. 25, 146–47n. 36, 151n. 7
journalism: and authorship, 85, 108; development of, 27; European, 85; tabloid, 27. *See also* newspapers
Jubert, Gérard, 147–48n. 41
Julia, Dominique, 135n. 22

Kamen, Henry, 138n. 39
Kendrick, Walter, 54–55, 138n. 37, 146nn. 32–33, 159n. 47, 160n. 52, 161n. 61, 178n. 79; and the invention of pornography, 15, 131n. 2, 132n. 5, 136–37n. 30
knowledge, democratization of, 22
Krakovitch, Odile, 170–71n. 35

La Barre, Chevalier de, 125–26; as reader of obscene publications, 126
La Bruyère, Jean de, 87, 171–72n. 42
LaCapra, Dominick, 180n. 6
Lachèvre, Frédéric, 157n. 35; on Claude Le Petit, 165n. 15; on *L'Ecole des filles,* 62–63, 151n. 2, 152n. 14, 153–54n. 22; on *Parnasse satirique,* 141n. 7, 142n. 9; on Théophile's sexuality, 146n. 35; on Théophile's trial, 43, 136n. 29, 141n. 6, 144n. 22, 147–48n. 41
La Croix, Philippe de, 101, 172n. 48
La Fontaine, Jean de, 87, 175n. 63, 180n. 8
La Grange, sieur de, *Registre,* 163–64n. 5, 169n. 29, 176n. 69, 177n. 76
Lapeire, Paul, 134n. 17, 149n. 45, 151n. 4
La Reynie, Nicolas de, 122–23, 138–39n. 41; appointed head of Parisian police, 22, 88, 138n. 40; as censor, 138n. 39, 170–71n. 35, 179n. 1; duties as head of police, 165n. 13, 179n. 84
Larson, Ruth, 161–62n. 62, 170n. 33
Latin: as international language of print culture, 67; as language for acceptable sexually transgressive publications, 155n. 27, 156n. 31; obscene vocabulary in translation, 5, 9; publication in, 68, 155n. 28, 155–56n. 30, 156n. 31; vocabulary of obscenity, 3, 5–6, 134n. 16. *See also* literature, Roman; Rome, ancient

Lawner, Lynne, 134n. 18
Lawrence, D. H., 2, 27, 124; and *Lady Chatterley's Lover*, 51–52, 80, 105, 180n. 6; on "survivals," 174n. 55
Lecompte, Henry, 117, 177–78n. 77
Le Maire, Nicolas, 12, 16
Le Petit, Claude, 62, 90–91, 149–50n. 49,
165nn. 15–17, 166n. 18
Le Roy Ladurie, Emmanuel, 181n. 17
lesbianism, representations of. *See* homosexuality, female
Lettres provinciales (Pascal), 151n. 6
Lewinsky, Monica, 1, 127, 180n. 10
Liaisons dangereuses, Les (Laclos), 15, 105
libel, obscene, 118–19, 157n. 35, 161n. 60
libelle, 157n. 35
libellus, 157n. 35
libraires. *See* booksellers
life, everyday, and modern obscene literature,
75, 77, 160n. 49
life, private, 115–16, 118–20, 133n. 10, 178n. 79
literature: feminocentric, 57; as religious
threat, 31
literature, Roman, influence on early modern
sexually transgressive poetry, 10, 47–48, 57–
58, 142n. 9, 146nn. 31–32. *See also* Catullus,
Gaius Valerius; Latin; Rome, ancient
literature, sexually transgressive, 3, 47, 133n. 9;
and authorship, 85; censorship of, 6, 10, 85,
124–25; for elite readers, 37, 133n. 9, 153n. 17;
reinvented, 57, 72, 85; in Rome, 160nn. 52–
53, 163n. 3; secularized, 50, 75, 77; uncontrolled circulation, 51–52, 145n. 29, 149nn.
44–45; vernacular, 58
livres philosophiques, 125
Loiselet, Jean-Louis, 163–64n. 5, 169n. 29
Longino, Helen, 160n. 53
Loret, Jean, 171n. 40
Lough, John, 131–32n. 4, 163n. 5, 175n. 63
Louis XIII: and censorship, 40, 59; and state
sponsorship of the arts, 164n. 8
Louis XIV: and Paris, 174n. 60, 176n. 70; reforms initiated by, 22, 85, 87, 174n. 60; and
state sponsorship of the arts, 87, 164n. 8;
support of Molière, 119, 171n. 40; and Versailles, 27, 100, 172n. 45
Louÿs, Pierre, 136n. 29
lust, in manuals for confessors, 158n. 39
Luther, Martin, 11, 164n. 7
Lutheranism: in France, 11; and print culture,
11, 60, 135n. 23
Luyne, Guillaume de, 109, 166–67n. 21, 171n.
38

Mahelot, Laurent, 174n. 58
Mainil, Jean, 155n. 29
Maintenon, Françoise d'Aubignac, Madame
de, 62
Manet, Edouard, 15, 127
manuscripts: approval of by censors, 11; sold by
writers, 162–63n. 2, 166n. 20, 175n. 63
Mapplethorpe, Robert, 15, 127
Marais theater, 170–71n. 35
marketing, literary, 120, 151–52n. 9, 157–58n. 38
marketplace, literary, 101, 175n. 63; centered on
Paris, 162–63n. 2. *See also* authors, and the
sales of their manuscripts; value, literary
markets, literary, mass, 3, 131–32n. 4, 151–52n.
9, 156n. 31
Martial (Marcus Valerius Martialis), 6, 9, 47,
57, 158–59n. 42, 163n. 3
Martin, Henri Jean, 88, 135n. 24, 144n. 19, 151n.
8, 155n. 28, 155–56n. 30, 156–57n. 34; on the
Parisian book trade, 166–67n. 21; on the
sales of manuscripts by authors, 175n. 63; on
the typography of *L'Ecole des femmes*, 173–
74n. 53
masculinity, definitions of, 128–29
masturbation, and reading, 153n. 19
Maugin, Edouard, 139n. 43
mauvais livres, 18, 123, 179n. 1
Mazarin, Cardinal Jules, and regulation of
print culture, 61, 87
Mellot, Jean-Dominique, 139n. 44
memorial reconstruction, 93, 109, 167n. 23
Mercure galant, Le, 99, 176n. 66
middle class, the, relation to modern literary
obscenity, 75, 78–79, 106, 111. *See also* bourgeoisie, the
Mignard, Nicolas, 112–13, 177n. 76
Milesius, Antoine, 132n. 8
Millanges, Simon, 9, 134n. 17, 143n. 14
Millot, Michel, 62, 64, 153n. 21, 153–54n. 22
Milton, John, 162n. 1
Molière, Jean-Baptiste Poquelin de: advertising his plays, 176n. 66; author's name, 94,
109–10, 167–68n. 25, 176n. 67; biography,
108–9, 115–16, 120, 178n. 78, 178–79n. 83;
box office receipts, 171n. 36; career, 85, 87,
91–97, 100; central figure in the French tradition, 85, 121; and collaboration, 84; collected works, 109–10, 120, 176nn. 67, 69;
comic style, 169n. 31; compared with
Shakespeare, 84–87, 95, 163–64n. 5; confrontation with censorship, 19, 65, 85, 88, 97,
107, 122, 164n. 9, 168n. 27, 171n. 36, 174–75n.
62; and cuckoldry, 101, 118–19; definition of

Molière, Jean-Baptiste Poquelin de
(*continued*)
literary value, 172–73n. 49, 174–75n. 62; definitions of obscenity, 105, 173n. 52; as director
of troupe, 93, 100; and double-entendres,
174n. 54; and *L'Ecole des femmes*, 88, 95–101,
172nn. 43–48; and *L'Ecole des filles*, 170n. 33;
and *L'Ecole des maris*, 93, 95, 167–68n. 25,
168n. 27, 177n. 72; and *Le Festin de pierre*
(Dom Juan), 88, 98, 122, 164n. 9, 167n. 23,
179n. 2; as first modern writer, 27, 84, 87,
109, 120–21, 162–63n. 2, 163–64n. 5, 167–
68n. 25; and the French court, 95, 100, 119,
164n. 6, 168–69n. 28, 171n. 40, 172n. 45;
helped create censorship of the stage, 170–
71n. 35; income, 86–87, 94, 101, 108, 163–
64n. 5, 169n. 29, 169–70n. 32, 175nn. 63, 64;
internationally known, 85, 95, 109–10, 165n.
14, 176–77n. 71; marketability, 109–10, 120,
175n. 63, 176–77n. 71; and memorial reconstruction, 167n. 23; and a new esthetic for
French comedy, 169n. 30; and *obscénité*, 13,
91, 100, 102–3, 117, 121, 173–74n. 53; obscenity as foundation of his authority, 3, 27, 84,
96–98, 110, 120–21; and patronage, 95; and
pirated editions of his works, 165n. 14, 166–
67n. 21; portrait, 112–16, 118, 120, 177n. 76,
177–78n. 77; and *Les Précieuses ridicules*,
166–67n. 21; as print author, 85–87, 92, 96,
162n. 1, 163–64n. 5, 166n. 19, 173–74n. 53;
private life invaded, 115–16, 118–19, 178nn.
79–82; and the publication of his manuscripts, 95, 175n. 63; and the punctuation of
his plays, 173–74n. 53; and the sale of his
plays, 163–64n. 5, 164n. 9, 175n. 63; and *s'encanailler*, 107, 174n. 61; sought to preserve
the orality of his works, 166n. 19, 166–67n.
21; as stage author, 86, 96; and state sponsorship, 96, 100, 169–70n. 32; and *Le
Tartuffe*, 80, 87, 106, 122, 170–71n. 35, 174–
75n. 62, 176–77n. 71; translations of
his works, 176–77n. 71. *See also* authors; *Critique de "L'Ecole des Femmes," La*; *Ecole des
femmes, L'*; *Impromptu de Versailles, L'*
Montaigne, Michel de, 85, 134n. 17, 152n. 12
Montfleury, Antoine Jacob, 101, 108, 112, 119,
170n. 33, 172n. 48, 175n. 63, 178–79n. 83; and
obscénité, 173–74n. 53; play set in a bookseller's shop, 174n. 54
Montgrédien, Georges, 172nn. 43, 46, 173–74n.
53, 174–75n. 62; on Molière's private life,
178n. 82
Montpensier, Anne-Louis d'Orléans,
duchesse de, 77, 153n. 20, 171n. 41

Mortimer, Ruth, 177n. 75
Moulton, Ian, 159–60n. 48
Moxon, John, 143n. 14
Müller, C. O., 136–37n. 30

name, author's, 94, 109. *See also* Foucault,
Michel, on the author's function; Molière,
author's name
nationalism, and print culture, 155n. 28. *See also*
Anderson, Benedict
Netherlands, the: controversial French books
printed in, 89–90, 151–52n. 9; newspapers
in, 171–72n. 42; plays staged in French in,
176–77n. 71; print culture in, 89, 165n. 12
Netz, Robert, 139n. 43, 180n. 6
Neuf-Villaine, Sieur de, 93, 167nn. 22–23
Newman, Jane, 135n. 21
news: in newspapers, 5, 21, 99; and obscenity,
108
newsmen, 21, 99, 101, 108, 120, 171–72n. 42;
changed Molière's biography, 118–20; as
prisoners in the Bastille, 175n. 64; and
"scoops," 22, 100, 172n. 43
newspapers: coverage of writers, 32, 99, 101,
108, 119–20, 140–41n. 3, 176–77n. 71; in Europe, 171–72n. 42; in France, 22, 108, 171n.
40, 171–72n. 42, 172n. 46; and photography,
130; and sexually transgressive literature, 58.
See also journalism
Nochlin, Linda, 159n. 44
nouvelle, 21, 99, 171n. 41
novel, the: appealed to new readerships, 16, 80;
modern, 57, 66–67, 81, 171n. 41, 172n. 44; and
the new literary economy, 175n. 63; and
pornography, 66

obscene: etymology, 134n. 16; history of the
word, 7, 132n. 7, 134n. 15; meaning of, 2, 6;
new usage in English, 76, 82, 125, 129–30,
131n. 1, 181nn. 16–18; used during the Renaissance, 8; used in censorship, 180n. 6
obscène: in French censorship, 126–27, 180n. 7;
in French today, 181n. 17; history of the
word, 10, 132n. 8, 135n. 20, 145–46n. 30; related to photography, 181n. 14
obscene, the, 173–74n. 53; as censorable category, 3, 55, 104, 123, 125; meaning in Latin, 6,
49; in the Middle Ages, 133–34n. 13; religious connotations, 49; status of, in the seventeenth century, 131n. 2; as transcultural
concept, 6
obscénité: and censorship, 100, 103–4, 180n. 7;
early usage, 5, 13, 45, 55, 123–24, 179n. 2;
Molière's use of, 15, 19, 100, 103, 105, 107,

173–74n. 53; and print, 15, 49, 53; relation to modern authorial status, 27; in the seventeenth century, 3, 5, 13–14

obscenities, primary, 9, 15, 34–35, 48, 71, 76, 105, 143n. 14, 149–50n. 49; and body parts, 42–43, 102–3, 138n. 38, 142n. 11; in English, 137n. 31; identified with modern literary obscenity, 53, 71, 76; in Latin, 137n. 31; lifting of taboo against, 180n. 10; when printable, 174n. 57. *See also* body, the

obscenity, 8; evolution of the term, 5, 46, 129–30; history of the word, 7, 123–25, 132n. 7; relation to ethical issues, 2, 129–30. See also *obscénité*

obscenity, literary: in antiquity, 132n. 6; and authorial status, 2, 8, 85, 99, 109, 120, 133n. 10; and body parts, 11, 49–50, 54, 71, 111; censorship of, 8, 16, 82–83, 123–24, 162n. 64, 179n. 85; circulation of, 27, 45, 52, 78–79, 107, 148n. 42; created in relation to censorship, 17, 23, 46, 51–52; as crime, 30, 124; definition of modern, 3, 20, 32, 54–55, 72, 75, 99, 107, 111, 159n. 46; as destabilizing force, 46, 81; in English law, 12, 82–83, 119, 124–25, 155n. 24, 162n. 64, 180n. 6; and ethical issues, 130; and female genitalia, 72–74, 102–3, 105, 111, 118, 159n. 46; and four-letter words, 72, 82–83; and French culture, 27; history of censorship of, 7, 12, 17, 30, 126–27; in Italy, 132n. 7, 135n. 25; legal history of, 24, 30, 69, 82–83, 121, 124–27, 155n. 24, 157n. 35, 179n. 85; as legal problem, 23, 83, 124–26, 136–37n. 30; and medical discourse, 143n. 14, 155n. 29; in the Middle Ages, 7–8, 133nn. 12–13; and the middle class, 75, 77, 79–81, 106; and modernity, 27, 59, 104, 107, 123; and Molière's portrait, 120; and the private lives of authors, 117–18, 120; produced for elite readers, 14, 17, 37, 63; produced in England, 135n. 24; produced in France, 135n. 25; prosecuted on religious grounds, 43, 125–27; reinvention of, 3, 54, 77, 124, 132n. 7, 133–34n. 13, 174n. 56; in the Renaissance, 8, 14, 132n. 7; Roman, 6, 49, 72, 111, 132n. 6; and sexual orientation, 32, 48–49, 51–52, 54–55, 128–29; as sin, 13, 30; and small publication formats, 69; as speech crime, 13, 45, 123; as threat to society, 3, 49, 107; and visual culture, 14–15, 126–28, 130, 136nn. 28–29, 180nn. 5–10, 180–81n. 13, 181nn. 14–15; and witnessing, 181n. 17

Olympia (Manet), 15

opinion, public, 98

Origine du monde, L' (Courbet), 73–74, 111, 127, 129, 159n. 44

Ovid (Publius Ovidius Naso), 2, 7, 85, 133n. 10, 133n. 13, 177n. 75

Palais-Royal, theater, 95, 163–64n. 5, 169n. 29

paper: poor quality, used to print obscene books, 37; recycling of books to make new, 153n. 21; taxes on, 89

Paris: Benjamin's view of, 4–5; as cultural capital, 4; in *L'Ecole des femmes*, 106–7; foreign visitors to, 110, 176n. 70; in the 1660s, 4, 107, 174n. 60; as setting for plays, 106–7, 168n. 27, 174n. 59; theaters in, 163–64n. 5

Parliament, the Parisian: authority over censorship, 13, 30, 123, 170–71n. 35; prosecution of *Parnasse satirique*, 43; prosecution of printers, 43; prosecution of Théophile, 50–51

parliaments, provincial, and censorship, 135n. 26, 140–41n. 3

Parnasse des poètes satiriques, Le, 33–37, 141n. 7; badly printed, 144n. 17; later editions of, 149n. 49; publication history of, 142n. 9; punctuation in, 144nn. 15–16, 149–50n. 49; why prosecuted, 39–40, 142n. 10

Pastoureau, Michel, 152n. 13

patronage, literary, 86

Peignot, Gabriel, 180n. 5

Pepys, Samuel: diary, 2, 78–79; early reader of literary obscenity, 27, 78–79, 159n. 45; on *L'Ecole des filles*, 154n. 23, 161n. 58

permission, 25, 139n. 43

photography: linked to obscenity, 181nn. 14–15; of war dead, 129–30, 181n. 14–15

Pia, Pascal, 33, 141–42n. 8

Picard, Raymond, 167–68n. 25, 169n. 29, 169–70n. 32

Pintard, René, 140–41n. 3

Piot, Louis, 62–63, 152n. 13

piracy, print, 93

Pizan, Christine de, 8, 98, 134n. 14, 138n. 38; precursor of feminists against pornography, 160n. 53

Plato, 76; on the danger of the theater, 7, 133n. 11

police, 5, 21–22, 138n. 40

police, modern: and the city's orderly functioning, 5, 107, 174n. 60; creation of, 5, 22; evolution of the concept, 22, 138n. 40; and the theater, 98, 170–71n. 35; use of portraits, 179n. 84. *See also* book police; La Reynie, Nicolas de

Pompeii, and sexually transgressive visual artifacts, 15, 136–37n. 30

population, concept of a, 77

pornographie, 5, 132n. 7, 136–37n. 30

pornography, 15, 75, 131n. 2, 132nn. 5, 7, 136–37n. 30

pornography: attempts to censor, 160n. 53; circulation of, 69, 74, 79–80, 128; definitions of, 75–76, 160n. 53; demand for, 57, 70, 74; explosion in the production of in the nineteenth century, 138n. 37; "feminist," 180–81n. 13; focus on female genitalia in, 72–74, 159n. 43; origins of, 131n. 2, 159n. 45; produced in England, 57, 66, 124, 132n. 7; produced in France, 57; tradition of, 66

portraits: in antiquity, 177n. 75; authors', 85, 112, 177n. 75; characters', 111–12; individualized, 112; Molière's, 85, 110, 111–15, 120; and obscenity, 120; self-, 177n. 75; use of by the police, 179n. 84

Pot, Olivier, 179n. 2

Pottinger, David, 23, 139–40n. 44, 167n. 24

press, modern, creation of, 5, 171–72n. 42. *See also* newspapers; tabloids

presses, printing, attempts to limit number of, 61–62

print culture: and authorship, 86–87, 94, 98; and the bourgeoisie, 81, 111, 177n. 74; involvement with censorship, 2, 4, 21, 89, 98; nationalization of, 69; and national languages, 67; obscenity and, 8, 45, 98–99; and social corruption, 45, 49–52, 174n. 58; and the standardization of texts, 112, 177n. 75; vernacular, 151n. 6. *See also* contamination, threat of social; obscenity, literary

printers: attempts to limit number of, 38, 61, 89, 152n. 10, 165n. 13; function of in France, 135n. 24; held responsible by censors, 17, 53, 140n. 2, 167n. 24; income, 163–64n. 5; responsible for the punctuation of authors' works, 35–36, 143nn. 13–14, 162n. 1, 173–74n. 53; shops in Paris, 152n. 10. *See also* booksellers

privacy. *See* life, private

privilege, 100; and censorship, 63–64, 121; history of the, 25–26, 39, 93, 139n. 43; Molière's understanding of the, 92–94, 166–67n. 21, 167–68n. 25, 171n. 38; obtained by authors in their name, 167–68n. 25; as regulatory principle, 65, 89; "tacit," 139–40n. 44

projects, publication, costs of, 156n. 32. *See also* formats, publication

promiscuity: sexual, 49–52; social, 148n. 42, 174n. 58. *See also* circulation, literary, uncontrolled; contamination, threat of social; *s'encanailler*

property, literary, 109; authors', 120; linked to propriety, 120

propriety, 120

prose, used in sexually transgressive literature, 66, 155n. 25

Protestantism: attempts to hinder spread via censorship, 38–40; and the censorship of images, 135–36n. 27; in France, 31; invasion of French print culture in the sixteenth century, 141n. 5, 155–56n. 30; and print culture, 31, 37–38, 145n. 27

pubic hair, representations of, 159n. 44

publication: in French, 155–56n. 30; in Latin in France, 68, 155n. 28, 155–56n. 30; religious, 155–56n. 30

publicity, 21

publics, for literature, 18; new, 51–52, 54, 57, 67, 69–70, 131–32n. 4, 149n. 44. *See also* readers

publishers. *See* booksellers

punctuation: and Molière's use of *obscénité*, 105; and primary obscenities, 15, 34, 36, 142n. 11, 142–43n. 12; printers responsible for, 143n. 13. *See also* ellipsis

Quinet, Gabriel, 173–74n. 53

Rabelais, François, 8, 19–20, 53, 57; censorship of, 18, 134n. 17

Racine, Jean, 94, 119, 169n. 30, 177n. 72, 178n. 82; income, 163–64n. 5, 169–70n. 32

Raimondi, Marcantonio, 9, 140n. 1, 161–62n. 62. *See also* Aretino, Pietro; *I Modi*

Rambouillet, Catherine de Vivonne, Marquise de, 162n. 63

Ranum, Orest, 164n. 8

Ravaisson-Mollien, François, 165–66n. 17, 179n. 1

readers: anonymous, 14, 131n. 3; bourgeois, 15, 57, 69, 78–79, 81, 131–32n. 4, 137n. 32, 154n. 23; elite male, 3, 17, 37, 47, 57, 78, 133n. 9, 153n. 17; female, 16, 20, 27, 57, 79–81, 131–32n. 4, 161n. 61; French seventeenth-century, 131–32n. 4, 157–58n. 38; lower-class, 4, 37, 51–52, 54, 57, 149nn. 44–45; male, 128–29; of newspapers, 99; numbers of, 157–58n. 38; of pornography, 74; solitary, 4, 131n. 3; worldly, 156n. 33

Rebuffé, Eustache, 91

reconstruction, memorial, 93, 109, 167n. 23

Reformation, the, 11, 135n. 21

reproduction, mechanical, 9

Rétif de la Bretonne, Nicolas, 136n. 30

Rey, Alain, 134n. 16

Rey-Flaud, Bernadette, 169n. 30
Ribou, Jean, 92–93, 166–67n. 21, 167n. 22, 171n. 38
Richardson, Samuel, 57
Richelet, Pierre, 179n. 2
Richelieu, Armand du Plessis, Cardinal de, and the regulation of print culture, 60–61, 87, 151n. 5
Richlin, Amy, 6, 19, 46, 49, 137n. 31, 146nn. 32, 34, 146–47n. 36, 147n. 37, 155n. 25, 160nn. 52–53; on double-entendres, 174n. 54; obscenity and the writer's private life, 178n. 79; on the treatment of female genitalia in Roman sexually transgressive literature, 72, 158–59n. 42; on women's lack of sexual desire in Latin literature, 161n. 56
Riddle, John, 160–61n. 54
rights, publication, 120. *See also* authors, and the sales of their manuscripts
Robic-de Baecque, Sylvie, 137–38n. 36
Robinet, Charles, 101, 105, 108, 110, 169n. 29, 175n. 63; as newsman, 172n. 46
Roche, Daniel, 137–38n. 36, 138–39n. 41, 139n. 42, 141n. 5, 165n. 13
Rochemont, sieur de, 179n. 2
Roeder, George, 181n. 15
Roman de la Rose, quarrel of, 8, 133–34n. 13
Romano, Giulio, 9
Rome, ancient: censorship in, 6, 135n. 22; comedy in, 118; portrayal of desire in, 20, 47–48, 111; taboo regarding portrayal of female genitalia, 158–59n. 42; toleration of sexually transgressive literature in, 6–7, 133n. 9. *See also* genitalia, female; Latin; literature, Roman
Ronsard, Pierre de, 8
Rou, Jean, 166n. 18
Roullé, Abbé Pierre, 170–71n. 35
ruelle, 162n. 63

Sade, Donatien Alphonse François, Marquis de, 159n. 43
Saint-Germain, Jacques, 138nn. 39, 40, 153n. 21, 174n. 60, 179n. 84
satire, political, in obscene literature, 74
Saturnalia, and obscenity, 6
Saugrain, Claude Marie, 179–80n. 4
Sauman, Alfred, 139n. 43
Saunders, David, 156n. 31, 179n. 85
Sauvy, Anne, 137n. 33, 138n. 39, 154–55n. 23
Scarron, Paul, 62, 67, 161n. 59, 173n. 50, 174n. 57
Schlafly, Phyllis, 76–77
Scudéry, Georges de, 145n. 24

Scudéry, Madeleine de, 66, 155n. 26, 171n. 41, 175n. 63
scurrilité, 169n. 31
Séguier, Pierre, 60, 91–92, 165–66n. 17
s'encanailler, 107, 174n. 61. *See also* contamination, threat of social; promiscuity, social
Sévigné, Marie de Rabutin-Chantal, Marquise de, 161nn. 58, 60
sex aids, 77, 82, 161n. 57
sexuality: history of scientific discourse on, 76; modern discourse of, 72; phallic representations of, 37, 47, 146n. 34, 150n. 50; portrayal of female, 20, 72–73, 76–77, 159n. 46; portrayal of male, 20, 146n. 34, 150n. 50, 159n. 46; public policy on the policing of, 77; secularization of, 17, 77
Shakespeare, William, 84–85, 87–88, 162n. 1, 163–64n. 5
Siegert, Bernhard, 143n. 14
Smet, Ingrid de, 155n. 27
sodomy, 46, 49, 52, 147–48n. 41, 149n. 47
Sonetti Lussuriosi (Aretino), 10, 29
Sorbonne, the, and censorship, 12, 39–40, 59, 123, 139n. 43, 151n. 3
Sorel, Charles, 53, 150n. 50
sponsorship, state, of the arts, 86–87, 96, 162n. 2, 164n. 6; sums received, 169–70n. 32
status, authorial: recognition of, 27, 85, 96, 133n. 10; related to obscenity law, 179n. 85
status, social: lack of, 52, 174n. 61; Théophile's, 52. See also *s'encanailler*
Steinberg, Leo, 142–43n. 12
Steinem, Gloria, 76, 160n. 53
Stone, Lawrence, 161n. 57
streets: in Molière's theater, 106–7, 174n. 58; Parisian, 107, 174n. 60
syphilis, 49, 146–47n. 36

tabloids, 27, 118–20
taboos, sexual: imposition of, 18–19, 46, 174n. 56; and obscenity, 10, 98, 135n. 20; shifting, 39, 98, 119, 128. *See also* decency, new standards for
Talvacchia, Bette, 18, 135–36n. 27, 136n. 28, 160n. 50
Tamizey de Larroque, Philippe, 165–66n. 17
Tanner, Tony, 170n. 34
Tenain, Madame de, 158n. 41
theaters, Parisian, 163–64n. 5, 169n. 29. *See also* Hôtel de Bourgogne, theater; Marais theater; Palais-Royal, theater
Thomas, Alan, 153n. 19

Thomas, Donald, 134n. 15, 142n. 9, 154n. 23, 157n. 35
Thompson, Roger, 82, 142n. 9
Trachtenberg, Alan, 181n. 14
trials: obscenity, 7, 121; press coverage of, 22, 32; Théophile de Viau's, 29, 32–34, 50–51; writers', 4, 10, 17, 23–24, 54–55, 63–65. *See also Ecole des filles, L'*; Le Petit, Claude; Viau, Théophile de
Trumbach, Randolf, 159n. 45

value, literary: new definition of, 101, 108–9; produced by obscenity, 108–9; tied to market concerns, 115. *See also* authors, and the sales of their manuscripts
Van de Walle, Etienne, 160–61n. 54
Vanini, Giulio, 140n. 3
Vergil (Publius Vergilius Maro), 163n. 3
Veyrin-Forrer, Jeanne, 145n. 26, 166–67n. 21
Viala, Alain, 135n. 22, 139–40n. 44, 157–58n. 38, 162–63n. 2, 164nn. 7–8; and privileges, 167–68n. 25
Viau, Théophile de, 13; author's name, 144n. 22; censorship of, 29, 43–44, 126; circulation of sexually transgressive images stopped by the trial of, 136n. 29; conversion, 31, 141n. 4; defense, 146n. 32, 147n. 40, 147–48n. 41, 149nn. 47–48; manuscript of trial proceedings, 147–48n. 41, 148n. 42; and the *Parnasse satirique*, 36; *Première journée*, 43, 145n. 24; in prison, 147n. 39; and the punctuation of primary obscenities, 143n. 13; sexuality, 32, 48, 145n. 25, 146n. 35, 146–47n. 36, 147–48n.

41; the "sodomite" sonnet, 27, 40–41, 43, 45–46, 48, 52, 147n. 38, 149n. 46; and syphilis, 146–47n. 36; trial, 22, 29, 32–34, 39, 50–53, 144n. 22, 147n. 40, 149n. 43
Vietnam, coverage of war in, 130; linked to *obscenity*'s evolution, 130, 181n. 17
Visconti, Primi, 179n. 2
Voltaire (François Marie Arouet), 125
voyeurism, 136n. 29, 160n. 49

war: English civil, 56–57, 88, 150–51n. 1, 164–65n. 10; and photography, 129–30; and print culture, 56–57, 82; related to *obscenity*, 129–30. *See also* Vietnam
Williams, Raymond, 132n. 5
women: access to pornography, 161n. 61; as authors of sexually transgressive literature, 158n. 41; as narrators of dialogues about love and sexuality, 76, 158n. 41, 161n. 56; portrayed as having control over their sexuality, 77, 81; portrayed in obscene literature as having a right to pleasure, 77; as readers of sexually transgressive literature, 79–80; writers who lived from their pen, 163–64n. 5. *See also* genitalia, female; sexuality, portrayal of female
words: "dirty," 1, 52, 85, 124; four-letter, 34–36, 49–50, 53, 71–72, 102–3, 127; moment of invention, 4–5; power of printed, 14, 41, 124; relation to things, 4, 15; shock value of, 124, 127–28
writing, "written," 84, 162n. 1. *See also* authors, print